QUEST
FOR PEACE

A Memoir

Han S. Park

CATHOLIC INSTITUTE OF
NORTHEAST ASIA PEACE

IMPRIMATUR

Uijeongbu, die 23 Mensis Decembris 2022

+ Petrus K. H. LEE

Episcopus Uijeongbuensis

Published by Catholic Institute of Northeast Asia Peace
  Address _ 111, Seongdong-ro, Tanhyeon-myeon, Paju-si, Gyeonggi-do,
        Republic of Korea
  E-mail _ publ-cinap@hanmail.net │ Tel _ +82) 31-850-8502
  ISBN _ 979-8-37247-859-6

Note:

The official names of North Korea and South Korea, respectively, are the Democratic People's Republic of Korea (DPRK) and the Republic of Korea (ROK). The abbreviations of these official names, the DPRK and ROK, will be used throughout the text.

The most important thing in life
is to not let the light in my heart go out.

Albert Schweitzer

Introduction:
My Obsession, My Hope

I was obsessed with peace. I still am. As long as I can remember, I have suffered with a severe longing for peace. I've spent my lifetime thinking, teaching, and researching to find an answer to the question, *Why can't we live together without killing each other?*

The many wars I experienced as a child left me frustrated, and those brutal scenes are still vividly etched in my mind to this day. The thoroughly anti-communist education I received during my school days made the pain of division even more miserable, only intensifying my longing for peace.

This book is written by the son of immigrants born in China in 1939, who survived the Chinese Civil War as a child and suffered the terrible horrors of the Korean War. It contains my life journey of trying to fulfill the vocation for peace and reunification.

As a professor employed at the University of Georgia for 45 years since 1970, I believe that the purpose of my scholarship is to solve problems—that is, to identify societal problems of any size, find their cause, and suggest a remedy. This definition of a scholar's mission has been my lifelong philosophy. For me, the issue to be solved was the inter-Korean problem—and I have been mourning for my entire life, believing it is my scholarly role and responsibility to conceptualize and design an ideal society able to resolve the military tensions and division of North and South Korea.

This book is a compilation of articles published in The Hankyoreh from March 2019 to December 2020 as a series entitled "Crazy for Peace." The first part, "The History We Lived, The History of Our Dreams," deals with the North Korean nuclear issue, beginning with the story of former US President Jimmy Carter's 1994 visit to Kim Il Sung in North Korea. The next part, "America, as Learned in America," covers what I came to understand about the United States from the time I moved there as a student in 1965 forward. "The Path to Understanding North Korea" shares my observations, studies, and realizations over dozens of visits to the DPRK, beginning in 1980. The final part, "Our Peace, Our Unification," introduces what I've learned of peace and the path to true unification while traveling back and forth between North and South Korea, as well as hosting various events and activities in the United States.

I hoped to convey that inter-Korean issues and unification should be approached from a "peace paradigm" rather than a "security paradigm," and I desired to explain the peace that has been my lifelong research topic—indeed, my life's purpose. When these articles were published in the newspaper, many readers responded, saying the series was provided "new information," and that they "learned a lot." Particularly rewarding was the fact that high-ranking officials and experts from North and South Korea—who study inter-Korean issues and play a direct or indirect role in the government's unification policy—said they gained a new perspective on peace and unification, giving generous reviews of the series as a good study.

After the Korean War, both South and North Korea became prisoners of systemic competition and the security paradigm, demonizing each other. I hope that I will be able to enjoy the thrill and joy of true peace and reunification of the Korean Peninsula in my lifetime. If achieving that goal proves too difficult, I hope to see a solid foundation laid for future peace and unification.

I would like to express my sincere gratitude to *The Hankyoreh* and Reporter Kim Kyung-Ae for providing the opportunity for me to first publish these articles and to the translators of this book from Korean to English, especially Jennifer Telfer for her final, refined editorial work.

Han S. Park

Augusta, Georgia

December 2022

| Table of Contents |

Part 4 › Our Peace, Our Unification

Part 1:
The History We Lived,
The History of Our Dreams

I was in a state of shock.
When I asked the elders around me why my father had been tortured,
they all replied that it was because he had no "strings to pull."
When I asked how I could get such "strings," they advised me to become a
member of the National Assembly. When I asked how to do that, they told
me I would need to become a good orator.
So, in middle school, I began to work on my public speaking skills.
I went to the mountain first thing each morning to practice.

Jimmy Carter's Trip to North Korea

In the spring of 1994, the Korean Peninsula was on the verge of war. In the United States, Bill Clinton's administration was finalizing plans

▲ Jimmy Carter's visit to the DPRK (June 15-18, 1994).
On June 17, Carter (left) and Kim Il Sung (right) held their second meeting on a Taedong River cruise ship. (Hankyoreh file photo)

to bomb North Korea's [1] Yongbyon nuclear complex. [2] The escalating crisis in Korea reached its dramatic turning point when Jimmy Carter[3] made a sudden visit to the DPRK. Jimmy Carter met with the DPRK leader, Kim Il Sung, in June. When Kim Il Sung promised to freeze North Korea's nuclear program. Jimmy Carter immediately went on CNN and made the DPRK's commitments public.

---

[1] Officially known as the Democratic People's Republic of Korea or the DPRK. These names will be used interchangeably with "North Korea" throughout this book.

[2] Yongbyon, or Nyongbyon (녕변핵시설), is a major North Korean nuclear facility north of Pyongyang.

[3] Jimmy Carter was US President from 1977-1981.

More than a decade after the end of his presidency, former President Jimmy Carter suddenly returned to the scene as the protagonist in this drama. Behind this headline lay a long history between the two of us.

◀ At a gathering commemorating the end of President Carter's term in 1980. (Photo courtesy of Han S. Park)

I came to know Jimmy Carter through a friend of mine named Howard Burnell. Howard graduated from the US Naval Academy in 1946 and served in the Navy for over 30 years. Wanting to continue his studies after discharge, he enrolled in graduate school at the University of Georgia where I taught. Because Howard was born in China, where his father had worked as a missionary, he was keenly interested in East Asia, particularly Korea and China. He sought me out as his academic adviser.

In the mid-1970s when Howard was my advisee, his former Naval Academy classmate, Jimmy Carter, was preparing to run for President of the United States. Carter had recently left office as Governor of Georgia, and, at that time, he had little knowledge of international politics. So, he decided to hire his close friend, Howard Burnell, as a foreign policy adviser. Eventually, as mentor to his international advisor, I came to know Jimmy Carter.

I began advising Carter on international politics, and he listened. A prime example was the case of withdrawing US troops stationed abroad. I believed that the longer the US maintained its military presence abroad the more anti-US sentiment would spread. In my dissertation, I emphasized how it was in the United States 'interest to withdraw its troops from other nations.

◀ Jimmy Carter (right), who visited Korea on June 29, 1979, caused a stir by revealing to Park Chung-hee (left) his plan to withdraw US troops from Korea. (Hankyoreh file photo)

Carter sympathized with my opinion and, during his first campaign for President in 1976, he pledged to withdraw US forces from South Korea[4]. The South Korean government responded quite sensitively. Ham Byung-chun,[5] special advisor on Foreign Affairs to then President Park Chung-hee,[6] learned of the young Korean professor who appeared to be "too close to Carter," and he didn't like that at all. Ham Byung-chun opened the Korean Consulate General in Atlanta, Georgia and sent a schoolmate of mine, from our days at Seoul National University, to serve as consul general. This former classmate was much older than me, and it seemed they used him to monitor me

---

[4] Officially known as the Republic of Korea or the ROK. These names will be used interchangeably with "South Korea" throughout this book.

[5] His name is written 함병춘 in Korean.

[6] Park Chung Hee (박정희) was an army general who took over South Korean leadership by coup in 1961 and acted as President until his assassination in 1979.

and intervene with me as necessary.

Carter's policy of withdrawing US forces from the ROK went directly against the interests of the military-industrial complex, a spigot on America's colossal money keg. Then as now, without financial backing, US politicians had no hope of being elected to office. Cut off from the political donations of the merchants of war, Carter lost his bid for reelection in 1980. When I tried to take responsibility for the fallout of my policy recommendation and apologized for his losing reelection, Carter told me not to feel sorry for him. He took full responsibility for the policy to withdraw US troops.

After failing to win a second term as President, he established the Carter Center in 1982 with the mission of "waging peace, fighting disease, and building hope." Because he faithfully lived out the founding spirit of the Center, Jimmy Carter became widely known as the President who did the most good after leaving office.

Returning to 1994, in the days leading up to Jimmy Carter's visit to the DPRK, I had been putting all of my energy toward averting war on the Korean peninsula. The nuclear crisis in North Korea began in the early 1990s. At that time, I put aside my other studies and focused on preventing a return to the horrors I had witnessed as a child during the Korean War.

Jimmy Carter was particularly interested in the denuclearization of the Korean Peninsula. He believed that the entire peninsula, not only the northern half, should be free of nuclear weapons, and that the US should remove all of its tactical nuclear weapons from South Korea.

Well aware of his perspective on this subject, I strongly recommended that he visit North Korea to meet with Kim Il Sung. I hoped that the strained dialogue between North Korea and the United States could resume, and that they would find an opening for peaceful resolution of the nuclear issue.

Carter liked the idea, but then-President Bill Clinton opposed such a visit. President Clinton saw the DPRK nuclear issue as something he should handle within his administration, not former President Carter. Although Carter was unable to visit the DPRK right away, he looked forward to the opportunity.

One day in 1994, Robert Gallucci, US State Department Special Envoy for the DPRK, visited the Carter home in Plains, Georgia. Gallucci's visit to such a small, rural town, five-hours from Atlanta, with no airport, suggested that President Clinton had a clear message to deliver to former President Carter.

Carter called me right after that meeting, asking for logistical help because Clinton had finally allowed him to visit the DPRK. He told me the purpose of his visit was to deliver President Clinton's "ultimatum" to Kim Il Sung. Everything was urgent. First, we needed an official invitation letter from the DPRK. I drafted an invitation letter in English and sent it off to North Korea. The DPRK government made some edits to the letter and faxed it back to me within 24 hours. For confidentiality reasons, I received the fax in my home basement, not at my school office. It was midnight. I immediately forwarded the fax to Carter and confirmed his receipt at dawn.

In the middle of all these preparations, Carter invited me to accompany him on the trip. Since he didn't have much knowledge of the DPRK's internal affairs, he asked me to explain what he needed to know on the way there. I would be lying if I said I had not wished to accompany him, but I was caught in a dilemma. "I am Korean, and also a US citizen. Should I sit next to President Carter while I'm there? Wouldn't that make me look like Ye Wanyong?[7] But, wouldn't it be awkward to sit next to Kim Il Sung?"

After tossing and turning all night, I decided to forego the chance to be there in person. Instead, I offered to write a detailed briefing about the DPRK for President Carter. Due to my frail physical constitution, I don't usually stay up all night, but I spent all night writing that briefing. Considering Carter's characteristic meticulousness, he must have studied my nearly 40-page briefing to the extent that he had memorized much of it before entering the DPRK.

When Jimmy Carter was on a plane flying over the Pacific Ocean, I received a phone call from another university schoolmate, Jung Jong-

◀ Jimmy Carter, his wife Rosalynn, and Ambassador to South Korea, James Rainey (far right), bid farewell to South Koreans before crossing the Military Demarcation Line. (*Hankyoreh* file photo)

---

[7] Ye Wanyong (이완용) served as Prime Minister of Korea in 1910, at the time when the Japanese were politically maneuvering to colonize Korea. He supported the Japanese and is considered a traitor to the Korean people, infamous for signing the Japan-Korea Annexation Treaty.

wook,[8] who then served as Senior Secretary for Foreign Affairs and National Security to South Korea's President. He asked me to talk Carter out of visiting the DPRK since the Kim Young-sam [9] administration didn't want him to go. I said that the plane Carter boarded had already left.

The Blue House then revised their plan and made me a new proposal. I should persuade Carter to visit Seoul before Pyongyang. They also wanted me to ask Carter to personally deliver a Blue House proposal for an Inter-Korean Summit to Kim Il Sung at their meeting. I forwarded the proposal to Carter, and he decided to change his plans. Instead of flying directly to Pyongyang, he chose to go to Seoul and to cross the 38th parallel into North Korea, by land. He received permission from the ROK, DPRK, and the United States to make it happen. It was an earth-shattering event.

---

[8] His name is written 정종욱 in Korean.
[9] Kim Young-sam (김영삼) was South Korea's seventh President from 1993-1998.

The US Government's Yongbyon Bombing Scenario

On June 16, 1994, Carter met with Kim Il Sung in Pyongyang. They agreed to "freeze the North Korean nuclear program," and Carter was supposed to report directly back to President Clinton. However, he instead made an international call from Pyongyang to Robert Gallucci at the White House, conveying both the details of that day's agreement and notifying Gallucci that he would announce the details publicly on an interview on CNN. And he did just that, unilaterally making his announcement to the world on cable news. He feared that if the contents of the agreement were not immediately made public, the US may instead move ahead with their plans to destroy Yongbyon. President Clinton was so perturbed by Carter's unilateral action that their relationship was cold for quite a while afterward.

◄ Returning across the Military Demarcation Line at Panmunjom, Jimmy Carter does not appear cheerful, perhaps because his relationship with President Clinton became strained after announcing the nuclear freeze agreement. (Hankyoreh file photo)

The Clinton administration had a plan to bomb the Yongbyon complex if Jimmy Carter and Kim Il Sung could not reach an agreement to freeze the North Korean nuclear program. To this day, quite a few South Koreans believe the nuclear issue could have been resolved if the US had bombed Yongbyon at that time. That dangerous idea is based solely on hatred without much knowledge about the reality of the DPRK. The Clinton administration had often peppered me with similar questions. Our dialogue went something like this:

> "How will North Korea respond when the US bombs Yongbyon?"
> "If the US bombs Yongbyon, the DPRK will inevitably launch a retaliatory attack."
> "How do you think the DPRK will retaliate?"
> "They will bomb US bases in Korea, Japan, and Guam."
> "Aren't there a lot of civilians living around those bases?"
> "Yes. Therefore, hundreds of thousands of lives will be lost if North Korea bombs the US bases. And then, the US will have to take severe moral responsibility for the damage in the international community."

In 1950, Pyongyang had a population of roughly one million people. During the Korean War, the US Air Force dropped about 10,000 bombs on Pyongyang—one bomb for every 100 people. In those days, extended families commonly lived together in a single house. If 10 people made up each family, we can estimate that there were 100,000 households in Pyongyang. The US bombardment turned everything to ashes. Countless people lost their lives. This is the historical backdrop to North Korea's intense hostility toward the United States.

Having witnessed the power of the US Air Force during the War,

Kim Il Sung spurred on the work of digging tunnels and building shelters as soon as the war was over. Some claim the DPRK became the best tunnel-digging country in the world. Also remarkable, Pyongyang's subway operates at a depth of 100 meters underground, running under the riverbed of the Daedong River. The subways were built very deep and wide, enabling them to double as huge air-raid shelters. In case of emergency, sirens go off and the citizens of Pyongyang swarm into these underground shelters, making it very difficult for the United States to identify bombing targets.

What about South Korea, the United States 'ally? In the Republic of Korea, everything is exposed above the ground. In Seoul along, there are millions of cars with tanks full of gasoline, diesel, and natural gas. If the DPRK bombs the ROK, those cars will explode. Also, in South Korea, most homes are heated by and cook with gas from public gas lines. If attacked, those gas lines would explode.

I explained all of this to President Carter, and repeated my warnings in the media, including on CNN. If the US bombed Yongbyon, although people in the North may not suffer great loss, millions of South Koreans, American allies, would be killed in retaliation. Beyond a shadow of a doubt, if war broke, the DPRK would have an advantage over the ROK, possibly even over the United States. Many progressives listened to my warnings and agreed with me.

On the other hand, South Korea's Kim Young-sam government didn't appear to have much interest in preventing war. While devoting himself to averting the outbreak of catastrophic war should have been his priority, he publicly opposed Jimmy Carter's visit to the DPRK.

Suddenly, on July 8th, less than a month after President Carter's visit to North Korea, President Kim Il Sung died. Carter wanted to return to Pyongyang to pay his condolences. A DPRK official, well known for his exemplary service to his government, read the thoughtfully written letter that Carter sent and was moved to tears. However, the DPRK refused Carter's respects, broadcasting a "principle of refusing foreign condolences" at Kim Il Sung's funeral. (I later had the opportunity to meet the councilor who wept after reading Carter's letter, and he took the opportunity to pay his respects to Carter in return.)

On the day of Kim Il Sung's death, I was in Rome. CNN asked me for an interview. Because CNN had a direct hotline to communicate with the DPRK, I asked the North Korean side if there was anything I could do if I came there right away. They replied that there was nothing to do there but to weep.

If not for President Jimmy Carter's visit in 1994, the first North Korean nuclear crisis could have escalated to war. Instead, it ended with the Geneva Agreement on October 21st. As an incentive for the DPRK freezing its nuclear development and in response to its severe and extended power shortage, the international community agreed to provide them two light-water reactors (LWRs).

However, the Geneva agreement, which was essentially the the last will and testament of Kim Il Sung, was essentially an agreement doomed to fail from the start. Because South Korea's Kim Young-sam government was convinced that without Kim Il Sung the DPRK would collapse within three months, the United States didn't even allocate a budget to implement the agreement. Consequently, all of the expenses related to installing the LWRs were handed over to Korea. Although South Korea eventually failed to implement the Geneva Agreement, all the US did was wait for the day the DPRK would collapse. The Obama administration's strategy of "strategic patience" was an extension of that same thinking. After the Soviet Union was dismantled and as they watched socialist countries in Eastern Europe collapse one after another, American presidential administrations thought that North Korea's collapse was just a matter of time.

However, the DPRK has still not collapsed. To the contrary, it appears to become more and more stable with time. I can roughly summarize the reason it did not collapse in the following five points:

▲ US Special Envoy to North Korea Robert Gallucci (left) and North Korea's First Vice Foreign Minister Kang Sok-ju (right) agree to freeze the North Korean nuclear program in exchange for US support for light-water reactors on October 21, 1994 in Geneva, Switzerland. (Hankyoreh file photo)

Firstly, while socialist countries in Eastern Europe remained largely dependent on the Soviet Union in political, economic, social and cultural spheres, the DPRK intentionally excluded the Soviet Union's ideological influence by promoting its own *Juche* ideology. Therefore, while socialist countries in Eastern Europe were directly affected by the dissolution of the Soviet Union, North Korea was able to avoid some of the shock.

Secondly, when a political system collapses, a so-called "legitimacy crisis" tends to occur during which public support for the government is withdrawn. However, the legitimacy of North Korea's system is not based in its economy, but upon *Juche* ideology. Therefore, even when their economy tumbled into severe recession, their system faced no immediate crisis of legitimacy. On the contrary, an even more consolidated sense of unity formed around the *Juche* idea.

Thirdly, for a *coup d'état* to successfully overthrow a political system, the forces opposing the government must be able to share secret information among themselves. However, the DPRK is a country where information is tightly controlled and all information is distributed transparently. Without the ability to share secret information, a coup would be doomed from the start.

Fourthly, North Korea bolsters its own system by waging a legitimacy war with South Korea. Without that comparison, it would be difficult for the DPRK to maintain its legitimacy. This strategy, denying the other (South Korea) to build and maintain one's own legitimacy is unique to North Korea, not found in other socialist countries.

Lastly, although it is well known that East Germany was reunified through absorption by West Germany, it is extremely unlikely that Korea could be reunified in the same way. This is because the situations in East Germany and in the DPRK are very different, as are the ones in West Germany and in the ROK. The East-West Germany and inter-Korean relations are very different, too. For example, West Germany and East Germany both have a strong sense of pride in their German identity. However, while North Korea is based on strong nationalism, in the South there is a growing rejection of or hostility towards nationalism. In short, unless the circumstances described above are significantly altered, I believe it is unlikely we will see the collapse of the DPRK in the near future.

In order to understand the DPRK's "secret" to successfully maintaining its system against all sorts of adversities, one must accurately understand the so-called "Military-First Politics" or *Songun*.[10] People often understand military-first politics as a structure through which the military exploits the people. If military-first politics had really been such a system, the DPRK would have collapsed decades ago. During the "Arduous March"[11] in the 1990s, when the Cold War ended and economic support from socialist allies was almost cut off while the US economic sanctions were strangling its neck, North Korea had no other way than to choose *Songun* for its survival strategy. It was a time of life or death for the DPRK, when it could find support from nowhere and was completely isolated.

---

[10] Military-First Politics or songun is written 선군정치 in Korean.
[11] The famine known as the Arduous March is written 고난의 행군 in Korean.

In the DPRK, when people faced severe economic difficulties, the military stepped forward to solve them. 90% of the people who worked on farmland were soldiers. There is also an office where soldiers are stationed to help the people in each neighborhood. So, if a faucet is leaking in some neighbor's house, one can call this military office for help. Soldiers have the expertise to solve various problems the people face. When soldiers help in this way, the people develop loyalty to the military. Until recently, all sons and daughters are required to serve 10 years in the military. Therefore, military-first politics in which the soldiers are positioned at the forefront of society, naturally help unite the soldiers and the people with one heart.

If war broke out in South Korea or the US, soldiers on leave must immediately return to their military bases. In the DPRK however, the soldier should return to his family and take charge of family protection. Their participation in war is not to occupy the battlefield, but to defend their hometown and family who lives there. If you fight for your family, you can't help fighting with everything you have. Their loyalty comes right from the heart, which is Kim Il Sung's legacy.

Starving Children and Human Rights

As part of the Geneva Agreement signed in October 1994, the United States promised to provide the DPRK with two 1,000-MegaWatt LWRs in exchange for its freezing the nuclear development at Yongbyon, and to provide 500,000 tons of heavy fuel per year, for generating electricity, until the reactors were completed. However, the United States did not honor this promise. The failure to deliver on its promise made North Korea's energy situation worse, leading to a terrible famine, known as the Arduous March, in the mid-1990s.

The devastation DPRK people suffered during this time is appallingly revealed in the fact that roughly 2 million people died of starvation. I visited several times during this Arduous March period. Each visit, I witnessed elementary and middle school students marching in the street, singing military songs with red scarfs around their necks. Theirs was literally an arduous march to overrule hunger with an iron will.

In 1998, Kim Jong Il set the military-first policy in motion, and the US strengthened economic sanctions against North Korea. The sanctions 'stated purpose was to prevent North Korea from developing nuclear and missile programs, and many countries in the international community actively participated in this US policy, including the United Nations. However, it is extremely unlikely that the DPRK will succumb to the US economic sanctions and comply with the United States 'will. As mentioned above, even if the DPRK's economic foundation is damaged by US economic sanctions, Juche ideology keeps the nation's fundamental legitimacy intact. This is why the US policy of resolving the nuclear issue by continually sanctioning the DPRK has failed.

I should note, however, that using food as a weapon is much more brutal than using nuclear deterrence. In international politics, nuclear weapons are understood not as a means of war but as a means of diplomatic negotiation. Paradoxically, the horrendously destructive power of nuclear weapons has limited their practical use. On the other hand, US sanctions become weapons of hunger that directly threaten the survival of human beings who must eat every day. In the 1990s, the American-led, United Nations Security Council's economic sanctions on Iraq, which lasted for 13 years, resulted in the starvation of approximately half a million children under the age of five. According to a 2018, UNICEF (United Nations Children's Fund) report, about 60,000 children were on the verge of starvation due to the US-led economic sanctions against North Korea.

When I visited a daycare center in the DPRK during the Arduous March, I witnessed children dying of starvation firsthand. When I asked my North Korean guides where the children's parents were, they replied that they were all dead. Think about it. Wouldn't parents with hungry children give up their own food to keep their children alive, even to the moment they themselves die of starvation? The sight of those children starving to death in the nursery was the most miserable sight I had ever seen.

I returned to my lodgings with the officials who were guiding me, but I couldn't shake the memories out of my mind. The images of dying children became even more vivid. I quietly locked the door and approached the DPRK officials, who were almost twice as tall as me. (I'm short. I've met two people in my life who are shorter than me, and they're Park Chung-hee and Deng Xiaoping.) I looked up and glared straight at them, punching them with all my might. Their glasses fell to the ground. I almost wailed, "Your stomach is plump! How the hell could you let the children in the nursery die like that!" The officials wrapped their arms around me to restrain me. Together we fell down to the floor and wept out loud. The sadness didn't diminish, no matter how long I cried.

◄ The scene just before the collapse of the second day of talks at the Metropole Hotel in Hanoi on February 28, 2019. (Hankyoreh file photo)

At the Hanoi Summit with the United States on February 28, 2019, Kim Jong Un asked the United States to "remove some of the UN sanctions, that is, items that interfere with the civilian economy and people's lives." Kim Jong Un's request must have been to alleviate North Korean people's suffering from hunger. But Trump rejected the request, and the US Congress welcomed the breakdown of the summit.

Americans criticized human rights abuses in North Korea and called for further strengthening economic sanctions against the DPRK. Against this backdrop, where 60,000 children were starving to death due to US economic sanctions, what are the "human rights" for which they were vehemently advocating?

While I was at the University of Georgia (UGA), I created and taught a human rights course for decades. In 1995, I established The Center for the Study of Global Issues (GLOBIS) to study and solve human rights issues outside the classroom. I have also struggled to properly establish the concept of human rights while discussing human rights issues with Jimmy Carter over the years. President Carter included human rights on his foreign policy agenda. From all I have studied, it seems that the concept of human rights in the United States reflects the values and interests of the countries that won World War II. In other words, their concept of human rights was not of the universal values of mankind, but the limited views of certain victorious nations, including the United States. The DPRK also has its own conception of human rights, which has certain advantages and disadvantages, just like the conceptual framework found in the United States. Human rights are not the purview of the United States or of Korea alone. There can be many conceptions of human rights.

I believe that human rights are largely based on three principles. Firstly, universalism. They are rights that every human being born into this world can enjoy. Therefore, it isn't true that the United States has human rights while North Korea does not. Secondly, inalienability. They are rights that you have from birth which no one can take away from you. Thirdly, entitlement. This means, for example, that if a child is starving in Pyongyang, I should feel it is my responsibility and not the child's.

Also, I believe that human rights, based on the birthright, non-transferability, and shared responsibility mentioned above, are largely composed of six dimensions. Firstly, a right to survival. It is a human right to maintain life, occupying the most important dimension of human rights. Secondly, a right to belonging. It is the right of a person to belong to a certain group and lead his or her life. Thirdly, a right to equality. This means that human beings have the right not to be discriminated against for any reason. Fourthly, a right to choice-making. The right of an individual or group to freely choose certain values. Fifthly, a right to love. It is the human right to love. For example, instead of marrying in consideration of the authority of the family to which they belong, humans are bound by the right to love that cannot be decided by the parents. In addition, the right of separated families to love each other can also be called the right to love. Sixthly, a right to nationhood. This refers to the human right to be freed from the restraints of time and space, specifically religious liberation or deliverance. Human rights can be fully realized when all of the above six dimensions are met.

The concrete form of the concept of human rights, which the United States have advocated as a universal value for mankind, can be found in the 1948 Universal Declaration of Human Rights. Article 1 of the Universal Declaration of Human Rights stipulates the inherent freedom and equality of all human beings. "Freedom" is the key-word of capitalism, while "equality" is that of socialism. Theoretically, they are incompatible. The reason they both were stipulated was intended to simultaneously satisfy the US and the Soviet Union, the victors in World War II. Article I was simply a juxtaposition of the freedom of the capitalist state of the United States and the equality of the socialist state of the Soviet Union. Therefore, we see that the concept of human rights advocated by the United States was incapable of being universally valued.

Out of the six dimensions of human rights that I just classified, the concept of human rights in the United States was constructed upon emphasizing only the right to choice-making. The right to choice that the United States highly values essentially means political freedom, and requires a democratic system to guarantee that freedom. On the other hand, among the rest of the six dimensions of human rights, the American concept of human rights has a fatal weakness which is that it neglects the right to survival, one of the most important rights. This is why the United States is constantly criticizing the human rights violations in the DPRK while completely ignoring the obvious fact that many North Korean children starve to death due to America's harsh economic sanctions.

The DPRK, which chose socialism, prioritizes the sovereignty of the State over individual human rights. This is based in the judgement that individual human rights can only be guaranteed (by the State) if the State's sovereignty is first guaranteed. Therefore, the right to individual choice is not prioritized in the DPRK's conception of human rights, whereas it is emphasized most strongly in the United

States. Conversely, the right to survival, the right to belonging, and the right to equality, all of which are highly valued human rights in the DPRK, are not as highly esteemed in the United States.

According to this analysis, we see that conceptions of human rights in the United States and the DPRK are relative to their own systems. No matter how strongly the US criticizes North Korea using its own concept of human rights, the criticism will not yield desired results because the DPRK's concept of human rights is completely different from that of the United States. If the United States, based upon Christianity, were to criticize Islam in Arab countries, would that criticism succeed in the Arab world?

As such, the ultimate reason the United States fails to achieve any remarkable results, despite its longstanding efforts to resolve the North Korean nuclear issue, lies in ideology that the United States takes for granted. Instead of endless intimidation, demonization, and driving countless North Korean people into a living hell, the US should make efforts to reform its own paradigm. If the United States truly thinks about the human rights of North Korean children on the verge of starvation, they could formulate and enact a new policy to peacefully resolve the North Korean nuclear issue.

CVID and Truth Behind the Dark Nighttime Satellite Photos

The nuclear crisis that began when North Korea withdrew from the Nuclear Non-Proliferation Treaty (NPT) in 1993 has yet to be resolved, 28 years later, in 2021. It is not that the United States, China, DPRK, and ROK haven't made efforts to solve the problem, nor that their efforts haven't been fruitful. For example, North Korea and the United States signed the Geneva Agreement in October 1994 and announced the September 19th Joint Statement in 2005. However, those achievements fell apart soon after, and despite repeatedly returning to negotiations, the nuclear crisis worsened. In other words, the more time spent trying to resolve the North Korean nuclear crisis, the worse the crisis became. Hasn't the DPRK now become a de facto nuclear state? How on earth are we to understand the bizarre paradox in which efforts to solve these problems have actually exacerbated them?

Since my first visit to North Korea in 1981, I have visited more than 50 times and have become painfully aware of one thing. People outside of North Korea look it in a totally different way than the people inside North Korea view the world. People looking from outside interpret the DPRK from the perspective to which they are accustomed, even forcing that perspective on North Koreans. It is impossible to properly understand the DPRK with that approach.

I coined the term "epistemic imperialism" to describe the act of resizing North Korea to fit one's own perspective. I have come to the conclusion that all solutions to the North Korean nuclear crisis designed according to epistemic imperialism will inevitably fail. I believe that epistemic imperialism is the real cause of 28 years of failed efforts to solve this problem.

My 2002 book, *North Korea: The Politics of Unconventional Wisdom*, is a comprehensive summary of the Juche ideology, learned through direct observation of North Korea's political culture and through serious discussions with scholars in the DPRK. Ten years after that, in 2012, I co-wrote and published North Korea Demystified with fellow scholars. The book argued that we should depart from the image of North Korea adapted according to our conventional wisdom. I published a Korean study of the DPRK entitled Thinking Beyond the Line in 2018, proposing how to better understand the DPRK.

It was just a coincidence that the titles of my books, published 10 years apart, converged into a common proposition. These books stressed the fact that North Korea must be understood beyond epistemic imperialism, and that the readers should, as closely as possible, know the way the people of North Korea approach the world. I conceptualized my research attitude with the term "empathy." This term, when translated into Korean, can be understood as an act of or putting oneself in another's shoes.[12]

---

[12] The closest Korean term to "empathy" is *yeokjisaji* (역지사지, 易地思之).

The United States is currently demanding CVID, which stands for "complete, verifiable, and irreversible dismantlement" of North Korea's nuclear program. There are other terms such as PVID, meaning "permanent, verifiable, and irreversible dismantlement, " and FFVD, meaning "final and fully verifiable dismantlement," but they are not very different from each other. The key is that CVID is a concept that typically reflects American epistemic imperialism. Above all, it is a concept that unilaterally forces the DPRK to unconditionally get rid of its nuclear weapons, while completely ignoring North Korea's motives for developing nuclear weapons in the first place. It is an unrealistic and unachievable foreign policy goal.

In order to realize "complete" denuclearization, the facilities in question must be inspected by the International Atomic Energy Agency (IAEA). IAEA inspections are categorized into routine and special inspections, with routine inspections being most frequently used. The DPRK would voluntarily report the location and the number of nuclear weapons, and the IAEA would visit to verify the reports. In some cases, the IAEA may only verify some of the locations reported. Trusting North Korea is prerequisite to the successful completion of a routine inspection.

However, at present, the IAEA and the United States do not trust North Korea. No matter how honestly the DPRK were to report on their nuclear activities, the USA and IAEA will not take them at their word. On the other hand, special inspections would be very difficult to implement. Special inspections involve not only inspection of locations the DPRK reported, but also of all suspected nuclear weapons facilities, according to the IAEA's own analysis. This essentially means that any location in North Korea would be subject to IAEA inspection. Would that level of inspection be possible? If the IAEA and the United States enforced special inspections, who knows but that the DPRK may not ignore foreign acts in violation of their national sovereignty, resulting in a gunfight.

"Verifiable" denuclearization is an even greater challenge. To achieve this, nuclear weapons experts must verify the areas North Korea reports. However, since the IAEA and the United States fundamentally distrust North Korea, they surely do not intend to verify only reported areas.

"Irreversible" denuclearization is also virtually impossible to achieve. The DPRK already possesses nuclear weapons. They have the expertise, the experience, and the raw materials necessary to manufacture them. Even if the DPRK dismantled all of their current nuclear weapons, it could feasibly rebuild its arsenal at any time. So how is "irreversible" denuclearization possible?

Combining these analyses, it is easy to recognize that CVID is conceptually and practically impossible. In fact, it precludes any

◀ The Team Spirit military exercises, begun in 1976 at the request of the Park Chung-hee regime and conducted every year until 1993, were ostensibly a defense operation— according to the motto in 1990, "ROK-US Partnership for Peacekeeping Exercises"—but served as an excuse for DPRK nuclear development in its own defense.

solution to the North Korean nuclear crisis from the start. In order to solve this problem, we must first accurately diagnose the reason they developed nuclear weapons in the first place. If we take an empathetic attitude, we can accurately make such a diagnosis.

I stayed in North Korea several times to observe what happened there during the Team Spirit military exercises (which took place every spring, from 1976-1993) in the South. Team Spirit was a US-ROK joint military exercise with the objective of attacking North Korea. It was the world's largest military exercise during the Cold War era, and it was held annually for about two months. The number of participating troops sometimes reached 200,000 to 300,000. When military training begins in the South, the DPRK immediately enters a state of war preparedness. Although it was just a training exercise, there was concern that the weapons could be turned on the DPRK at any time. In a state of war, daily life comes to a full stop. Since the training is mainly conducted during peak farming season, North Koreans have no choice but to abandon farming during the period.

After repeatedly experiencing that vicious cycle, and desperately seeking a way to liberate themselves from its threat, North Korea finally settled on nuclear weapons as their solution. Moreover, as North Korea witnessed Muammar Gaddafi's death after surrendering his nuclear weapons, and how the USA butchered Saddam Hussein like an animal death, despite not possessing nuclear weapons, they became more and more convinced that nuclear weapons were their answer.

During Team Spirit military training, I visited the homes of North

Korean professors and ordinary residents to observe how they responded. At night, they turn off the lights all at once and close the curtains. They do all they can to block any light from escaping. The government authorities have forbidden any light to leak out. The entire nation is immediately enveloped in pitch-black darkness. I have never witnessed an ordinary North Korean night as dark as those nights.

If you have ever seen one of the NASA satellite photos of the Korean Peninsula at night, which have been widely circulated in the media, there is a clear contrast between the darkness in North Korea and South Korea, which is as bright as daytime. People marvel that the DPRK is so dark and wonder about the extent of the electricity shortage. While South Korea, with an abundance of electricity, appears as bright as broad daylight. "Isn't South Korea heavenly compared to hellish North Korea?" Such articles distort the reality of the DPRK to the extent that I can't help but laugh, if not get angry, because of what I witnessed while staying in North Korea during the Team Spirit military exercises.

Whenever I had a conversation with a North Korean scholar or high-level political leader during the military exercises, I used to wonder if

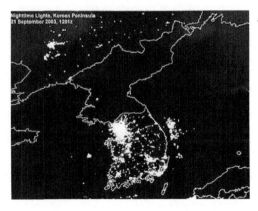

◀ In 2005, US Secretary of Defense, Donald Rumsfeld placed a nighttime satellite photo of the Korean Peninsula on a table in the Oval Office. The photo is thought to have been taken by NASA satellite in September 2003. (*Hankyoreh* file photo)

the DPRK might ever attack the ROK first. High-level North Korean leaders were very concerned about a scenario in which they would be unable to respond to a preemptive attack, despite the fact that they had prepared a powerful standing army in case of an attack by the United States. Hearing them share, my heart sank at the thought that they might launch a preemptive attack out of fear of an American attack. The ancient Greek historian Thucydides emphasized three times in The History of the Peloponnesian Wars that Sparta attacked Athens out of fear of the latter's expansion in the region.

As long as the nuclear standoff between the DPRK and the United States persists, I believe it is possible that North Korea could launch a preemptive strike. Even after the Team Spirit exercises officially ended in 1993, ROK-US joint military exercises have continued, only with different names, to this day. I personally witnessed that the war readiness situation in North Korea has not changed much, either.

Another surprising fact is that when I come from North Korea into South Korea, I find a completely different world. Even during the Team Spirit military exercises in South Korea, there was no sense that war was possible. In contrast to North Korea, which has been repeatedly driven into a state of war, South Koreans were completely unaware of the serious tension between the DPRK and the United States. Even more, South Korea was unaware of the extreme fear that the North feels from the United States or of the possibility of their committing a preemptive strike based upon that fear.

What has taken the place of that awareness in the South was "red-baiting," completely out of touch with the reality in the DPRK. People even seemed to believe that such ideological scapegoating was a patriotic act. Can such vacuous discourse prevent renewed outbreak of devastating war on the Korean Peninsula? If war breaks out on the Korean Peninsula again, will they simply curse "evil" North Korea for the violence?

To seriously consider taking the first step to peace on the Korean Peninsula, I would like to remind us of something Bertrand Russell once said, "War does not determine who is right—only who is left."

Kim Il Sung's Paradoxical Legacy

At the second summit between the United States and the DPRK, Donald Trump announced that the US and the IAEA would completely dismantle North Korea's nuclear program through special inspections, by which they would investigate all suspected nuclear facilities at will. He even demanded that North Korea's nuclear scientists and engineers only work commercially.

Reuters' coverage said that Trumps demands must have been borrowed from the "Libya model" that John Bolton had been advocating. The Libya model, which demanded disarmament first and offered compensation afterwards, ended in the tragic death of Muammar Gaddafi. Since the US breached its agreement in that case, North Korea has always rejected the Lybia model. In their first summit in Singapore in June 2018, Trump distanced himself from Bolton's position and never called for the Libya model. So, why did he change course and propose the Libya model at the Hanoi Summit? Why did he suddenly demand CVID from North Korea, when it is both theoretically and practically improbable?

Perhaps, knowing that the DPRK would reject the Libya model, Trump was looking for a way out—an option that prevented resolution of the North Korean nuclear problem. In other words, it is possible that the US pushed North Korea into rejecting a plan that was doomed to failure. Leaving the nuclear issue unresolved, and thus indefinitely maintaining the current state of military tensions on the Korean Peninsula, serves the exact interests of the Trump-dominated, "deep state" government of the United States. The deep state is a group of hidden, but powerful, influencers who rake in astronomical profits by selling weapons. Such profitable weapons deals with South Korea only happen steadily alongside escalation of military tensions on the Korean Peninsula.

It is not easy to get an accurate view of the deep state. It appears to be operated by people with abundant experience in information and technology, great financial influence, and military power. The deep state undermines the formal system of government, destroying its normal working logic. In Korean, I translate deep state as "seismic state," noting its hidden explosive power. If the US deep state continues to play an outsized role in government, it will eventually reach the point of destroying American democracy and the rule of law.

Even Trump couldn't control the deep state. In hiring Bolton, who has been called the deep state's "shadow President," Trump must have intended to take control, but his attempt was doomed from the start. From my point of view, Bolton is nothing more than a deep state pawn. According to a Reuters' report, the yellow envelope that Bolton carried at the Hanoi Summit contained a document reflecting deep state interests, which, rather than promote an agreement with North Korea, were intended to induce North Korea's categorical rejection of US proposals. The deep state uses North Korea's existence as a boogeyman to maintained its own power.

There is an even more serious problem in South Korea's policies toward the US and North Korea. South Korea always seeks to resolve the North Korean nuclear issue in cooperation with the US. So, just like the United States, South Korea emphasizes the need for complete denuclearization. That means CVID, a direct import from the United States. In addition to that, South Korea sees North Korean denuclearization and the denuclearization of the Korean Peninsula as two different things. The former means CVID of North Korea, while the latter denuclearization of the entire Korean Peninsula is separate. The reason South Korea distinguishes the former from the latter is because they understand that the latter is an unrealistic goal that does not fit the US' global and East Asian strategies.

The idea of separating the DPRK's denuclearization from that of the rest of the Korean Peninsula is an Americanized idea that only reflects US interests. To North Koreans, the very idea of distinguishing the denuclearization of the DPRK from that of the rest of the Korean Peninsula is regarded as a "fantasy." The notion of denuclearizing the DPRK does not exist as a stand-alone concept in North Korean minds; there is only the concept of denuclearization of the whole Korean Peninsula. I personally discussed this with numerous scholars in North Korea to confirm. I asked them over and over again,

"What specifically do you mean by denuclearization? Does that mean we should even get rid of nuclear weapons on the American mainland?"

North Korean scholars responded unanimously that they argue for denuclearization "that encompasses the denuclearization of North

Korea, the denuclearization of the US forces stationed in Korea, and the denuclearization of US nuclear aircraft carriers stationed in the seas surrounding the Korean Peninsula." The DPRK has never talked about the denuclearization of their land alone—not in any official statements—but have consistently insisted on denuclearization of the entire Korean Peninsula. During his second meeting with Japanese Prime Minister Junichiro Koizumi in May 2004, Kim Jong Il said:

> The United States is asking us to surrender our nuclear weapons unconditionally, just like Iraq. We can not meet such demands. If the United States attacks us with nuclear weapons, we will not just give up and suffer. If we let our weapons go, the fate of Iraq awaits us.

Kim Jong Il's concerns played out in Lybia's case. Responding to the United States' request, Libya embarked on "complete denuclearization" in 2003, dismantling all of their weapons of mass destruction. In 2006, the US State Department normalized diplomatic relations with Libya and upgraded the existing liaison office to an embassy. And then, the US launched "Operation Odyssey Dawn," bombing Libya in March 2011. In October, Lybian rebels, backed by the US-led NATO forces, captured and killed Muammar Gaddafi. After witnessing the tragic end of Lybia's regime, how could the DPRK accept any proposal meaning nothing more than their own unilateral disarmament? South Korea's solution to the nuclear issue, based on ROK-US cooperation, is just as unrealistic as the American solution.

If we look more closely at the nature of North Korea, we can better understand just how unrealistic the US-ROK solution is. The DPRK is a country built upon a very strong national pride. Its constitution was designed to resist foreign oppression. Therefore, the stronger the pressure placed on North Korea, the stronger the opposition from within.

You would be convinced of this if you read North Korean history textbooks. North Korea's national pride or strong nationalist spirit is mainly cultivated by teaching ancient Korean history from the Gojoseon and Goguryeo dynasties,[13] because North Korea believes those were the eras in which the Korean people's[14] political spirit was most vigorously expressed. North Korean students learn the indomitable spirit of resistance and fervent national pride while studying how Goguryeo resolutely repelled invasions by the two strongest world powers of the time, the Sui and Tang dynasties.[15] The DPRK strives to maintain the same spirit in its current confrontation with the United States. Therefore, it is unimaginable and unrealistic to expect the DPRK to accept CVID as proposed by the United States.

A certain Professor K, who studied history at the Juche Academy of Sciences in Pyongyang, invited me to attend several academic conferences where I closely observed the trends in North Korean historical research and confirmed that Goguryeo was particularly important in their historical studies. Rather than emphasize heroic individuals of the period (such as Euljimundeok, King Gwanggaeto

---

[13] Gojoseon (고조선, 古朝鮮) and Goguryeo (고구려, 高句麗) dynasties

[14] Korean or "Han" ethnic group is written 한민족 in Korean and 韓民族 in Chinese/Hanja.

[15] Sui (수나라, 隋) and Tang (당나라, 唐) dynasties

the Great, and Yeongaesomun), [16] North Korean historians emphasized how the people used their collective capabilities to overcome national crises. Joseon Warriors, [17] a compilation of the Korean people's history, was also written based on the people's collective perspective.

When Professor K heard that I was born in Manchuria, [18] he asked me whether my father, grandfather, and ancestors were also born in Manchuria. I was initially confused by his question, not sure where it was leading. The professor was trying to find out if I had descended from Goguryeo. When I twice visited the tomb of King Dongmyeonggseong, [19] I could not help feeling as if I had inherited the Goguryeo spirit. In short, North Korea's strong nationalism is the embodiment of the ancient Goguryeo spirit, still very much alive on the Peninsula.

There is one more thing to keep in mind when South Korea calls for North Korea's complete denuclearization. The ROK and DPRK have engaged in fierce, national competition since the modern founding of their countries. I use the term *legitimacy war* to conceptualize this system competition. The ROK self-identifies as the only legitimate government on the Korean Peninsula, completely excluding the DPRK, and the DPRK does the same. The reason that North Korea developed nuclear weapons in the first place was to secure military

---

[16] Euljimundeok (을지문덕, 乙支文德), King Gwanggaeto the Great (광개토대왕, 廣開土), and Yeongaesomun (연개소문, 淵蓋蘇文)

[17] The history book, *Joseon Warriors,* is entitled 조선전사 in Korean.

[18] Northeastern China, the provinces along the DPRK's northern border

[19] King Dongmyeonggseong (동명성왕, also called King Jumong or King Chumo) was the founding King of the Goguryeo dynasty. His tomb is located in Pyongyang, North Korea.

means to ensure its security. In his 2018 New Year's address, Kim Jong Un declared the completion their national nuclear force. In other words, he declared that by possessing nuclear weapons, the DPRK had secured military means to ensure its own safety. Since then, North Korea has used nuclear weapons as a means of confirming its legitimacy and to claim that their system was superior to that of South Korea. Therefore, South Korea demanding North Korea's complete denuclearization is equivalent to demanding they give up the very thing securing their national system. Can you imagine?

For peaceful resolution of the North Korean nuclear issue, we must pay attention to Kim Il Sung's paradoxical legacy on nuclear weapons. Therein lies a clue to accurately understand what motivated their nuclear development. A certain Professor C from North Korea, with whom I had many academic exchanges over the years, was able to give me a detailed explanation of why Kim Il Sung turned to nuclear weapons. Having fought in the anti-Japanese armed struggle, Kim Il Sung was deeply impressed by nuclear power when he saw Japan immediately capitulate in response to the atomic bombings. Kim Il Sung was convinced that if only he had nuclear weapons, he could repel even the most powerful foreign aggression, securing his nation once and for all. As his nation suffered ruthless bombings by the US during the Korean War, the necessity of obtaining nuclear weapons was engraved even more deeply in his heart. So, beginning in 1958, he sent young scholars to the Soviet Union to study nuclear physics. That a was the beginning of North Korea's journey to develop nuclear weapons.

Watching the entire nation of Japan being scorched under atomic bombings, Kim Il Sung witnessed not only the immense power of the bombs, but also the devastation they can cause. He came to believe that nuclear weapons should not be used on the Korean Peninsula under any circumstances. To that end, he was convinced that "the denuclearization of the Korean Peninsula" was necessary in order to eliminate all nuclear weapons from the Peninsula. In other words, Kim Il Sung was conflicted about possessing and dispossessing nuclear weapons, pursuing both lines of reasoning simultaneously.

His reasoning seemed contradictory, but in reality it was highly logical and practical. Kim Il Sung thought that nuclear weapons could be abandoned at any time, in the event that a political arrangement was established to reliably guarantee the DPRK's security. This is the context in which North Korea has repeatedly states that "denuclearization is the legacy of our predecessors." If we pay attention to Kim Il Sung's paradoxical legacy on nuclear weapons, we recognize that North Korea's denuclearization can only be realized when certain political safeguards—such as establishing DPRK-US diplomatic ties, a multilateral non-aggression treaty, etc.—are first set in place.

I have a dream. I dream of the moment when North Korea's security is guaranteed and the Korean Peninsula is fully denuclearized. The moment when the DPRK rejoins the NPT and persuades other countries with nuclear ambitions to denuclearize, moving throughout the international arena in close cooperation with global powers, including South Korea and the United States. The moment when this country, which has been regarded as a "rouge" and "evil" nation, contributes to the peace of mankind by leading the global denuclearization and non-proliferation movement. I dream of the moment when North Korea is rightfully seen as a normal state and member of the international community.

Longing for Peace has Afflicted Me Since Childhood

I have lived in the United States for over fifty years, and during the past twenty, I was able to travel to North Korea more than fifty times. The distance from the United States to Pyongyang, via Beijing, and then back to the United States is the distance around the globe. So, I have orbited the Earth more than fifty times. I didn't travel there on vacation. I didn't even go with the support of the South Korean government. I paid all of my own expenses from the pittance of a University professor's salary.

My first visit took place in the summer of 1981. To understand the DPRK accurately, I thought it necessary to understand the *Juche* idea from their viewpoint, rather than mine. In the United States at that time, when the conservative Republican candidate, Ronald Reagan, had just defeated the incumbent Jimmy Carter for President, Cold War tensions were running high. At such a time, visiting North Korea felt as fearful as walking alone into the jaws of death.

In fact, as I waited at the Atlanta Airport for my first ever flight to the DPRK, I was seized with fright. After much deliberation about my journey, I bought a life insurance policy for my three children for 3 million dollars. I also asked my colleague at the University of Georgia

(UGA), Professor Dean Rusk, to routinely check up on my safety. He was a professor of international law at UGA, who had formerly served the Kennedy and Johnson administrations for 9 years as Secretary of State.

Why would I visit North Korea? I don't think a sane person would have made that trip. Looking back, if I were to diagnose my own mental illness, I would say I was afflicted with an obsession with peace. Even now, memories of the cruel landscape in Manchuria, where I spent my childhood, flood my mind.

All three of my grandfather's brothers were farmers in Korea's Gyeongsang Province. In 1911, the year after Korea was forcibly annexed by the empire of Japan, they migrated to Manchuria. Because the fertile lands north of the Yalu and Tumen Rivers had already been occupied by people from Korea's Pyeongan and Hamgyeong Provinces, my relatives went further north and settled in Harbin, in China's Heilongjiang Province.[20] Soon my father joined them. My parents were married around 1931. My mother was also a Korean migrant who left her home in Gyeongsang Province. I was born in 1939, the third of three sons and three daughters. I was a very week baby, to the extent that I learned to walk after my sister, who was two years younger than me. My head was relatively large, earning me the nickname "improper fraction."

My grandfather didn't allow me to speak Chinese or Japanese at home. My father worked as a Korean language teacher at a Korean elementary school, and he also interpreted Chinese and Japanese in

---

[20] China's Heilongjiang province is written 黑龙江省 in Chinese.

the Japanese courts. The Korean elementary school I attended had only one classroom. First graders sat in the front row, second graders in the row behind them, and the third graders in the back. Shortly after entering school, I skipped grades twice and sat in the third row earlier than the rest.

Two unforgettable memories from my childhood in Manchuria are still etched in my mind. The first of those memories were the brutal massacres perpetrated during the Chinese Civil War between the Kuomintang and the Communist Party.[21] The other indelible memory was the sight of Chinese bodies piled here and there, dead from opium overdose. During the Chinese Civil War, people were not equipped with modern weapons. They slashed each other to death with knives, sickles, bamboo spears, or whatever they could lay their hands on. The scenes I witnessed taught me that human life was literally no more important than that of a fly. Although the level of cruelty was beyond what my young mind could comprehend, it became routine, normalized as the backdrop to my childhood.

The majority of Koreans in Manchuria supported Mao Zedong wholeheartedly. Most of the Koreans who migrated to Manchuria had no choice but to live as tenant farmers. Chinese landlords charged farmers 70% of their profits as rent, whereas the Japanese landlords, who emerged after Japanese colonial rule came to Manchukuo,[22] charged 85%. It was natural that Korean immigrants, subjected to severe exploitation and expropriation, harbored feelings against their

---

[21] China's Civil War is written 国共内战 in Chinese.
[22] Manchuria was called Manchukuo (满洲国 in Chinese), during Japanese colonial rule.

landowners. While Chiang Kai-shek [23] essentially represented the interests of Chinese landowners, Mao Zedong,[24] walking the socialist path, insisted on the "abolition of private property." Rather than using the term "working class," a standard in socialism, he used the term the Chinese "people." By doing so, he modified the socialism imported from the West into a "Chinese-style socialism" that particularly responded to the reality of Chinese peasants living in extreme poverty. Soon enough, Chinese peasants and Korean people in Manchuria determined to support Mao Zedong. Even among our relatives, there were quite a few strong young men who joined Mao's People's Liberation Army.

The missions carried out by Koreans in Manchuria lay the foundation for a special relationship between North Korea and China. Mao Zedong gave preferential treatment to Korean people in Manchuria. During the Korean War, China dispatched an estimated 100,000 "reinforcements to resist America and aid the DPRK." The reinforcements included many Korean people still living in Manchuria, and their purpose was to liberate their country by driving the United States from the Korean peninsula. Mao Zedong also sent his eldest son, Mao Anying,[25] to the war. On November 25, 1950, Mao Anying was killed when an American fighter dropped a napalm bomb on Daeyu District, Dongchang County, North Pyongan Province. He was buried at the Veterans Cemetery of the Chinese People's Volunteer

---

[23] Chiang Kai-shek (蔣介石) led the Kuomintang, also called the Chinese Nationalist Party.
[24] Mao Zedong (毛澤東) led the Communist Party.
[25] Mao Anying (毛岸英) was the son of Mao Zedong and a soldier who fought and died in the Korean War.

Army located in Hoechang County, South Pyongan Province. The fact that North Korea remains one of China's most important allies exemplifies the special relationship formed in the upheaval of Chinese modern history.

In an April 7, 2017 interview with Fox Business, after the US-China Summit with Xi Jinping,[26] President Trump said that he and President Xi had prioritized talks about the North Korean issue, and since the United States could not tolerate the DPRK's nuclear and missile programs, China must help the United States. In response, President Xi explained it would not be easy because of the special relationship between China and the Korean Peninsula, which has existed for thousands of years. Nevertheless, on April 21st, Trump posted on Twitter that due to China being North Korea's economic lifeline, while it may not be easy, if China wanted to solve the North Korean problem, they could. On April 22nd, China made a firm statement in response:

> If the ROK and US forces cross the 38th parallel and invade North Korea on the ground, trying to overthrow the North Korean regime, we will immediately engage in military intervention. China cannot accept the overthrow of the North Korean regime and the Unification of the Korean Peninsula by means of force. China will hold on to this Maginot Line to the end at all costs.

ROK President Park Geun-hye[27] attended Chinese Victory Day celebrations in Beijing, China on September 3, 2015. She was there

---

[26] Xi Jinping (习近平) has been President of China since 2013.
[27] Park Geun-hye (박근혜) was the 11th President of the ROK from 2013 until her impeachment in 2017.

because the South Korean government's policy toward North Korea at the time was to work through China to pressure North Korea into denuclearization. However, could the same China which would later reject Trump's proposal, accept Park Geun-hye's proposal and deny their special relationship with the DPRK? So, as a signal to China, the Park administration closed the Kaesong Industrial Complex overnight and pushed ahead to deploy the United States' missile defense system, THAAD (Terminal High Altitude Area Defense) in south Korea, despite China's vehement opposition. To this day, in 2019, the political and historical legacy of the Park government's "misjudgment" remains a heartrending tribulation on the Korean Peninsula.

Seeing the corpses of opium addicts scattered across Manchuria as a child plunged me into deep anguish. 100 years had passed since the Opium War broke out in 1840. British troops never reached Manchuria, yet nevertheless, there was opium everywhere. Opium infiltrated China so deeply that more than 27% of Chinese men were addicted to it. At that time, China had roughly 60 million people, an estimated 20 million of whom were opium addicts. From early childhood, I witnessed with my own eyes that opium was a weapon as lethal as guns and swords. Opium was a far more barbaric weapon, in that it paralyzed the spirit of a nation.

Surprisingly, I didn't know of any Korean people addicted to opium in Manchuria. No one prohibited opium, nor was there a crackdown against it. To this day, I know of no opium addiction in North Korea.

After the collapse of the Qing dynasty in 1912, the Sun Yuan[28] and Chiang Kai-shek regimes found that opium had widely been distributed. It was Mao Zedong who eradicated opium addiction from China. He declared that opium, paralyzing the national spirit of China, was a very serious weapon. Any Chinese person caught selling opium was put to death without exceptions. Mao Zedong regarded those fellow Chinese trying to get ahead through partnership with foreign powers as the lowest class, and proposed the concept of "the people"[29] as an alternative. He believed that the people, armed with the spirit of anti-foreign nationalism, should become the protagonists of a "revolutionized China." That was the context of the great work to relieve 20 million Chinese people who had been addicted to opium for the past hundred years.

As is well known, America is a country built by the British. Currently, the United States is the world's largest arms seller. The way the United States makes an astronomical profit by selling arms is similar to the way the British built its fortune by selling opium, based

◄ Chinese people, high on drugs in an "opium den." (Hankyoreh file photo)

---

[28] Sun Yuan is written 孫文 in Chinese.
[29] The People is written 人民 in Chinese.

in the degenerate spirit of capitalism. Just as opium corrupted the national spirit of consuming countries, weapons also deplete the self-defense capabilities of importing countries.

The fact that South Korea is one of the world's largest importers of US arms is problematic. In 2015, the Stockholm International Peace Research Institute (SIPRI) reported that South Korea was the number one importer of US arms over the previous five years. A major driver behind this reality is the ROK's security policy, or should I say "security paranoia,"[30] which blindly obeys the United States and regards North Korea as its "main enemy."[31] American defense companies never transfer their core technology to South Korea. Unless the ROK fundamentally reforms its current security policy, it will forever be subordinated to the US defense industry. The US' deep state, dominated by the "defense" industry, is steadily destroying the foundations of American democracy and Constitutional order.

Let us also note that pursuing security with tremendously destructive, US-made weapons actually creates more insecurity on the Korean Peninsula. Imagine South Korea goes to war with North Korea, a nuclear armed state, using the weapons they have incessantly imported from the United States. Is there any conceivable scenario where only North Koreans get killed and all South Koreans emerge unscathed? South Korea's severe addiction to weapons made-in-the-USA is no different from China's severe addiction to opium traded by

---

[30] Han S. Park's "security paranoia" is written 안보병 安保病 in Korean and Chinese/Hanja, respectively.

[31] Administrations of the ROK government who are closely aligned with US foreign policy use the term "main enemy" (주적, 主敵) to describe the ROK's relationship with the DPRK.

the British at end of the 19th Century. Korean people in Manchuria managed to maintain sufficient mental fortitude to prevent succumbing to opium addiction, however, I question whether South Korea is mentally strong enough to recognize their own addiction to US weaponry.

We should look back on how the Chinese people overcame a century of opium addiction. Abandoning the current security policies, which can never actually guarantee South Korea's safety, to create a new paradigm of security which promises both peace and prosperity for all Korean people - this should be the most important and urgent task for those of us living in this era.

Liberation, Homecoming, and Return to War

August 15, 1945! The news of the liberation was spreading fast in Harbin, China. Many Korean people living in Manchuria began to return home. Our family of eight also started home. We traveled south from Harbin and crossed the Tumen River on a Chinese merchant ferry. Then we boarded a train headed to Pyongyang. The train was jam-packed, with people even riding on the roof. When the train entered a tunnel, however, we could hear screaming from the roof. Coming out of the tunnel, there was silence, as it seemed everyone on the roof of the train had disappeared.

When we reached Pyongyang, my parents got an "enemy house"[32] that the Japanese had left behind. What a plight it would have been for a family of eight, including my grandmother, to live in a refugee camp in Pyongyang. People living in the refugee camps shared small food rations between them. However, our family who chose to stay in an enemy house, had to find ways to get food for ourselves. My mother went out daily to find work as a day laborer. My father was the first one to leave Pyongyang. He headed back to Daegu, in Gyeongsang

---

[32] Houses left by the Japanese after Korea's liberation were called enemy houses or 적산가옥, 敵産家屋 in Korean and Chinese/Hanja, respectively.

province, looking for a place for us all to live.

My brother and I went to the Pyongyang Racecourse every day to buy pureed soybean, which they used as horse feed. I went there so often that one day, one of the staff asked me how many horses I had. Not wanting to reveal the details about our family's desperate situation, I responded, "A couple of them."

Our family lived on pureed soybean porridge for over a year. I didn't know what rice tasted like. My brother and I also collected firewood from the stakes at the racetrack. We dug them up with a shovel, dried them, and used what parts hadn't rotted to build our fires.

In 1946, when I was seven years old, I returned to school, re-entering the first grade at Pyongyang Elementary School. They taught me many songs at school. All of them were songs that praised Kim Il Sung. I used to walk the streets of Pyongyang humming "the Song of General Kim Il Sung" that began with "the bloody traces of the stems of Mt. Changbai." It wasn't just me; all the kids my age were humming the same song. By 1946, his opponents had fled to China, and Kim Il Sung had already established his absolute status. North Korea stood in stark contrast to South Korea at the time, which was an absolute feeding frenzy of various political leaders.

In 1945, the United States and the Soviet Union demarcated the 38th parallel to jointly receive Japan's surrender. I heard this firsthand story from Dean Rusk, who worked on the demarcation of the 38th parallel from the American side. At that time, the Soviet Union had little

◀ Citizens marching in support of appointing Kim Il Sung as leader before the DPRK's government was established in 1948. (*Hankyoreh* file photo)

ambition for the Korean Peninsula and took a passive attitude toward trusteeship, unlike the United States. Rusk said that the Soviet Union would have accepted any military demarcation line (MDL), even if the US had connected the line from Wonsan to Pyongyang, instead of across the 38th parallel. Rusk also told me he understood the demarcation of the 38th parallel as a provisional measure. Even he never expected it to last this long. It seemed clear from the outset that the United States had a strong strategic interest in the Korean Peninsula, which may have been the reason why the US implemented a thorough trusteeship in   South Korea, unlike the Soviet Union.

To prevent the division of the Korean Peninsula, Kim Il Sung's first action was to block the general election to be held in the south on May 10, 1948. So that year, from April 19th to 24th, a special meeting, the so-called "Ssuk Island Council" (South-North meeting),[33] was held on Ssuk Island in the middle of the Daedong River in Pyongyang. Kim Gu and Kim Kyu-sik[34] from the south attended, although Syngman Rhee[35] did not. Kim Il Sung expected that the two representatives

---

[33] The "Ssuk Island Council" was called 쑥섬협의회 in Korean.

[34] Kim Gu is written 김구, and Kim Kyu-sik is written 김규식 in Korean.

[35] Syngman Rhee (이승만) became the first President of South Korea from 1948-1960.

from South Korea would be able to block the May 10th election, but they said that they could not. Kim Il Sung also failed to grasp the details of Syngman Rhee's secret connection with the United States. Eventually, the Ssuk Island Council broke down and the Korean Peninsula was divided.

My family crossed the 38th parallel in the lush summer of 1948. We chose the summer so we could easily hide in the green overgrowth while the Americans were on guard. After meticulously calculating the time it took for troops to patrol back and forth, we decided to make our crossing. As soon as the sentry disappeared from our sight, we ran for all we were worth, even my grandmother, who had difficulty moving around.

Fortunately, we all crossed the 38th parallel in one piece and managed to reach a refugee camp in Kaesong. (Kaesong is located south of the 38th parallel. Only later, when the Korean War armistice was signed, did the MDL get moved south of the 38th parallel, making Kaesong part of the North.) We stayed in the refugee camp in Kaesong for a couple of months. The sanitary conditions there were unspeakably bad, and I contracted smallpox. I remember how itchy my body was, but I was forbidden from even touching it because scratching would give me pockmarks. On rainy days, I took off my clothes and stood with my head facing the dreary sky. The raindrops somewhat relieved the itching, but I still have a pockmark on my nose.

Eventually, we all made it to Daegu and settled in Daemyeong district. My father had managed to rent a one-room house there, for our family of eight. In 1948, I began school at Namsan Elementary, redoing the first grade yet again. I was nine years old. After school, I would go to the street to sell apples and roasted chestnuts. In the midst of our hardship, our grandmother became ill with dementia. To have more space to care for Grandmother, we moved to Suchang neighborhood. Our new home had two rooms.

I wanted to transfer to a school in our new neighborhood, because it was such a long commute from Suchang to Daemyeong. But "for the honor" of Namsan Elementary school, because teachers said I was such an "intelligent and good student," they wouldn't let me go. So, I bought a used, adult-sized bicycle to make the long trip faster. The bike was so big for me that I had to put one arm over the seat, only one hand on the handlebars, and pedal with just one foot on the side, while carrying my backpack on the back of the bike. I was a weak boy, and it was such a strenuous job to make that long ride on an adult bicycle, so I was often tardy.

In the 5th grade, there was a kid in my class who was older than the rest of us. He was a bit of a bully. He would coerce his classmates to open their lunch boxes each day and take the most delicious food. One time, he took a boiled egg from my lunch box. In winter, when we put our lunch boxes on the stove to keep it warm, he would put his own lunch box closest to the heat.

I hated him so much, but I didn't dare fight him head-on because I knew I was too weak. No one in my class dared to cross him. So, I put my brain to work. For a few days, I followed him after school to learn his routine. I discovered the place along the way where his friends turned off, and he continued alone. One day I hid near that place with a baseball bat in hand. The moment he walked past me, I ambushed him, striking the back of his head with the bat. He stumbled and fell with a thud. I ran home as fast as my legs would carry me, not once looking back. I stared at the ceiling all night, unable to sleep, wondering what I would do if he had died.

When I went to school the next day, he was there. He was actually laughing, telling his friends about getting hit in the head the day before. I couldn't have been more relieved to see him in the classroom like that. From that day forward, I treated him nicely. I often gave him my boiled eggs. I even gave him the prized camera I treasured. The strong guy began protecting me, the weakling of the class. We ended up becoming close friends, but in the back of my mind, I always regretted what I had done to him.

Years passed. As a senior in high school, I confessed to him that I was the one who had struck him in the back of the head. He didn't believe me. He looked me in the face and insisted that there was no way it could have been me. He was grinning in his insistence, so I just laughed. That's how "the case of the baseball bat ambush" ended.

When I look back on my elementary school years, the most unforgettable element of all was, of course, the Korean War. The war erupted when I was in the third grade. Because I had been so terrified by the violence of the Chinese Civil War in Manchuria, returning home after Liberation meant finding a safe haven, free from war. But what awaited us in my hometown was more violence. The definitive element of the Korean War was the bombing sprees of US fighter planes. US bombs indiscriminately killed everything in sight. These weapons were on a whole different dimension from the primitive weapons used in the Chinese Civil War.

I remember cows startled by the bombs, how they ran around on the roadside; people fleeing the bombardments of fighter jets, wretchedly falling to the ground; corpses strewn about here and there; families holding each other, wailing over the dead bodies of their loved ones. As a child I could not escape these images reflected in my vision over and over. That led me to decide, *I will devote myself to preventing war as long as I live.* I do not expect to ever recover from this longing for peace that has afflicted me since childhood.

The number of American casualties in the Korean War was relatively small, because the US military focused on an air force strategy. However, the Korean War was the first war in American history that America couldn't win. The US wanted to cover up that fact. So, they didn't even call it a war, instead, calling it the "Korean Conflict." Only after their defeat in Vietnam did the United States officially begin to use the term "Korean War."

What can we possibly learn from the war? So far, researchers have mainly studied the origin or cause of its outbreak. They usually visit the Library of Congress, or some other treasure trove of historical documents, and make lots of photocopies. Then, they read, interpret the material, and publish something on their Korean War studies, usually about as thick as a wooden pillow. The width of a book is generally regarded as a criterion for evaluating the writer's academic achievement. So, in many cases, authors of these thick books replete with references are given academic awards.

Although I have read countless such books, I have yet to discover the true origin or cause of the Korean War. In order to determine a cause, it is necessary to *explain* the outbreak according to the social sciences' strict principles of causation. The countless Korean War research papers that I have come across offer nothing more than a *description* of the outbreak of the Korean War by combining vast amounts of historical material in one way or another. One cannot determine the cause through description. If different researchers use the same data, they may interpret it in another way, drawing different conclusions.

William Dray, a historical philosopher, once reflected that despite over a hundred years of tremendous effort to determine the cause of the American Civil War, the debate has not ended. Similarly, people still debate the cause of the Cold War. These debates continue due to researchers crude research methods. Nevertheless, they impute the crudely identified *cause* of the Korean War to the DPRK and condemn it. Or, they impute the cause to South Korea and condemn it. Or, they impute it to the Soviet Union or the United States and condemn the respective nation, becoming a source of endlessly induced hatred and hostility on the Korean Peninsula.

What we really need to learn from the Korean War is the fact that we have yet to break free from the fetters that the war inflicted on us. The Division that was passed on from the Korean War; the extreme hostility between the two Koreas; the increasing polarization within the South, so often blamed on the North; the as-yet-unatoned-for genocide of civilians during the Korean War; the unresolved separation of families; the persistent problem of being guilty by association with anyone branded a "commie"—these have all left our collective consciousness and soul inadvertently brainwashed into a "culture of division." Our academic agility will have to be devoted to the work of facing up to, analyzing, and dismantling these problems.

War Orphans and Civilian Massacre

During my elementary and middle school years, I had two unforgettable experiences. Looking back, I realize they have dominated my life ever since. One of them was my time with Kim Tae-won, a friend, orphaned by the war. The other was seeing my father come home half-dead, after being tortured at the police station.

▲ Author's family photo with his father (Park Yeong-seok) and mother (Lee Dong-soo) seated in the front center, three sons and three daughters, eldest brother-in-law, nieces and nephews, taken circa 1957/1958. The author is in the back row, on the far right. (Photo courtesy of Han shik Park)

Kim Tae-won was born in North Korea as a son of a doctor, but he lost both of his parents in the US bombings during the war. He became a war orphan overnight. An American soldier found him crying alone on the street and later placed him in an American-run orphanage, called the Convent of St. Paul of Chartres. It was in Daegu, near Namsan Elementary School, which I attended.

After Kim Tae-won and I became friends, I often went to the orphanage where he lived. Most of the caregivers were nuns, and they

◀ 400 inmates preparing to make kimchi during the Korean War at the White Lily Orphanage, St. Paul of Chartes Convent in Daegu. (Photo from St. Paul of Chartes Convent's website)

looked after the orphans with all their heart. Even to a child's eyes, though, the orphans were living in destitute surroundings. Seeing orphans squatting and eating made me feel such profound pity for them that I decided to become a social worker in the future. Tae-won and I enrolled in Gyeongbuk Middle School together. Because I was so delicately built, I had to be carried on a stretcher to enter the entrance examination hall, whereas Tae-won was always big and hearty. We became so close that we talked about our dreams, which included walking together on America's Broadway when we grew up.

During the war, a certain Professor Lee from Kyungpook National University was sent to teach math classes at Kyungpook Middle School. As class leader, each time we had morning assembly in the school yard, I stood in front of the class with my back to the principal. One day, Professor Lee included, "Guess the principal's height," on our exam. Naturally, I couldn't guess the answer. Because I always got a perfect score, I acutely felt the injustice of that question. So I said as much to the professor, "I don't think the question is fair. Can you guess my height?"

As soon as I finished speaking, the professor began to beat me like a madman. Soon, I was covered in blood, and I felt like I was going to die. Still furious, the professor shouted, "Who is his best friend?"

Kim Tae-won raised his hand without hesitation and came forward. Tae-won was beaten ruthlessly, too. Although he was much more muscular than me, he couldn't hold out for long and collapsed.

After graduating from high school, Tae-won enlisted in the Air Force. Shortly thereafter, we learned he had died. We heard various rumors about how he died, but none were ever verified. My dear friend's death brought me sorrow beyond words. I was bitter, so resentful of the war that stole the life of such a smart and capable young man.

I love singing so much that I have a karaoke room in my house. Whenever I miss Tae-won, I sing Cho Yong-pil's song, "My Friend," even if I can't make it all the way through, due to the lump in my throat and the tears pouring down my cheeks.

The Korean War also stole the lives of so many noncombatants. The Association for Bereaved Families of the Korean War estimates that 1 million civilians were slaughtered. I particularly pay attention to the massacres of civilians by the US and South Korean military, such as the Yeo-Sun Incident, the Jeju April 3rd Incident, the National Bodo League Massacre,[36] and the Geochang Massacre, among others. Why on earth did the US and South Korean forces kill civilians on such a large scale—not even in enemy territory, but on their own side of the division? Korean social scientists are inevitably tasked with explaining, not simply describing, the civilian massacres repeatedly

---

[36] National Bodo League is written 국민보도연맹, 國民保導聯盟 in Korean and Chinese/Hanja, respectively.

perpetrated in modern Korean history.

US and South Korean military excuse civilian massacres through "red-baiting," alleging the civilians were "reds" or "commies," derogatory terms meaning Communists. When a Communist party member, or any member of the People's Army, hiding in the mountains came by night to a nearby village to ask for food, the villagers had no choice but to give it to them, for their own survival. However, then the US and South Korean military would massacre those villagers, denouncing all of them as "collaborators."

◀ A scene from *Red Room* (레드룸), a documentary about the Bodo League Massacre.

Such massacres of civilians were unprecedented in the history of world warfare. Even during the Chinese Civil War, which I experienced firsthand in Manchuria, Chiang Kai-shek's Kuomintang Army never massacred Chinese civilians for providing food to Mao Zedong's People's Revolutionary Army, and vice versa. Neither side committed mass killing of civilians.

I believe there are three factors which can explain the massacres of civilians perpetrated by the US and South Korean military during the Korean War. The most important factor is found in Harry Truman's Christian view of good and evil. In the Christian view of good and evil, the Communists were demonized for denying God. Like the indigenous Americans needed to be wiped out to conform with the Puritan understanding of good and evil, so Communists had to be killed in the name of God.

The second factor was the Japanese Governor-General of Korea. After Japanese surrender to the Americans, John Reed Hodge, Truman's commander of the US military government in Korea, chose to reinstate the Japanese Governor-General to carry out the US military administration of Korea. Americans didn't trust the Committee for Preparation of Korean Independence that had been prepared by Lyuh Woon-hyung,[37] because they thought it was made up of "commies."

The third factor was Syngman Rhee. His power base was centered in the United States. Because of his weak power base in South Korea, Rhee learned how the Japanese had maintained control of Koreans. The Japanese Governor-General of Korea considered Koreans "bad seeds," who were unaffected by torture and pain. Therefore, they believed the only way to control them was by killing insubordinate Koreans to make an example of them.

From the viewpoint of the Truman administration and the US military government in Korea, if Koreans, a race similar to indigenous Americans, had "turned red" (gone Communist), they had become "evil" and could never be saved. Syngman Rhee actively responded to the US military government interests by boldly practicing the

---

[37] To transition Korean people to self-rule after liberation from Japan, Lyuh Woon-hyung (여운형) organized the Committee for Preparation of Korean Independence (조선건국준비위원회) which established people's committees throughout the country.

control methods he learned from the Japanese Governor-General of Korea.

As the Korean War was intensifying and the slaughter of innocent civilians spread across the country, my father was red-baited as a Communist. During the Japanese colonial era, he had immigrated to Harbin, China from Cheongdo, North Gyeongsang Province. After liberation, he returned to Korea through Pyongyang and settled in Daegu. His life history seemed to match the narrative of a Communist, so he was accused.

One day, the police arrested my father, took him to the station, and tortured him. My mother and older sister couldn't do anything but pace at home, anxiously waiting for my father's return. That evening, a police car stopped in front of our house. They hurled my father from the car like discarded luggage. He lay in the yard, his body covered in blood. He looked like a corpse.

I was in a state of shock. When I asked the elders around me why my father had been tortured, they all replied that it was because he had no "strings to pull." When I asked how I could get such "strings," they advised me to become a member of the National Assembly. When I asked how to do that, they told me I would need to become a good orator.

The need to have "strings" was the moment I changed my dream from becoming a social worker to becoming a politician. So, in middle school, I began to work on my public speaking. I went to the mountain first thing each morning to practice. I also listened to addresses by lawmakers many times, meticulously studying their speeches and oration styles. Syngman Rhee's speech sounded the worst. His Korean was sparse, to say the least, making him sound like a foreigner speaking in Korean. I participated in many speech contests and won a number of prizes. I donated all the prize money to newspaper companies. Before filling up my hungry stomach, I thought about my friend Tae-won. I hoped that my new skills would be of use to people in need just like him.

My oratorical skills improved by leaps and bounds, and I earned the nickname "King of Eloquence" in Daegu. Later, when a scholar named Yang Ho-min[38] ran for the National Assembly, I was invited to give speeches endorsing him. Other people also offered me opportunities to give speeches in public. I always wrote my own manuscripts, mainly about preventing war and maintaining peace at all times. I told my audiences that the weapon of single-heartedness was more terrifying than the atomic bomb. Although I was only starting middle school and barely 4 foot 3 inches, I was so obsessed with peace that I tackled such heavy subjects as war and peace at public oratory events.

▲ The author, as a 3rd grade student at Gyeongbuk Middle School, speaking on the theme of "peace" at Daegu Station plaza. (Photo courtesy of Han Shik Park)

---

[38] Yang Ho-min is written 양호민 in Korean.

In 1975, while teaching at the UGA, I received an urgent call that my father was critically ill. I immediately returned to Korea. I sat by his side and talked with him at length over the course of three days. Our conversation seemed to help him, because his condition temporarily improved. My father had lived as part of a separated family his whole life, and he asked me to find his grandfather in Manchuria. Then, he urged me not to return to South Korea before Unification, but to stay in the United States and devote myself to Unification. My father's words became his last will and testament to me, a milestone that set my life on a course of concern for the issues of separated families and work toward peace and Unification. Although I received a few good job offers to come to South Korea, I stayed in the United States.

My father suffered in fear his whole life long. He could never get a job; he had no choice but to earn his living by doing small jobs at home. My mother did the same, living off of what she could earn sewing. My father never told me why he was tortured at the police station, and too late, I came to understand the intentions he carried so deeply in his thoughts. His final wish that I not return to South Korea before unification was connected to his desire to protect his children from the stigma of being red-baited a "commie's kid." When I understood this, my heart sank.

Humanity sometimes lays the blame for certain misdeeds on the victim of the crime, something called "victim blaming." A prime example is the case of General Chun Doo-hwan.[39] After killing thousands of Gwangju citizens in May 1980, he framed the victims as a "communist mob" and portrayed himself as a patriot defending the nation from Communists, although his own government perpetrated the massacre. Such deceptions have circulated widely in our society for more than 40 years. Just like my father, millions of the bereaved who survived civilian killings in South Korea have lived, are living, and will continue to live lives fraught with resentment and terror. How could such an indescribable deception dominate our thinking for so long and with such intensity?

I believe scholars should play their part at this point—to explain scientifically the most painful realities of our time and to consistently guide the way out of them. I believe these are two prime reasons for scholarship.

---

[39] General Chun Doo-hwan (전두환) was an ROK military leader who took power by coup in 1979 and went on to become South Korea's fifth President from 1980-1988.

Meeting my Life Partner and Lifelong Mentor

During high school, I formed deep, lifelong bonds with two people. I met my wife, who became my constant companion through my life's odyssey. I also met Seo Young-hoon, who has been a constant source of inspiration. Thanks to him, I came to understand the harsh conditions under which the *Zainichi* Koreans[40] live, and I was able to meet Ham Seok-heon,[41] my lifelong spiritual mentor.

My wife, Juhn Seong-won, was the sister of Juhn Seong-gyun, a medical student at Kyungpook National University and advisor to my high school's YMCA club ("HiY") of which I was a member since my freshman year in 1956. Seong-gyun was five or six years older than me. As I became friends with Seong-gyun, often visiting his home, his sister, Seong-won, caught my eye.

Juhn Seong-gyun's father, my eventual father-in-law, Juhn Ho-yeol, was the doctor who led Gwangje Hospital in Daegu. Both father and son admired and sought to follow the example of Albert Schweitzer. My father-in-law visited villages with no doctors, driving a

---

[40] *Zainichi* (재일동포, 在日韓人) is a Japanese term for Korean people living in Japan.
[41] Ham Seok-heon (함석헌, also romanized "Ham Sok Hon") was a scholar and voice for human rights and nonviolence in Korea. He is sometimes called the "Gandhi of Korea."

motorcycle made-in-Germany with a sidecar full of medicine. In the mid-1950s, after the War, Korean society was essentially a gigantic hospital ward, overflowing with all kinds of diseases. Because I was already afflicted with a terminal longing for peace, he seemed even more respectable in my eyes. I saw him as the "Korean Schweitzer." He also sincerely cared about me and used to incessantly share with me his thoughts on the meaning of life. Seong-gyun, who later became a professor of medicine at the University of Minnesota, followed a similar path as his father, with the same spirit. He founded the "Reverence for Life Club" in 1958, which is still actively carrying on the spirit of Dr. Schweitzer. In 2017, Juhn Seong-gyun was awarded the Seo Jae-pil Medical Award.

Born as an only son, my father-in-law had 13 children. He dreamed of opening a general hospital and encouraged most of his children to study medicine. After graduating from Gyeongbuk Girls 'High School, this dream of his greatly influenced my future wife's decision to enter Pharmacy school at Ewha Women's University in 1959. That same year, I entered the Department of Political Science at Seoul National University.

Seong-won liked sports, and rode a bicycle very well. Thanks to my early days commuting to school by bicycle, my biking skills were not far behind her. In college, we often went on biking dates. Seong-won started biking from Sinchon, and I, from Dongsung-dong, and we met in Jongno. I can still vividly remember the image of Seong-won approaching me from afar, with the brightest smile I've ever seen. Together, we headed straight for Taereung. Seongwon preferred to read, and I preferred to think. We talked and talked about philosophy, religion, art, life, and love. We also talked about our dream of studying abroad in the United States. In 1964, we engraved a super-mathematical formula, "$1+1=1$," on our engagement rings and embarked on our life's odyssey together as one.

▲ Engagement ceremony in Daegu in 1964, before moving abroad for studies. (Photo courtesy of Han Shik Park)

During middle and high school, I was the head of our local Youth Red Cross. From an early age, I was attracted to the humanitarianism of Henri Dunant, the founder of the Red Cross, who helped the wounded on the battlefield without discrimination. At that time, Lee Beom-seok was the head of the South Korean Red Cross, and Seo Young-hoon was the head of the Youth Red Cross. In the summer, the Youth Red Cross held a "Summer Cadres Training" by the Han River. One of the trainings 'regular programs was an oratory contest, and I once won first place in that contest with my speech entitled "The Bomb of Single-hearted Unity."

Thanks to my speech, I became friends with Seo Young-hoon. He was well educated in the fields of religion, faith, philosophy, etc. I was so interested in religious studies and philosophy that I once thought about changing my major to religious philosophy, although I finally settled on studying politics. I really enjoyed listening to him and asking him questions. I wanted us to be good friends, and to follow him for the rest of my life.

◀ Seo Young-hoon lectures during a summer class for youth Red Cross officers in 1964. Seo was active since the early days of the Korean Red Cross in 1953 and served as the president from 2000 to 2003. (Photo courtesy of the Youth Red Cross)

Japan. In order to participate, I had to take an English test. Since I enjoyed studying English, I passed the test without any problem and was selected as a delegate to the conference. I later found out that among the five male and five female students who had been selected for the Korean delegation, eight of us were from Seoul, one from Incheon, and then me, the only delegate from Daegu.

We headed to Japan under Seo Young-hoon's guidance in 1956, when I was a freshman at Gyeongbuk High School. I was so excited and happy to participate in an international conference. It was my first experience flying on an airplane. I must have looked like a show-off wearing my crew cut and sunglasses at Yeouido Airport in Seoul. My mother traveled all the way from Daegu to send me off.

◀ The author and his mother (Lee Dong-soo) at the airport, right before leaving for Japan to participate in the International Youth Red Cross Leadership Workshop. (Photo courtesy of Han-shik Park)

◀ During the International Youth Red Cross Leadership Workshop, Han Shik Park had a one-on-one discussion with the U.S. representative (right) thanks to his excellent English skills. (Photo courtesy of the Youth Red Cross)

Joy was not the only emotion that set my heart fluttering as we departed for Japan. Traveling reminded me of the Korean-Chinese expatriates in far-away Manchuria. I grew up witnessing the harsh realities of life that my parents and grandparents faced there. I still had heart-rending memories from my childhood in Manchuria, so questions filled my mind. How many overseas Koreans live in Japan? What kind of life do they live?

After the International Youth Red Cross Conference in Tokyo, I contacted Korea University in Japan. I said I wanted to know how Koreans in Japan lived. Then, an old gentleman from the *Chongryon*[42] came to visit me in person. He was very friendly, buying me a delicious meal along with some stamps as a souvenir. He also explained in detail the current situation of Korea University and the Korean residents in Japan.

The more I got to know about the living conditions of the *Zainichi*, the more I came to realize that the situation of the Korean-Chinese living in China was better. China allows a considerable degree of autonomy for Korean-Chinese. There are two major paths open to the children of Korean-Chinese. One path is to get into one of the prestigious universities classified as China's "key universities" to advance into the elite of Chinese society. Another path is to study at Yanbian University and become an elite Korean-Chinese. However, the *Zainichi* didn't have such autonomy in Japanese society. Japan effectively treats the *Zainichi* as lower-class citizens.

After liberation, the *Zainichi* felt the need to teach their children the language and history of their home country. They intended to establish a school for Koreans to preserve their national identity. However, progress came to a halt due to Japanese non-cooperation and obstruction. Kim Il Sung, a staunch nationalist, gave his full support to the education programs of the *Zainichi* beginning in 1955. The DPRK built schools for the Koreans in Japan and provided all

---

[42] *Chongryon* (조총련, 在日朝鮮人總聯盟) stands for the General Association of Korean Residents in Japan.

school supplies free of charge.

Therefore, even now, Koreans in Japan have tremendous respect and gratitude for Kim Il Sung. This is the reason why Korean schools in Japan regularly send their students on field trips to North Korea. Also, *Zainichi* operating pachinko parlors and bulgogi restaurants in Japan regularly remit cash they earn to the DPRK. For its part, the DPRK has a deep appreciation for the way the *Zainichi* return the favor.

◄ Zainichi Koreans protested in 1948, when Japanese authorities issued an order to shut down Korean schools, including Korean language schools established right after liberation. (Photo courtesy of the Korean Residents' Archives)

Rhee Syngman rejected the *Zainichi* who received assistance from Kim Il Sung's regime. Far from helping his countrymen who were struggling in their painful existence in Japan, Rhee was extremely hostile to them, accusing them of being supported by Kim Il Sung. In the same way he branded the bereaved families of murdered South Korean civilians as "commies" or "reds" after the Korean War, he extended his red-baiting policy towards the *Zainichi*. In short, the *Zainichi* Koreans, victims of Japanese imperialism, have once again fallen prey to an unjust system, this time in the name of the Korean Peninsula's fierce inter-Korean "war of legitimacy," a systemic competition in which the ROK and DPRK each claim that they are the only legitimate government on the Peninsula.

Our countrymen in Japan have lived and are living a difficult life, resisting this inter-Korean legitimacy war. There are about 30,000 Koreans classified as *Joseonjeok*, a temporary nationality assigned to Koreans in Japan by the US military government in 1947.[43] There remains a portion of *Zainichi* who still retain their *Joseonjeok* status, because they think that choosing either South or North Korean nationality would be the same as accepting the Division of their country as a *fait accompli*. It seems to me that these Koreans are the ones who most ardently aspire to the Unification of the two Koreas. The only way to comfort their troubled souls is to reunify Korea as soon as possible.

When I turn my eyes to the Korean diaspora in the United States, where I live, my heart sinks more deeply. A few years ago, the Korean American National Coordinating Council (KANCC) based in New York and the New York chapter of the Peaceful Unification Advisory Council (PUAC NY) asked me to give them a lecture around the same time. KANCC is an organization on friendly terms with the DPRK, whereas PUAC NY is one that was established by the ROK government. At the time I was invited to share, the *zeitgeist* on the Korean Peninsula was reconciliation. Inter-Korean summits were being held one after another in Panmunjom. I thought that it would be good if I could encourage that spirit on the grassroots level. Noting that the KANCC and PUAC NY were both headquartered in New

---

[43] *Joseonjok* is written 조선족, 朝鮮籍 in Korean and Chinese/Hanja, respectively, and roughly means "Joseon Domicile" or "from Korea."

York, I made the condition that I would take the podium if the two organizations could agree to jointly host my lecture. Representatives of both groups agreed to that proposal, but I heard nothing more from either of them since then. The inter-Korean legitimacy war and the political conflict in South Korea is present in the community of 2.5 million Korean Americans, too.

PUAC was founded in 1981 by the Chun Doo-hwan's government as an organization opposing the Korean Workers 'Party (KWP). However, the characteristics of the PUAC and the KWP are completely different. This is because the KWP is the organization forming the basis of the DPRK's socialist system, whereas the PUAC is merely an advisory body to the ROK's President. The PUAC was established without their leadership knowing exactly the nature of the KWP. In the end, the PUAC has grown into an institutional foundation leading the inter-Korean legitimacy war in the international community. However, in order to pave the way for peace and the unification on the Korean Peninsula, we must theoretically dismantle the conceptual framework of the inter-Korean legitimacy war and break all practices of coercive inter-Korean system competition that exist within this framework.

Wandering in the Sea of Ideology

My entire family, cramped into a room in Namsan-dong, Daegu, held their breath and listened to the radio. The announcer's roaring voice slowly read through a list of 400 numbers. We almost stopped breathing. Suddenly, all my family shouted, "Hurray!" Even my soft-spoken father, who rarely expressed his feelings, spoke up in a low voice, smiling, "Go get a bottle of *makgeolli*."[44]

My examination number had just been announced on the radio. In those days, Seoul National University's admission numbers were broadcast on the radio. Even now, I can't forget the exhilarated look on my father's face.

However, after beginning my studies at the Department of Political Science at Seoul National University in 1959, my college life could be described as a time of spiritual wandering. I began with high expectations, only to feel lost and disheartened after entering the classroom the first day of the semester, because most of the lecture consisted of adjuring students to simply memorize details of various political systems.

I wanted to *reason* politically. I was interested in the complex thought processes that gave birth to specific political systems. I could

---

[44] *Makgeolli* is Korean rice wine.

not find myself interested at all in lectures that simply required us to memorize the outcome - which were the political systems - skipping the entire political reasoning process.

Leaving the Political Science classroom behind, I began to wander about a wider world. I began to ask philosophical questions. What is the ultimate essence of Science? This question I repeated to myself redirected my steps to the Philosophy lecture hall, where I encountered a lecture that caught my attention. It was a Philosophy lecture by Professor Park Jong-hong. I was particularly fascinated by his teaching on dialectic reasoning.

Dialectic reasoning sees the relationship between thesis and antithesis as interdependent, rather than mutually exclusive. Therefore, it emphasizes a paradox, that the essence of thesis is antithesis, and vice versa. It was similar to the ancient Eastern logic of Yin and Yang, in that Yin is impregnated with Yang, and vice versa. According to the paradox of the dialectic, the essence of freedom, as emphasized in capitalism, lay in equality, as emphasized in socialism, and conversely, the essence of equality lay in freedom. In the same vein, wouldn't it be true that the essence of South Korea is in the North, and the essence of North Korea is in the South? I have come to believe there is truth in the paradox of the dialectic.

I continued to study dialectics, years later when I went to the United States. When I was in Professor Park's classroom, I didn't understand from where the driving force for the transition from thesis to antithesis came. I found out, only after studying Western dialectical reasoning in the United States, that the driving force is the "internal contradiction." I attentively followed the logic that thesis would transition to antithesis in the process of the thesis 'overcoming its own internal contradiction. Capitalism, for example, would suffer the internal contradictions through which distributional justice is disrupted as the gap between rich and poor widens. Then, in the process of overcoming those internal contradictions, the capitalist system necessarily converts itself to socialism, based on classlessness and equal distribution. Before long, I was captivated by the logic of dialectical materialism.

The dialectic that I studied during my University years became the intellectual foundation for the "Dialectical Unification Theory" that I later developed. I believe that the ROK and DPRK are paradoxical systems, impregnated in each other, and thus, can be unified dialectically while overcoming their own internal contradictions, respectively.

Another subject that fascinated me as I explored the philosophy classrooms was the philosophy of religion. I was deeply moved, in particular, by the dialectical theologian Reinhold Niebuhr's writings, such as *Moral Man and Immoral Society: A Study in Ethics and Politics* and *The Children of Light and the Children of Darkness*. I even thought about changing my major to Comparative Philosophy of Religion for quite a while.

My interest in religious philosophy once led me to discover and become curious about the Unification Church near Seoul National University. How would they interpret the Bible? I went to the Unification Church every morning and listened to Sun Myung

Moon's[45] sermons. Although the Unification Church was widely regarded as heretical, I couldn't have cared less.

What caught my attention was the framework of the Unification Church's "principle," which was a unique blend of familism and nationalism. The familistic nature of the Unification Church appealed to Western society where families had disintegrated. Later, while studying Juche ideology, I discovered that its basic framework was also made up of familism and nationalism. From my perspective, there was an "elective affinity" between the principle of the Unification Church and the *Juche* ideology.

Meanwhile, I became friends with a Mennonite missionary from the United States. Mennonites try to thoroughly incorporate anti-war, pacifism into their daily lives, abiding by the conscientious objection to military service, for instance. In the United States, where the law at the time mandated conscription into the military, Mennonites were exempted from military service if they volunteered abroad during the period of their military service. When I came in contact with Mennonites, I noticed the way they pursued peace through a lifestyle of thorough separation of politics and religion.

The ultimate reason that Europe fell into glut of religious wars for more than a century following the Reformation was because politics and religion were too closely interconnected. Europe was transformed into a sea of blood in the process using political and physical coercion to force one's religious belief on others. After over 100 years of

---

[45] Sun Myung Moon (문선명) was a Korean religious leader and founder of the Unification Church.

religious warfare, Europe came to realize that a peaceful future was only possible by separating politics and religion.

However, many politicians in South Korea conduct politics according to their Christian beliefs these days, and quite a number of spiritual leaders defend their preferred politicians religiously before their congregations. ROK politics is returning to the period of European religious warfare in the 17th century. Rather than becoming a "promised land," such political regression will degenerate the Korean Peninsula into a "land of violence" as it did in Europe a few centuries ago. Have we completely forgotten that under the Christian view of good versus evil, Harry Truman, the Northwest Youth Corps, and others slaughtered as many as 1 million civilians after the Korean War?

▲ Hankyoreh file photo

My warmest memory, enriching my college days, was attending Kyungdong Church with Seong-won for four years. Listening to Pastor Kang Won-yong's [46] sermons, I learned two things; one was that peace and unification were impossible without dialogue, and the other was that intellectual engagement in our social reality was important.

According to Pastor Kang Won-yong's teaching, I established my

---

[46] Pastor Kang Won-yong's name is written 강원용 in Korean.

own dialogue theory. I consider the essence of dialogue as an exchange of values. If steadily accumulated, the exchange of values opens up the horizon for mutual understanding. As mutual understanding is achieved, a new community is developed where differences can coexist. Many people wonder what I did when I went to North Korea. The answer I can give them is that, in line with my own dialogue theory, I had conversations with as many people as possible there. I wanted to understand the DPRK, and I did so based on pure academic interest.

I spent my lifetime studying and teaching mainstream American social science to my students. In the process, however, I found that mainstream social science in the United States was incapable of explaining real problems. After diagnosing such ills philosophically, I tried to establish a new social science theory. Published in 2017, the 500-page book entitled *Globalization: Blessing or Curse?* is a compilation of my efforts in that direction. My rationale in this book was that social science exists to solve the prevailing problems of the day, and to provide the detailed academic reasoning necessary to make such solutions feasible. All of my North Korean studies and comments to the press were based on the social science theory that I constructed.

Another thing I will never forget during college was getting to know Ham Seok-heon.[47] One day, I visited Seo Young-hoon's house, and Mr. Ham was there. If I remember correctly, they were having an

---

[47] Ham Seok-heon (함석헌, also romanized "Ham Sok Hon") was a scholar and voice for human rights and nonviolence in Korea. He is sometimes called the "Gandhi of Korea."

editorial meeting for the publication *Sasang Gye*[48] with Jang Jun-ha and others. In those days, Mr. Ham gave weekly lectures at the Daesung Building in Myeong-dong where the Young Korean Academy's[49] office was located. I rarely missed those lectures, and I fell in love with his ideas. I visited Mr. Ham's house, too, and his farm[50] in Cheonan. Watching him crawling around on the floor with his grandchildren on his back, I came to know him as a very ordinary, down-to-earth person.

One day, I followed Mr. Ham as he worked his farm with a cow-drawn walking plow. I asked him a question about which I had been wondering. "You have always taught us how to live. I would also like to ask you how we should die."

He answered right away, "The best death would be if I fell down dead now, in the middle of my work in this field."

Ham's answer left me in deep contemplation for quite a while.

The biggest lesson I learned from my relationship with Mr. Ham was a "religious openness" that infinitely expands the scope of Christian belief. Mr. Ham expressed his own religious conversion in this way:

> [I] thought that Christianity was the only true religion, and that Christianity was found only in the Bible... [But]

---

[48] *Sasang Gye* (사상계, 思想界) was a monthly, current affairs magazine published from 1953-1970.

[49] The Young Korean Academy (흥사단, 興士團) was an organization established by Ahn Chang Ho in 1913, after Korea was colonised by the Japanese, to raise up moral, democratic leaders for the future.

[50] Ham Seok-Heon's farm was called Ssi-Al Farm (씨알농장).

the fruit of all religions (truth) is one... Due to the changing times, we need to broaden our Christian faith... It is a narrow ideology that only asserts itself while denying others... The thought that salvation exists only in Christianity is a limited one. Buddhism, Hinduism, and Confucianism are all high beliefs. As I have come to see it, Christianity is not the only ideology that works in this day and age.

In order to understand Ham's religious openness rightly, imagine different hiking trails that reach the highest peak of a mountain. The mountain peak symbolizes religious truth, and the various hiking trails symbolize various religions such as Christianity, Buddhism, and Confucianism. We can climb to the mountain peak using different hiking trails. Although varied, they all meet together at the peak of the mountain. There is one shared view from the mountain peak. In other words, although the religious means are different, in the end, each means leads to one religious truth.

One case that dramatically symbolizes Mr. Ham's religious openness was his 1950's publication *Korean History from a Biblical Perspective* which was republished several years later under the revised title, *Korean History from the Perspective of Meaning.*[51] Mr. Ham explained his reason as follows:

> If there is a heaven, wouldn't it be a place we all go together! ...What will save the righteous, sinners, civilized and barbarians all together? ...So, I used the word meaning. It is okay if you don't believe in God

---

[51] *Korean History from the Perspective of Meaning* was entitled 뜻으로 본 한국역사 in Korean. *Ddeut* (뜻) is a Korean word that simultaneously conveys "meaning" or "will."

because you can't, but belief is not possible without meaning... Even if you lose, having meaning is enough, and if you do not have meaning, winning is nothing. That's why I used the word meaning. Meaning is truly everyone's religion.

Mr. Ham understood the meaning of Korean history as a "history of hardship." He found meaning in the suffering itself:

> The history of suffering appears on its own. The self is its own reason. The self (自) is the reason (由). Freedom (自由) means arising from oneself. Therefore, suffering (고苦는) is the fundamental principle of life. Freedom is reached through suffering.

Although I accepted Ham's paradox of suffering, that "we reach freedom through suffering," I disagreed that such suffering should reach the extent of undermining human dignity. Therefore, rather than finding meaning in suffering itself, I thought we should find it in overcoming what makes us suffer. When I reflect on Korean history with this in mind, Korean people seem like human "bobo dolls," always bouncing back. Five thousand years of Korean history tells the story of how Korean people never yielded to any foreign force for long.

April 19th and the People's Democracy Movement

The April 19th Movement broke out in 1960, when I was a sophomore in college. I helped with the English translation of various statements prepared by the Seoul National University's College of Liberal Arts and Sciences. I marched on the front line of the protesters on the Dongsung-dong campus. Our ranks swelled into a throng before we swarmed the school gate, shouting, "Down with the government of Syngman Rhee!"

As soon as we began rushing the gate, the riot police, who were standing in front of us, swung their bats ruthlessly and pressed down on the protesters. My arm was broken as I raised it to shield myself from the police blows. From that time, I could no longer play the violin, which I used to enjoy. But in the heat of the moment, I continued protesting, not even recognizing the pain in my arm.

As we moved out of Dongsung-dong and headed toward Jongno, we met Korea University students moving in from Dongdaemun. We joined them and flocked to Gyeongmudae[52]. At Gyeongmudae, I also stood on the front line of the demonstrators as we pushed a culvert ahead of us to advance. The police opened fire. All around me, my

---

[52] South Korea's Presidential residence at the time

classmates starting falling in their tracks.

Because I was short enough to hide behind the culvert, I avoided being shot. But, in that field of death, I couldn't keep my mind clear. After some time, I came to my senses and found myself lying in the grass, having somehow crossed over the high mud wall in Hyoja-dong. I had no memory of how I got over the wall. It appeared I was able to display supernatural strength in that life threatening situation.

After getting up, I removed and discarded my university uniform, because the police were indiscriminately arresting any students in school uniforms. (Later, when my uniform and name badge were found, Seoul National University assumed I was dead.) Only when I

▲ Around 9 am on April 19, 1960, students from Seoul National University's college of liberal arts led some 3,000 of their fellow students from the colleges of law, fine arts, pharmacy, medicine, veterinary science, and dentistry in breaking through police lines to charge the meeting hall on Taepyeong-ro. (Photo courtesy of the April 19 Revolution Memorial Library)

started walking helplessly towards the house where I stayed did I realize that my broken arm was swollen and throbbing. I started to feel pain.

Ham Seok-heon understood the meaning of Korean history as a history of suffering. But, as I said earlier, I think we should rather find the meaning in the act of overcoming difficulties that cause suffering. In my view, April 19th was a typical example in modern history of realizing meaning by overcoming hardships.

April 19th is usually understood as a revolution. But, it was neither a workers 'revolution from below, nor was it a revolution from above by military coup. In my view, April 19th was a revolution from the side led by the people, or *minjung*.[53]

It is not easy to accurately define this concept of *minjung*. I think it could be considered similar to what is embodied in the phrase "We the people" in the first sentence of the US Constitution. It's an established fact that the protests on April 19th were led by college students. However, many university professors, high school students, and other ordinary people also joined the ranks led by the students. *Minjung* in this context should be a concept that encompasses them all.

The United States, which, for the first time in human history, opened an era of participatory democracy, places the legitimacy of democracy in the people's hands (people's sovereignty). As President Abraham Lincoln stressed, the United States' "government of the people, by the

---

[53] *Minjung* is written 민중 and 民衆 in Korean and Chinese/Hanja, respectively.

people, and for the people" endows the people with sovereignty through democratic elections. Additionally, if the government violates the people's sovereignty, the Declaration of Independence of 1776 justified their resistance to such government as follows:

> We hold these truths to be self-evident, that all men are created equal, that they are endowed by their Creator with certain unalienable Rights, that among these are Life, Liberty and the pursuit of Happiness. That to secure these rights, Governments are instituted among Men, deriving their just powers from the consent of the governed, That whenever any Form of Government becomes destructive of these ends, it is the Right of the People to alter or to abolish it, and to institute new Government, laying its foundation on such principles and organizing its powers in such form, as to them shall seem most likely to effect their Safety and Happiness.

In my opinion, the values pursued by the April 19th Movement were "autonomy, democracy, and the people's livelihood." We demanded that Syngman Rhee's administration make those things the foundation of their governance. However, the administration flat out rejected them. It rejected autonomy by relying too much on the United States, democracy by countless repeated massacres and fraudulent elections, and the people's livelihoods by ignoring our economy in grave crisis.

The people rejected the pseudo legitimacy of Syngman Rhee's government through nonviolent means. Just as the American Revolution was a struggle by the people to regain their rights from the British government, so the April 19th Revolution was the people's struggle to regain their rights from the Syngman Rhee regime.

However, unlike the American Revolution, the April 19th Revolution was unique and unprecedented anywhere else in the world. It was a popular revolution led by University students and a historical event, concretely realizing the will of the Korean people who mobilized themselves to overcome the hardship imposed on them throughout history.

▲ On June 20, 1961, President Yun Posun announced his resignation in the presence of Army Chief of Staff Jang Do-young and Major General Park Chung-hee, and finally left office on March 22 of the following year. (*Hankyoreh* file photo)

The university students who led ordinary people during the struggle did not start their movement with an ambition for power. In fact, they immediately returned to college after Syngman Rhee was ousted. The consequent power vacuum in the political arena had to be filled by established politicians. Unfortunately, after the April 19th movement, the Chang Myon[54] government became entangled in an intense power struggle and was incapable of adequately accommodating the people's needs. The Chang Myon government's political incompetence eventually provided an excuse for a military coup on May 16th. In a moment, the people's will from April 19th, won with their own blood, was trampled relentlessly by General Park Chung-hee's military strike.

Park Chung-hee's 18-year military dictatorship and Syngman Rhee's 12-year dictatorship were toppled in a similar way. Since Park Chung-hee came to power by military coup, he was incapable of securing the political legitimacy from the beginning. Park Chung-hee chose to maintain his regime through complete dependence on the United States. Although Park was once a member of South Korea's Labor Party, he defected and became subservient to the United States' power. His administration pushed forward fierce anti-communist policies backed by the US. The United States was supporting the economies of anti-communist countries as a way to counter communism on a global scale. Park Chung-hee followed the US-led economic development plan, actively serving the aims of US foreign policy. To ensure his regime's political legitimacy, Park embarked on a so-called "Modernization of the Fatherland," becoming a poster child of the United States 'anti-communist global strategy.

However, to Korean people, the values of autonomy and democracy that Park Chung-hee was violating were so precious that they could not be replaced on the basis of the people's livelihood alone. In the

---

[54] After Syngman Rhee's ouster, Chang Myon (장면, 張勉) was elected Prime Minister of the Second Republic of Korea, South Korea's brief attempt at parliamentary governance, in 1960.

end, university students from Busan and Masan led the *minjung* to vigorously challenge the legitimacy of Park Chung-hee's regime. This Busan-Masan People's Uprising became the context in which Park Chung-hee was assassinated by the then-director of the KCIA, Kim Jae-gyu on October 26, 1979. Again, Korean people tried to overcome the hardships imposed on them by challenging the legitimacy of a regime and replacing the dictator, just as they had done with the Syngman Rhee regime.

The Busan-Masan People's Uprising led to *Seoul Spring* in 1980, followed by yet another political power vacuum. The Choi Kyu-hah[55] interim government needed to carefully navigate that risky period. And it was necessary for the powerful presidential candidates, known as the "three Kims," to actively cooperate with Choi Kyu-hah's interim government. However, their top concern was winning the presidential race. So, they independently prepared for the presidential election, without consulting or cooperating with the interim government.

A more serious problem was that Choi Kyu-hah's interim government was so politically incompetent that it could not prevent General Chun Doo-hwan's military coup. Chun Doo-hwan, known as General Park Chung-hee's adopted son, seized military control through a *coup d'état* on December 12th, ruthlessly suppressed the May 18th Gwangju People's Uprising, and rode on to take the Presidency. The people's will, expressed first in the April 19th Movement and carried on by the Busan-Masan and May 18th

---

[55] Choi Kyu-hah (최규하) was the fourth South Korean President from 1979-1980.

Gwangju Uprisings, was again trampled by another General. It was *déjà vu* of General Park Chung-hee's May 16th military coup.

When I look back on the May 18th Gwangju People's Uprising, two things immediately come to mind. I first think of the role played by Cardinal Kim Sou-hwan.56 Second, I remember that Chun Doo-hwan branded the Gwangju Uprising as the work of rogue commies under orders from the DPRK. As the news spread that Chun Doo-hwan was using military force to suppress the people of Gwangju, Cardinal Kim sent a letter and some condolence money to the Archdiocese of Gwangju. His letter also promised to find a way to stop Chun Doo-hwan's armed coercion. In fact, Cardinal Kim met with Chun Doo-hwan at the security house in Gungjeong-dong, Seoul, on May 20, 1980, and requested him to refrain from using armed force. During the June Uprising in 1987, when riot police rushed in to arrest students protesting inside of Myeong-dong Cathedral, the Cardinal shouted to the police, "To arrest the students, you must trample me first, and then the priests, and then the nuns!"

Cardinal Kim was an indomitable figure who directly confronted General Chun Do-hwan. However, I saw a totally different side of him on the occasions when we met in person. Cardinal Kim had a truly gentle personality, as suggested by his nickname, "Silly Kim Sou-hwan." He spoke quietly, in a low voice, and listened with patient attention to what others had to say. His political interests were to infinitely embrace the victims of political violence, the complete

---

56 Cardinal Kim Sou-hwan (김수환, 金壽煥) was the Catholic Bishop of Masan (1966-1968) and the Archbishop of Seoul (1968-1998).

opposite of catering to political power. His is a model for all religious people in Korea to follow.

Despite Cardinal Kim's disapproval, General Chun ruthlessly massacred the people of Gwangju. Adding insult to injury, he branded the people in Gwangju "reds" and used the massacre to market himself as a patriot combatting communist enemies. He followed the path of Syngman Rhee. Just as Rhee had slaughtered civilians accused of being communist, Park Chung-hee repeatedly committed extra-judicial murders and faithfully followed his predecessor's tactic of blaming the victims.

Countless South Korean politicians, intellectuals, and journalists accepted Chun Doo-hwan's propaganda. They continue accepting it

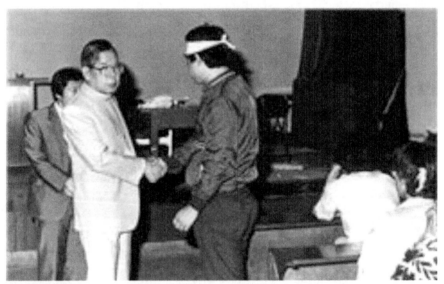

▲ Cardinal Kim Sou-hwan at the time of the torture and death of Park Jong-chul. Among the testimonies of the late Cardinal Kim, one entitled *May 18th and Catholic Witness* (5·18 과 천주교 증언록) was published in 2013 by Gwangju Diocese's Catholic Justice and Peace Committee on the 33rd anniversary of the May 18th Gwangju Uprising.

and will accept similar propaganda in the future. Despite the objective fact that North Korea had nothing to do with the Gwangju People's Uprising, the misled South Korean people treat citizens of Gwangju as if they are communist rogues. An Chi-hwan, a popular Korean singer, shudders at this social condition and cries out his lament in a song entitled "Reds":

> No logic necessary.
> No one need take responsibility.
> Just insist they are reds...
> When you want to wipe out
> Those who offend you like thorns in your eye,
> Just insist they are reds.[57]

The Soviet Union, China, the DPRK, and other nations which chose socialism as their regime's ideology, all have red flags. To this day in the West, China is called "Red China." Socialism was presented as an alternative system to solve the problem of a gap between the rich and the poor in capitalism. China, Vietnam, and the DPRK are among the countries classified as socialist. In Europe, democratic socialist systems compensate for the shortcomings of democracy by embracing the strengths of socialism.

Traditionally, the United States was a country that completely rejected socialism. However, with the recent collapse of the American middle class, politicians like Bernie Sanders have proposed socialist programs to advocate for middle class relief. Sanders emerged as a powerful presidential candidate, emphasizing healthcare for all, free

---

[57] From the song "Reds" (빨갱이) by An Chi-hwan (안치환).

college education, and a livable minimum wage. If we blindly embrace anti-socialist logic, we would have to reject all socialist countries such as China, Vietnam, and the DPRK, as well as social democracies in Europe and American democratic socialists, like Bernie Sanders.

My father lived his whole life in unspeakable pain, because he had been framed as a *red*. He couldn't get a decent job; he could not face the world with honor. Alcohol was his one and only friend, and he left this world too soon. There must be many other people in Korean society who lived a life just like my father. In order for our society to become healthy, instead of rejecting socialism blindly and outright, we should examine it rationally and sensibly. We should nurture a society that discerns socialism's strengths and weaknesses. Only then will we be freed from the red-baiting that has bound our souls, and open up a horizon for peaceful coexistence and Unification of the two Koreas.

The demands of the April 19th movement have yet to be fully realized in our society. Through the June Uprising in 1987, Korean people won the right to a direct popular presidential election. However, the political division between opposition party candidates Kim Young-sam and Kim Dae-jung split the vote, paving the way for Roh Tae-woo [58] (Chun Doo-hwan's close colleague) to be elected President with only 36.6 percent of the popular vote. Ever since the April 19th movement, the limitations of Korean politics to adequately

---

[58] Roh Tae-woo (노태우) was an ROK army general and South Korea's sixth President from 1988-1993.

accommodate the wishes of the people have been revealed again and again.

In light of these limitations, will the Moon Jae-in[59] government, born as a result of the "Candlelight Revolution"[60] in 2017, be able to respond appropriately to the aspirations of the people? There are still avenues to institutionalize the values of autonomy, democracy, and the people's livelihood—as proposed since the April 19th Movement—to strengthen the foundation for democracy and unification of the peninsula. It remains to be seen if South Korea's government will live up to the will of the people.

---

[59] Moon Jae-in (문재인) was the twelfth President of South Korea, from 2017-2022.
[60] The Candlelight Revolution (촛불혁명) was a series of protests beginning in 2016, leading to President Park Geun-hye's impeachment and Moon Jae-in's election in 2017.

Part 2:
America,
as Learned in America

I came to the United States of America to study peace.
However, as soon as I arrived, I had to experience the Vietnam War,
and no matter how much I searched the university library,
I could not find the peace study materials I was seeking.
The place was full of war studies instead...
What did I have to learn in America?

Starting Life in Washington D.C. with $100

In 1965, I went to study in the United States with my fiancee, Juhn Seong-won. Seong-won received a letter of admission to George Washington University, and I, to American University. There were only fifty dollars in Seong-won's pocket and another fifty in mine.

It was not that we had no money. The Park Chung-hee regime had prohibited traveling abroad with more than fifty dollars. Korea's foreign exchange reserves must have been very low at that time. In any case, limiting a foreign traveler's money to fifty dollars actually prohibited most people from going abroad. On top of that, in order to study abroad, one had to pass the English and Korean history tests administered by the state, and, by design, the test pass rates were very low.

As I look back on those days, studying abroad was a reckless thing for the two of us to do. Seong-won also risked her life, relying solely on penniless me. Among the graduates from the political science department at Seoul National University at the time, I was the only student who ended up studying in the United States.

There were two main reasons why I had such unrealistic dreams under such difficult circumstances. Firstly, I wanted to be loyal to my parents. My father's lifelong wish, who had lived a difficult life branded as "a red," was to find his grandparents in Manchuria. His expressed will to me at the moment of his death was that I should find his parents. At that time, China was called a "Bamboo Curtain" and the Soviet Union, an "Iron Curtain," so there seemed to be no way to find my grandparents from South Korea. But if I were to go to America, wouldn't I be able to find a way? At that time, such a nebulous idea was the very force guiding my life-changing decision.

Secondly, there were academic reasons. In order to cure the longing for peace, which so strongly afflicted me since childhood, I felt it necessary to conduct deeper research on war and peace and the challenge of unifying the Korean Peninsula. I really wandered intellectually during my time at Seoul National University, and realized that my longing for peace could not be cured in Korea.

Arriving in Washington D.C., the capital of the United States, with Seong-won felt like entering a desert, as if we had been stranded on a remote island, far out in the ocean. We were in urgent need of food, but we had no money. In order to survive financially, Seong-won and I rushed to get married. Consolidating two rooms into one saved us 50% on lodging.

Our wedding was held at Washington Korean Church,[61] a Korean Methodist Church on April 24, 1965. The senior Pastor Hwang Jae-kyung officiated. We went to New York on our honeymoon. Seong-won and I went all the way to the top of the Empire State Building

---

[61] Hwabu Korean Church or 화부 한인교회

hand-in-hand and took a picture together in front of the Statue of Liberty. I walked a few blocks on Broadway alone, thinking of my dear friend, Kim Tae-won, with whom I had once dreamt of walking there and whose memory I still held close. There I was, drenched in nostalgia.

▲ The newlyweds in front of the Statue of Liberty during their honeymoon in 1965. (Photo courtesy of Han Shik Park)

We started our life as newlyweds in a single room for 75 dollars a month. In April 1967, our eldest daughter Joo-young was born. Because milk delivery service was costly, I ran to the store every morning to buy milk. One day, at 7 am, I went to a store called "7 Up," and found it closed. I pounded hard on the door. As the owner cautiously opened the door and peeked out, I pointed to the sign that read, "7 Up" and yelled, "Why the hell is the store closed? It's past 7 o'clock!"

The owner rolled her eyes and glowered at me. Suddenly, it came to me. The sign didn't mean the store opened at 7 am! It turned out to be the name of a beverage brand. If that scene had played out nowadays, the owner might have come out with a gun!

Once, I saw a dog on a can at the supermarket and bought it home happily, thinking that people in the States were also eating dog meat. I even nodded in approval when my wife and I first tasted that "dog-meat broth." I have made countless mistakes living overseas.

The America I witnessed in 1965 was an industrial one, still in its infancy. There were far more production workers than service workers. There were no color televisions—let alone cell phones. The United States did not reach the zenith of its industrialization until 1969.

I needed a car to live in America, so I bought a 9-year-old Chevrolet for 200 dollars. I loved that car so much. I parked it on the roadside in front of the house and washed it often with a bucketful of water, humming and full of joy. I gave it such good care that I was able to sell it for 225 dollars, even after driving it for about a year.

I needed a job right away to make a living. My wife found a full-time job with no problem, because she had studied pharmacology in South Korea. I also had to move fast. I went straight to a job agency. When I was asked what skills I had, I replied that I had none. In that case, the agent said there were not many job options, and asked if I would try being a "bus boy." I accepted willingly, thinking they were talking about a bus conductor. But it was not a bus company to which the agent took me, but a restaurant. It wasn't until then that I realized a "busboy" was a person who cleared dishes from restaurant tables, not a bus conductor. In any case, I had to start working; I was in a dire situation. The thing was that all the dishware was porcelain and too heavy for me to handle. I was forced to find a new job.

The second job I got was an elevator boy. In those days, elevators did not move automatically as they do today; someone had to manually operate them from inside. The working hours allotted to me were from 11 p.m. to 8 a.m. the next morning. The job was satisfactory. There were few guests at that time, so I could study and read all night. On the other hand, the pay was too low. I couldn't maintain the job for long because the tuition for one semester alone was over 700 dollars.

The third job I took on was a taxi driver. I was drawn in by the story that I could make a lot of money by driving a taxi. I had to take the driver's license test. There were no problems in passing the written test, but I failed the practical test twice. In the practical exam, for example, I had to explain the route from the airport to the State Department. I had not been in the United States long, and I was unfamiliar with the area, so I had no choice but to give up the taxi driver job.

My fourth job was a hotel telephone operator. When the hotel received calls, the operator had to connect the calls to each room. So, the operator had to speak English well. I was hired because I said I spoke English well. However, when I started working, I found it difficult to understand English spoken over the phone. At one point, I had to understand a long sentence in incomprehensible pronunciation. Even after asking several times, I failed to grasp the meaning. I had no choice but to reply that I understood and hung up the phone. I later found out that it was an obituary that had to be delivered most urgently. I got fired after two days.

The fifth job I found was a waiter at a Chinese restaurant called "Zenith." Many State Department officials came there, since it was located near the US State Department. I worked with some interesting middle-aged ladies. There was no minimum wage, and I could only accept tips.

In the beginning, I was in charge of five tables. At lunchtime, customers swarmed in and the tables filled up in no time. I took all the orders from all five tables and put them all in the kitchen at once. For example, I placed the orders for 10 bowls of fried rice, 9 bowls of beef stir-fry, 8 bowls of fried shrimp, and 4 bowls of sweet and sour pork simultaneously. Then the kitchen made the food I ordered first, because there was a lot of it. When the food came out, I delivered it to the five tables with lightning speed. I was small in stature and moved with great agility. As a result, the customer turnover at my five tables was very fast.

The boss liked it as more food was sold, and my tips poured in. He gradually increased the number of tables I served while, the number of tables the middle-aged waitresses served decreased. They were too big to move as fast as I did, and they took orders one table at a time. As the tips they received decreased in inverse proportion to those I received, complaints began to pile up.

Demonstrating socialist spirit, I resolved the complaints of the waitresses in an instant. I called them all and suggested we split our tips equally. "Why don't we put each tip we get into a bin instead of our own pockets? Then, after work, take all the money out of the bin and distribute it equally?"

As soon as I finished my talk, the waitresses grinned from ear to ear. I was the most popular among those who worked at the place, and with sales rising day by day, the owner was pleased with me. I, too, was very happy, although my income decreased.

One day, a gentleman in a neat suit sat down at my table. After talking with him for a while, he seemed to me to be a professor from

Korea. He found out that I was studying in the United States after graduating from the Department of Political Science at Seoul National University. He might have felt bad for me. After he left, I returned to the table and found 20 dollars hidden under the plate. It was a very large tip. Zenith's food cost about 1 or 2 dollars, and the tip was usually about 25 cents. That was more than 10 percent, so quite a bit already. The moment I saw the twenty-dollar tip, that didn't fit the bill at all, I felt like he'd trampled upon my human dignity. I immediately grabbed that tip and ran after the customer. He was walking a distance away from me. I ran at full speed, stopped the customer, and, breathing heavily, said:

"I understand how you feel, sir. Thank you, but you tipped too much. I just want 25 cents."

As I turned around with the 25 cents in my hand, my legs felt heavy. I felt miserable, with the 20 dollars flitting around my mind.

Another day, young guys came by, chatting with their girlfriends. As soon as they sat down at my table, they ordered me to pour the tea, tossing their weight about. I declined because I was busy. After they ate, they left a tip of only one cent and walked out. I felt an indescribable sense of shame. I immediately threw that one cent on the table at the backs of the guys and shouted:

"Hey, kids! Here's your fortune! Take it and beat it!"

Still upset, I threw off my serving clothes and went home. Then the manager came to my house and pleaded with me to come back to work because without me, sales would not rise.

Living off of tips, I thought more deeply about America's unique tipping culture. In the United States, only restaurant workers and taxi drivers are tipped. I have never seen a tipping culture like that of the US in any other part of the world I have visited, including Europe. After much thought, I came to the conclusion that tipping originated in American slavery. Slaves were fed and cared for by their masters during slavery, but after their emancipation, they had to feed themselves. All they knew to do was to work at a familiar restaurant or farm, or as a driver. And so, tipping became a part of the culture. Former slave owners became tipping customers.

It is often said that in America every honest occupation deserves to be valued. Having lived on tips, however, I came to realize that there is some work that is not valued. I also came to believe that under no circumstance should human dignity be trampled upon in the workplace. I was shocked to learn the word *gapjil*[62] has recently gained popularity in South Korea. Does this mean that Korean culture has attributes of a "culture of slavery?"

---

[62] *Gapjil* (갑질) can be understood to mean "a power trip," "arrogant behavior," or "throwing one's weight around," such as when a boss treats his or her subordinates with disrespect due to their lower position.

Philosophical Reflection on American Behavioralism

The setbacks I faced in America were not only related to the fact that there were high class jobs and low class jobs. Leaving behind the gruesome experiences of Chinese Civil War and the Korean War, I went to the United States to study peace. Instead, I soon encountered the Vietnam War. *Isn't the United States a country whose founding ideology is the Christian spirit of 'love your enemies?' If a country was built to love its enemies, shouldn't it be the most peaceful country on earth?* Although I arrived with those expectations, the US military waded into the Vietnam War by bombing North Vietnam in February of that same year. *Gosh, another war? Why do I have to face war everywhere I go?*

It wasn't just that. Around that time, so-called "behavioralism" was just rapidly gaining popularity in the American political science community. In that atmosphere, I inevitably had some curiosity and hopes for behavioralism. However, the more I studied, the more I realized that, despite my fervent desire, I would not find any intellectual remedy for my longing for peace in behavioralism. Rather, it stifled my academic interest and was a more serious problem than my classroom disappointment at Seoul National University. I became an "academic orphan" again in the United States. My life abroad began with an academic struggle with behavioralism, which could not explain peace.

Behavioralism was born in the context of the Cold War. The Cold War began as an ideological confrontation between two nuclear states—the USA and the Soviet Union (USSR)—and divided the whole world into democratic and socialist camps, heightening military tensions and bringing humanity to the edge of annihilation. The United States could not peer through the "iron curtain" to predict Soviet behavior. In such uncertain circumstances, there was no way to escape fearing the USSR. Then social scientists stepped in. They were convinced that scientific methods could not only explain but also predict the behavior of the Soviet Union. They hoped that by reducing uncertainty surrounding Soviet behavior, it would also be possible to escape from the fear the Soviet Union was causing.

David Easton, who led the behavioralist revolution, published *The Political System* in 1953. Easton tried to predict the behavior of the political system by borrowing the "input-output model" of natural science. He regarded the inside of the Soviet political system during the Cold War as a "black box," because it could not be directly observed, and judged that by observing the input and output of that black box, it was possible to infer the dynamics inside the USSR's political system.

Gabriel Almond, considered a master of behavioralism, went a step further. He dissected the black box from the perspective of structural functionalism. Believing in the objectivity of natural science, he was convinced that all political systems were also structured to perform some universal functions. In other words, he argued, when inputs—such as political socialization, profit expression, and political communication—are put into political systems, the internal political system's capacity, transformation, maintenance, and adaptation functions will all produce similar results—such as legislative, administrative, and judicial functions. Of course, the path from input to output may be different depending on the historical, cultural, and political particularities of each country. However, Almond believed in the philosophy of modernization theory, that the structures and functions of all political systems eventually evolved to converge with the American democratic system. He was convinced in a universal law of history which set that course.

Gabriel Almond's structural functionalism was an adaptation of sociologist Talcott Parsons 'structural functionalism. Parsons argued that all social systems, including political systems, function to maintain their own structures, and he referred to such a function as a "pattern variable." Parsons said that pattern variables can be aggregated into five types. He referred to traditional societies as those that operate centered on ascribed status, functionally mixed obligations, particular values, clique orientation, and affective orientation, however, societies that operate centered on the polar opposites he referred to as modern. In Parsons 'view, human history was a series of processes through which the patterns performed in the traditional society was transformed into the ones performed in the modern society. He understood "modern society" as Western society, typified by American democracy. In the end, he was a leader in the modernization theory with "Western prejudice."

Nevertheless, the vision of behavioralism was not realized. The behavioralism method could not explain—much less predict—the behavior of the Soviet Union. Easton then published a paper in 1969 entitled "The New Revolution in Political Science." Easton acknowledged that behavioralism, which began with the goal of explaining and predicting political behavior, had failed, and emphasized that political science should be required to focus its research on solving pressing issues of the day.

However, Easton's proposal was rejected in American academia because, by the time Easton took a post-behavioralism position, behavioralism had grown to the point that it dominated academia. The Cold War ended with the collapse of the Soviet Union in late 1989. No scholar in the United States predicted the end of the Cold War, clearly exemplifying the "intellectual retardation" of American academia, which inertially adhered to behavioralism although it had been clearly revealed long before that behavioralism could neither explain nor predict the patterns of human behavior.

I entered a PhD program at the University of Minnesota and tried to diagnose the problems of behavioralism philosophically, while intensively taking lectures on philosophy of science by professors such as Herbert Feigl and May Broadbeck. In my view, the decisive reason that behavioralism could neither explain nor predict human behavior was because it adopted methods from the natural sciences.

Even from a commonsensical point of view, humans, the subject of behavioralism, as opposed to nature, the subject of natural science, are ontologically different. For example, humans are beings who seek the meaning of life, whereas nature does not seek such meaning. Humans may commit suicide when they lose meaning in life regardless of how much money they have, but that is not possible in the world of nature. Nevertheless, behavioralism borrowed its methodology from natural sciences and conducted research on humans who seek meaning, as if they were nature, that cannot pursue meaning. In other words, rather than openly seeking research tools suitable for the purpose, the research purpose was artificially framed in the tools that had been prefixed. This was the point where all the predicaments into which behavioralism fell were conceived.

The first problem with behavioralism is that it created an artificial formula, a mechanical view of man, that can be studied through logic of natural sciences. For example, behavioralism regarded humans as rationally behaving animals. Here, human rationality was understood as acting mechanically according to economic interests. Since economic benefits can be measured quantitatively, they can be analyzed mathematically. But isn't it true that human beings don't only follow economic interests? For example, can religious wars be explained by economic interests alone?

Secondly, behavioralism presupposed a methodological individualism that regards the arithmetic aggregation of individuals as a society. However, the historical heritage, cultural characteristics, and public values shared by society exist beyond such aggregation of individuals. Jean-Jacques Rousseau also stressed that the "general will" of a society exists beyond the arithmetic addition of its members.

Nevertheless, by adhering to methodological individualism, behavioralism banished the values that governed all members of society. How can one study society properly while ignoring such values?

Thirdly, behavioralism focused only on quantitatively measurable data by employing statistics and probability theory as important research tools, and excluded qualitative values that were difficult to measure, such as happiness, justice, and peace, from the study subjects. Behavioralism completely eliminated the need for social responsibility for such qualitative values. Rather, it convinced people that any ideal science had to thoroughly ignore such values to faithfully serve its value neutrality.

Fourthly, behavioralism also drove out human contemplation. In order to solve social problems, one must first be able to identify the problems, and for that, first establish a concept of an "ideal" society (having no problems). Only then can the problems of an abnormal society be clearly identified in the light of the concept of an ideal society. In order to establish the concept of an ideal society, it is necessary to deeply reflect on philosophy, history, and ethics, especially the nature of humanity. However, focusing exclusively on mathematical rationality, behavioralism ignored this and became oblivious to humanity. As a result, it lost the ability to independently conceptualize an ideal society. What kind of social ideal could we teach, and how could we educate thinkers to realize such an ideal through behavioralism?

Fifthly, the behavioralist mindset contributed to accelerating the arms race. As you know, war is a human business. In other words, war is one of the means to achieve human political ends. This is why diplomatic negotiations and political compromises are carried out even in the midst of war. However, because behavioralism pays attention to objects instead of humans, the essence of war was transformed from humans to weapons. Thus, it expelled human politics and diplomacy, giving birth to the belief that war can only be won by accumulating more powerful weapons than one's enemy. In which case, one's adversary would do the same. A weapons-centered view of war, that left out humans, inevitably led to an endless arms race.

Remember that the United States was defeated in the Vietnam War despite having the most powerful military force on the planet. Although the US was not defeated on the battlefield in Vietnam, it was defeated politically. This clearly exemplified the eternal truth that war is not waged by weaponry alone but through human political judgment.

Nevertheless, the US still has not given up on the "romantic" habit of forcing ruthless wars with advanced weapons—produced by its military-industrial complex—while downplaying politics and diplomacy. All one could expect from this romantic habit of working up the political nature of war is political defeat. In fact, hasn't the US also lost the wars in Iraq and Afghanistan? In his 500 page book, *Why We Lost*, Daniel Bolger, who served as a three-star general in both wars, analyzed that the US was destined to lose because of its blind trust in spreadsheet data and abstract theories.

Sixthly, another serious problem that can be found in the American behavioralism approach to war is its obsession with the body count. One of my indelible memories after coming to the States in 1965 was the daily televised report of the number of Vietnam War dead. Looking at the chart comparing the Vietnamese and US number of soldiers killed in action, the number of Vietnamese casualties was always overwhelmingly high. Just looking at the chart each day, it seemed like the US was winning the Vietnam War. Behavioralism managed to conceal the political nature of the war behind statistical casualty reports.

Later, as a graduate school professor at the University of Georgia, I taught behavioralism for decades as a required course. In a lecture called "Methodology of Political Science: Philosophical Reflections," I reminded the students of behavioralism's limitations, as explained above. However, when I visited South Korea, I found behavioralism was even more rampant there than in the US. It even seemed to have reached the point that no one there was even aware how it was dominating the social sciences.

▲ Lecturing on "Methodology of Political Science: Philosophical Reflections" at the University of Georgia's Department of International Relations. (Photo courtesy of Han Shik Park)

The Cold War in Korea, Intellectual Colony of the United States

Although the Cold War, on a global scale, is over, the Cold War on the Korean Peninsula still remains unshaken. The Cold War fostered fear, anxiety, and distrust, creating a *security paradigm* in which an arms race became inevitable. However, with the collapse of the Soviet Union in the late 1980s, the Cold War came to an end. We expected the Cold War on the Korean Peninsula to end soon thereafter, but that expectation has yet to be realized. I can't help but ask the question, "Why has the 'security paradigm 'that is constraining our lives so strongly persisted on the Korean Peninsula?" There seem to be several reasons. I believe that one of the important factors is the behavioralist mindset transplanted into Korea.

As I said earlier, when attending the Department of Political Science at Seoul National University, I was shockingly disillusioned at the educational method that exclusively focused on memorizing various political systems. However, whenever I visited Korea while working as a professor in the States, my disappointment only grew. Seeing almost everything from the United States being imported uncritically, I got the impression that even the deep-rooted evils of behavioralism were packaged as "advanced studies."

For example, the Korean academic community evaluates the ability of scholars by quantitatively measuring their number of published papers rather than the quality of their individual papers, a copy of the behavioralist mindset of the US at face value. I often argued this at faculty meetings at UGA. "Even the eminent sociologist Max Weber would have been rejected if he had applied for 'tenure 'at the University of Georgia in his forties, because Weber was a scholar known for the excellent quality of his papers, not for their quantity."

Although American behavioralism went philosophically bankrupt, Korean scholars forced it into the Korean psychic world. I call such a phenomenon epistemic imperialism, because behavioralism has penetrated the Korean psyche and pioneered an "intellectual colony" there. One of the malignant tumors that thrives in that colony is the Cold War on the Korean Peninsula.

The DPRK exists in the middle of the Cold War on the Korean Peninsula. This does not mean that North Korea was the cause of the Cold War, but that almost all aspects of the Cold War exist in direct or indirect connection to the DPRK. When the Soviet Union collapsed, the socialist countries in Eastern Europe that had been dependent on the Soviet Union soon followed suit, one after another. However, since North Korea had never been completely occupied by the Soviet Union, it was able to survive. To understand why the Cold War continues on the Korean Peninsula, understanding the DPRK is of supreme importance.

I am extremely skeptical of the South Korean academy's research methodology related to North Korea. Research on the DPRK conducted in the ROK is done in a manner nearly identical to the behavioralist Cold War research that was conducted in the United States. Just as it was not easy for the US to observe the Soviet Union from within, it is not easy for us to observe the interior of North Korea. Just as American social scientists considered the Soviet Union a "black box" and tried to infer the inner dynamics by observing the input and output of the black box, South Korean researchers on North Korea have, similarly, mainstreamed studies inferring the internal dynamics of the DPRK by analyzing North Korean defector interviews as primary sources or fragments of observed data. Just as the behavioralist Cold War research in the US failed, the ROK's behavioralist research on the DPRK is bound to fail.

Let's take an example. After the United States and South Korea donate food to North Korea, they monitor satellite images of DPRK military trucks transporting the food. Based on those photos, they claim that the North Korean army is stealing food that should be delivered to the people, further reinforcing their prior distrust of North Korea.

However, this is nothing more than a misjudgment based in complete ignorance. When I was in North Korea, I confirmed that military trucks are their only means of transportation. Additionally, the DPRK army operates as a business—an independent, for-profit system. They also independently manage proceeds from overseas weapon sales. The military can always secure enough provisions. If food donated from a foreign country were sent to the military, the soldiers would ask why it was given to them and request it sent to their family members, because the military always has abundant provisions. They don't have another option, because failure to provide abundantly for the military would result in dissatisfaction among their family members and a depletion of troop morale.

I should also note that the testimony of North Korean defectors cannot be considered objective data. The ontological status of North Korean defectors alone makes it impossible for them to have an objective understanding of the DPRK. Even calling their action "defecting from North Korea" reveals a value judgment, that they hate and reject the DPRK. How could we expect a person who fundamentally rejects the nation to speak fairly about it? As Max Weber once urged, "Whenever the person of science introduces his personal value judgment, a full understanding of the facts ceases."

There is yet a more serious problem. I am personally acquainted with Hwang Jang-yop,[63] as we spoke many times when I met him in North Korea before his exile. He himself told me that most defector stories were based on scripts from the ROK's Agency for National Security Planning (NSP) or the National Intelligence Service (NIS). Nevertheless, the reality is that many North Korea researchers in South Korea, posing as "experts" on DPRK-related issues, write academic books based on the testimonies of North Korean defectors and publish based on their personal value judgments about the DPRK.

What I would like to convey to South Korean researchers of North Korea is that behavioralism itself is fundamentally flawed. Behavioralist research can only be conducted when there are

---

[63] Hwang Jang-yop is written 황장엽 in Korean.

measurable observational data. However, acquiring a lot of data does not guarantee an accurate understanding of the DPRK. The English philosopher Alfred North Whitehead once observed that millions of people have seen apples falling, but only Newton devised the law of gravitation. Millions have seen lamps sway from side to side in temples and churches, but only Galileo's observation led to a mathematical scheme similar to that of Newton's.

Likewise, millions of people have visited the United States, and many more have lived there, but only those attaining to high standards of intellectual insight and conceptual ability wrote immortal pieces based on their observations, such as Alexis de Tocqueville's *Democracy in America* or Max Weber's great treatise, *The Protestant Ethic and the Spirit of Capitalism*. Would an unlicensed doctor be able to accurately diagnose a patient's disease, even if he placed his stethoscope to the affected area?

Nevertheless, these "unlicensed doctors" who do not possess a standard of intellectual insight or conceptual ability comparable to Newton, Galileo, de Tocqueville or Weber, keep visiting North Korea and meeting a variety of people. They walk here and there, taking pictures, or recording videos. And then, after returning to South Korea, they present themselves as "experts," writing books and traveling all over the ROK, giving lecture after lecture on North Korea. In short, this is nothing more than scientific blasphemy. The highest levels of scientific specialization are never born that way. A more serious problem is that their actions drastically misrepresent the DPRK, thereby contributing to widely-rooted prejudice against North Korea in South Korean society. Arguably, such prejudice is a serious impediment to peace and unification on the Korean Peninsula.

Many people say that I became an expert on the DPRK simply because I visited there so often. But, I feel humiliated every time I hear that, because I cannot equate the number of my visits to my understanding. Travelers pack their gear carefully before departure. So do I. Before departure for North Korea, I securely pack the theoretical propositions I've developed through academic research and my own imagination. For example, I make a theoretical proposition that "all political systems are in danger of collapse when faced with a crisis of legitimacy. The key to legitimacy is not economic interests, but ideological values and spirit." While in the DPRK, I carefully observe its society in comparison to my theoretical proposition. The reason why the DPRK did not collapse, despite the economic crisis, is confirmed in detail. After such observations, I come to the conclusion that my theoretical proposition is correct and that theory that North Korea will collapse is wrong. The first chapter, "Will the DPRK Really Collapse?", in my 2018 publication Thinking Beyond the Line[64] was written through such a process. My visits to the DPRK were a series of participant observations to empirically verify, revise, and supplement my prior theoretical propositions.

---

[64] Published in Korean, under the title 선을 넘어 생각한다

The behavioralist way of thinking is deeply embedded even in the so-called "Sunshine Policy."[65] Of course, I am not unaware of the "great" achievements of the Sunshine Policy, which contributed to paving the way for peace and unification on the Korean Peninsula. I met Kim Dae-jung numerous times and had many conversations on topics such as peace and unification on the Korean Peninsula. While acknowledging the achievements of the Sunshine Policy, I believe that efforts to overcome its limitations are also necessary.

◀ The author visited the Blue House several times in the late 1990s, when President Kim Dae-jung (left) was in office, to discuss the Sunshine Policy. (Photo courtesy of Han Shik Park)

One of the key premises underlying the Sunshine Policy is that the DPRK is an "abnormal state." Therefore, the policy intended to transform it into a "normal state" by strengthening peaceful exchanges and cooperation. The normal state, presupposed by the Sunshine Policy, was a democratic political system and a capitalist economic system, as exemplified by the United States. However, such a premise, taken for granted in the Sunshine Policy, is ultimately derived from "Western prejudice" shared by several theories of American behavioralism, such as David Easton's political system theory, Gabriel Almond's structural functionalism, and Talcott Parsons' modernization theory—which have all empirically failed. The

<hr />

[65] The Sunshine Policy (햇볕정책) was the ROK's policy toward the DPRK during the Kim Dae-jung and Roh Moo-hyun presidencies between 1998 and 2008.

Sunshine Policy could not achieve its desired goal. It could not change North Korea's political and economic systems at all.

We can reference the annual joint military exercises conducted by ROK-US alliance, the inter-Korean arms race, and the North Korean nuclear issue as examples which clearly show that the Cold War remains at a standstill on the Korean Peninsula. Political behavioralism has also deeply permeated the logic behind these actions. Following behavioralist thinking, the US was obsessed with the number of casualties in the Vietnam War—valuing materials over humans and focusing on counting the dead, rather than paying attention to the political decisions of the North Vietnamese commanders. Although the United States was not defeated on the battlefield, it failed to achieve its political goals in the Vietnam War.

▲ The Pyongyang subway, which opened in 1973–a year before the subway in South Korea, has 3 lines and 17 stations connecting the city center to the western side of the Daedong River (pictured left). Each station (like the busiest one, Glory Spation, pictured center) boasts a wide plaza and high dome ceiling modeled after Moscow and doubles as an emergency shelter where citizens of Pyongyang can evacuate. One must ride a steep escalator to enter (pictured right). (Photo courtesy of the Ministry of Unification)

If war were waged against the DPRK, using the ROK-US military training methods that have so far failed to dispel behavioralist reasoning, there is a high possibility they would lose the war—even in terms of numbering casualties—because the DPRK has underground air defense shelters and subways that can withstand atomic bombing. The Pyongyang subway operates at an average depth of 100 meters underground, passing below the Daedong River. From my observations, all 17 subway stations in downtown Pyongyang are arranged two kilometers apart, and each subway station is wide and spacious, like a playground. The underground stations are cool in summer and warm in winter, making them perfect places for many people to relax. One can even enjoy reading a book while riding the escalator 130 to 150 meters underground to catch the subway. Pyongyang's air defense shelters and subways can accommodate all of Pyongyang's two million people.

The US Central Intelligence Agency (CIA) is well aware of these facts. While on the other hand, Seoul is vulnerable if a war broke out. North Korean bombs could ignite the gas pipelines winding throughout the city like a spiderweb, not to mention the many automobiles and fuel tanks. Turning Seoul into a "sea of fire" was not an idle threat. Edward Timperlake, a military expert and former US Navy fighter pilot who served at the Pentagon (Department of Defense) once argued that if South Korea and the United States waged a ground war with North Korea, they would be defeated before they even start.

At this time, we must prioritize the understanding that the US' behavioralism approach to war plays a definitive role in indefinitely prolonging the Cold War on the Korean Peninsula, by cleverly promoting an arms race between the two Koreas. While the US appears to be negotiating with North Korea to resolve the North Korean nuclear issue, in reality, it is preventing North Korea from giving up its nuclear weapons by beginning with the unrealistic demand for "complete, verifiable and irreversible dismantlement." At the same time, the US prevents South Korea from developing its own nuclear weapons on the grounds that the US nuclear umbrella protects them. In which case, the ROK purchases more advanced conventional weapons from the US military-industrial complex, out of fear of the DPRK's nuclear arsenal. In fact, the United States uses the ROK-US joint military exercises as a way to promote new, state-of-the-art, American weapons to South Korea, and the rest of the world.

South Korea has been brainwashed by the behavioralist mindset and believes it can only live in safety by endlessly buying American-made weapons. In this climate, the arms race escalates, without an end in sight.

The Vietnam War and ROK Armed Forces

It was November 2nd, 1965, in the midst of the Vietnam War. A 31-year-old Quaker, named Norman Morrison, committed suicide right in front of the US Department of Defense. Even more shocking was the fact that Morrison attempted to burn himself with his own 1-year-old daughter, Emily, whom he was clutching tight while setting himself on fire. Fortunately, a passerby rushed in and took Emily away. To unambiguously convey his anti-Vietnam War message, Morrison chose a location where Defense Secretary Robert McNamara could look down from his office and see. The entire country was horrified at his chosen death, leaving behind his wife, one son, and two daughters. Anti-war campaigns intensified.

I was also in shock. After I arrived in Washington in March 1965, my life, which had been tied up hectically to studying and working part-time, stopped in an instant. When I woke up, my feet were carrying me towards the site of his self immolation. The scene where Morrison disappeared left me in deep thought and indescribable sadness. Morrison's death dramatically demonstrated that there was no justification for America's involvement in the Vietnam War. Still, isn't South Korea sending large numbers of Korean troops along with the US? How could dispatching the Korean army be legitimized?

War is a means chosen to protect the lives and property of the people and territory of a state. However, Vietnam never threatened the lives and property of the American people or invaded the US territory. Moreover, the US prefers the term "Vietnam Conflict" to the "Vietnam War," because it wishes to emphasize that it was simply helping South Vietnam, not engaged in American-initiated warfare. Such deceptive terminology tells us that the US itself does not recognize the legitimacy of the Vietnam War. Haven't we already pointed out that the US prefers to call the Korean War, the first war the United States did not win, the "Korean Conflict" instead of the "Korean War?"

Vietnam was a French colony since 1858. In 1940, it also came under Japanese colonial rule. However, with the end of World War II, the withdrawal of France and Japan created a power vacuum. Ho Chi Minh founded the Indochina Communist Party with the support of the Comintern in 1930, and infiltrated Vietnam in 1941, launching a liberation movement centered on the Viet Minh (League for the Independence of Vietnam). He declared the independence of the Democratic Republic of Vietnam(North Vietnam) in 1945 and took office as President of the government. Fearing that Vietnam would trigger a communist transformation of Indochina, the United States supported Ngo Dinh Diem and placed him as President of the Republic of Vietnam(South Vietnam) in October 1955. Vietnam had been divided.

Ngo Dinh Diem suffered from corruption and a crisis of legitimacy before he was assassinated on November 2, 1963. On November 22nd of the same year, John Kennedy was assassinated in Dallas, Texas. The Soviet Union, seeing a golden opportunity to include Vietnam in its own scope of influence, started large-scale military aid to Ho Chi Minh. Lyndon Johnson, who succeeded Kennedy as President, began sending large US troop deployments to Vietnam in 1965. The US-Soviet proxy war has begun. The United States sent a total of 500,000 troops to the Vietnam War, and 58,315 were killed in battle.

It is noteworthy that the US military massacred about 2 million Vietnamese civilians and even used chemical and biological weapons, a deadly tactical herbicide called "Agent Orange." It can be argued that the massacre of civilians was inevitable because many Vietnamese farmed during the day and engaged in guerrilla activities at night. It should be pointed out, however, that the United States has never used biological or chemical weapons against white people. The US used chemical and biological weapons only against peoples of color. It was the same with the Indian Wars and with the Korean War. Racism is imprinted in America's "genes." The fact that the US dropped the atomic bomb on Japan, not on Germany, during World War II cannot be explained without racism.

During the Vietnam War, the daily casualties report spread the message across the United States that youth engaged in warfare would die. A frenzy to dodge military service arose among young people. The US sent draft warrants to about 16 million young people, but only half a million responded. The children of many American politicians avoided military service. Even well known leaders like Donald Trump,

Bill Clinton, George W. Bush, Dick Cheney and famous people like John Wayne and Muhammad Ali avoided military service for various reasons. Between 40,000 and 50,000 people fled to Canada or went abroad to study.

The US government extended the existing policy of delaying conscription until after college graduation to until after graduate school graduation. As a result, the competition for graduate school admission skyrocketed, with acceptance ratios, which had usually been about 2 to 1, falling to 7 to 1. When I entered the doctoral program at the Graduate School of Political Science, the University of Minnesota, I was barely able to pass because hundreds of candidates flocked to apply for only 16 openings.

Universities led the way on US anti-Vietnam war protests. When I saw those demonstrations, I had a strange feeling, *Wait, did they import this from the Korean universities?* The way they organized the protests was exactly the same as those I had witnessed during the April 19 Movement back in Seoul, where I had been one of those students stood on the front lines of the rally at Seoul National University

There were also differences, of course. In Korea, the police brutally suppressed the April 19th protests. In the States, however, it was the military that invaded University campuses and forcefully suppressed the rioters. For example, American soldiers opened fire on anti-war protesters at Kent State University on May 4th, 1970. Four students were killed and nine were injured. Seeing the military culture look so familiar shocked me, so intensely that I could feel it through my skin.

Another difference between Korea and the USA was the responses

▲ The Millions of Vietnamese, US and Korean soldiers, and their descendents to the third and fourth generations have suffered hereditary sequelae due to the defoliant sprayed by the US military during the Vietnam War. In 1976, a child walks around naked in an ancient pastoral area in Vietnam's Ga Mau region that was devastated by Agent Orange. (Photo courtesy of the Vietnam War Museum)

from religious groups. Korean Christianity actively defended the Vietnam War under the pretext of anti-communism. On the contrary, in the United States, progressive Christians, including Quakers, actively carried out anti-war campaigns. Also, during the April 19th Movement, although Korean university professors participated in the march, they did not take the lead, whereas in the United States, many university professors fought at the forefront of the anti-war demonstrations, preaching the highest level of anti-war theory. For example, Mulford Sibley, a professor of political philosophy at the University of Minnesota, whom I respect academically, famously developed a strong anti-war movement from the perspective of "just war." Having fully honed my protest skills during the April 19th Movement, I also strongly criticized the injustice of the Vietnam War alongside Professor Sibley.

◀ On May 4, 1970, Ohio National Guard troops entered the campus of Kent State University and attacked anti-war protesters. (Photo courtesy of Kent State University website)

Wars must be justified in purpose, process, and result. Firstly, the purpose of war must be just. However, the Vietnam War waged by the United States was aimed at killing people. The war process must also be fair. However, the United States slaughtered numerous civilians in the Vietnam War and even used chemical and biological weapons. The outcome of the war should be able to contribute to history. But the Vietnam War is a war that the United States does not want to remember. In short, the Vietnam War lost legitimacy in each stage.

The Vietnam War finally ended in 1975. As soon as Jimmy Carter became president in 1977, he granted a general pardon to all young people who had avoided participating in the War. Very few disagreed, because very few Americans recognized the legitimacy of the Vietnam War.

Park Chung-hee dispatched a large Korean troop deployment to the warfronts in Vietnam. The US had to "import" foreign troops to fill the void, as more than 15 million young Americans avoided military service. Korea responded first. South Korea sent a total of 320,000 people between 1965 and 1973, and 5,099 got killed. South Korea sent the second largest number of troops after the United States.

Why did Korea send troops to Vietnam? We take the dispatch of troops for granted, but from the point of view of the Vietnamese, who never invaded Korea, it was unthinkable. Park Chung-hee justified participation in the Vietnam War for "Korea's security." At that time, even elementary school students were fed up with hearing a popular war-mongering song ("Here Come the White Tigers") about the White Tiger Corps that participated in the War. The lyrics began with these lines, "You're defending our fatherland for liberty and unification. You were chosen in the name of your country. You, warriors of the White Tiger Division."

▲ President Lyndon Johnson invited President Park Chung-hee to visit on May 16, 1965 and requested the deployment of a Korean military division to Vietnam. President Park Chung-hee received a welcome ceremony on Broadway in Manhattan, New York on May 18th, after a car parade in Washington (left). "Powell," by photojournalist Jung Beom-tae, captures her mother's sad expression (right). (*Hankyoreh* file photo; Photo from *Jung Beom-tae Photo Book,* courtesy of the National Archives of Korea)

During the 1967 presidential campaign, Park Chung-hee persuaded the people about Vietnam with the following logic: if South Korean troops were not sent to Vietnam, the US would move American troops stationed in Korea to Vietnam, leading to fear that North Korea would invade South Korea. The lyrics of the song about the White Tiger Corps were taking at face value the "domino theory" propagated by the United States. That is, if Vietnam became communist, all of East Asia would become communist, one nation after another. However, the domino theory was nothing more than an illusion completely separated from the concrete political reality of East Asia. Could it be that so many intellectuals, college students, and Christians in the United States participated in such a fierce anti-war movement all because they did not know about the domino theory?

Ultimately, what Park Chung-hee wanted was money. The total revenue earned from dispatching the South Korean military was estimated at about 235.56 million dollars. About 80 percent of total revenue, or 195.11 million dollars, was remitted directly to the South Korean government. The Korean government used that money for economic development. Of course, I have no intention of putting aside the economy or devaluing the sacrificed lives of young Koreans who died in the Vietnam War.

However, I cannot find any justification for the act of exchanging the lives of young fellow Koreans for money. Was dispatching troops to the Vietnam War really the only way for South Korea to make money at that time? Couldn't it have been possible to get a loan from an international financial institution and make money legitimately through a variety of diplomatic activities? The reason the United States lost the Vietnam War was because the war did not gain legitimacy in the eyes of the American people. When even the legitimacy of the war is in question, it simply is not just if not questioning the legitimacy of economic actions.

I have dubbed the increasingly fetishistic American democracy "Moneytalkcracy: When money talks, people listen." Today, America has become a money-worshiping society. Money became the saint of all religions. Hence, "when money speaks, people listen." From my point of view, democracy in Korea has also been reduced to a moneytalkcracy for a long time. I wonder, "Does the Vietnam War mean anything more to Korea than its so-called 'special demand economy'?"

Trump and Moon Jae-in are driving North Korea into a corner to make it denuclearize, not forgetting to promise a rosy future, if only it surrenders its nuclear weapons. They paint North Korea as a land of opportunity, promising possibilities of future economic success. They said the same during the Sunshine Policy. Because both the United States and South Korea are so caught up in their own moneytalkcracy, they believed that offering economic incentives would entice North Korea to listen to them, too.

Slavery, America's First Original Sin

I came to America to study peace. However, as soon as I arrived in the United States, I had to experience the Vietnam War. No matter how much I searched the university library, I could not find the peace studies for which I was looking. It was full of war studies. I turned my attention to American history. I was surprised to discover that America's history was full of warfare. Very few US Presidents have held office during peace time. The Vietnam War was just one of many episodes of American warfare history. This was utterly disconcerting.

I put my peace studies on hold and looked into why America's history has been so full of war. Countless books detail the wars fought by the United States, but I was unable to find records that clearly answered my questions. So what should I study in America? My frustration only increased.

As I conducted independent research, I came to the conclusion that the ultimate cause of the United States 'war disease was their "original sin." In Christian theology, original sin refers to the indelible sin that Adam and Eve committed by disobeying God's will and eating the forbidden fruit. From my point of view, America's original sin consisted of two major parts; one was race-based, institutionalized slavery, and the other was robbing the indigenous peoples of North America of their land by force. The United States has not been able to wash away its original sin to this day.

Rather, the legacy of its original sin has spread and become entrenched throughout America's psychic culture. From slavery came modern racism, and from indigenous conquests came today's militarism. The combination of the two continue to promote American warfare. This war disease is chronic and malignant, such as that it cannot be cured. I reached the conclusion that if one doesn't understand America's original sin, one cannot really understand America.

In the 16th and 17th centuries, British merchants sold approximately 5 million African people to American farmers as slaves. The "ideal" slaves were Black men in their mid-20s, who sold for about $1,200 each. The next most preferred slaves were pregnant Black women. Many such women of childbearing age gave birth to children of white owners. Black slaves mixed with white blood were sold for a higher price.

About 4 million Black slaves were sold in the Deep South (Georgia, North and South Carolina, Alabama, Louisiana, Mississippi, and Florida), and about 1 million Black slaves were sold throughout the rest of the United States. In the Deep South, slaves worked mainly in the cotton fields. There was a labor quota. Male slaves had to harvest 80 pounds of cotton a day, and female slaves, 70 pounds. If they didn't fulfill their quota, they were whipped until their backs bled. Cotton harvested in the Deep South was mainly sold to England. At that time, England was the mecca of the world's textile industry.

As is well known, slaves in the United States were liberated at the end of the four-year Civil War (1860–64). The Civil War was sparked by contrasting cultures and different interests between the North and the South. The North was a commercial and industrial society, where Presbyterian and Methodist churches flourished. They advocated emancipation, and supported the federal government. The South, on the other hand, was an agricultural society and tended to be Baptist. They opposed emancipation, and supported the local states. Harriet Beecher Stowe's novel *Uncle Tom's Cabin*, which exposed the horrors of slavery, became particularly important as one of the catalysts leading up to the war. The Civil War served as an opportunity to free the slaves, but it also deepened the conflict between the South and the North, and reinforced white supremacy.

White people don't like to work in so-called "3D industries," meaning dangerous, dirty, and demeaning work. Prior to the Civil War, this labor was mainly performed by Black slaves. After emancipation, people of color such as Mexicans, Latinos, and Asians were gradually engaged in the 3D industry. In line with the trend, racism against Black people was gradually transformed into white supremacy, which regarded all people of color as inferior.

Efforts to solve the problem of racial discrimination against Black people in American society steadily developed. The best example is the civil rights movement led by Martin Luther King, Jr (1929-68). I was deeply moved as I looked back on the life of Reverend King and read his writings. How could the writings of a short-lived 39-year-old communicate such profound truth? Whenever I read his writings, I often felt as if I were hearing God's voice. In 1983, President Ronald

Reagan signed an executive order that made King's birthday a national holiday in the United States. In 2000, 17 years later, finally all 50 states in the United States accepted that executive order. George Washington and Martin Luther King are the only two individuals in the United States whose birthdays are designated as national holidays.

▲ In March 1965, Rev. King led the Selma to Mongtomery march and called for the Civil Rights Act to ban racial segregation in public places, working with Rosa Parks, who brought Mongtomery, Alabama's unconstitutional segregated bus policy to public attention. (Hankyoreh file photo)

"Affirmative Action" was another effort to solve the problem of racial discrimination against Americans of African descent. This is a policy to ease admission requirements for African Americans according to the autonomous judgment of each university. This sparked dissatisfaction with white students. For example, in 1978, a student named Alan Bakke sued the University of California Davis School of Medicine, to which he had applied, when he was denied because of affirmative action measures. This controversial case ended in the US Supreme Court with a ruling in Bakke's favor. Then, many students of Asian descent who had been rejected after applying to Harvard University, also filed a class action lawsuit against the university based on measures to correct racial discrimination. The court ruled in favor of Harvard University, interpreting that the measures to correct racism were prepared to improve the treatment of African American people who had historically been enslaved. That's a reasonable interpretation.

Founded in 1785, the University of Georgia was the first state university in the United States and is currently regarded as one of the most prestigious universities in the southeast. During my work there, I was the only person of color among the 2,000 or so professors. White professors glanced at me curiously as they passed me. Every time they did, I felt like a monkey in the zoo.

The white professors were relatively kind to me and made a lot of concessions. For example, when they opened the door, they told me to go in first, or when we ran into each other on the street, we greeted each other with friendly smiles. However, when it came to financial issues, they changed their attitude and became completely stingy.

Among the students I was teaching in graduate school, there was a Korean student who served as the president of Yonsei University's student body. Due to financial difficulties, he was working part-time at the house of an older white professor from Harvard University. One day, because the student's grades weren't so good, I called him and asked him why. He said that the older professor gave him too much work, so he couldn't find time to study. Shortly thereafter, during a faculty meeting to evaluate student scholarships, the judges eliminated my student from the list of the candidates after seeing his grades. I made an open request to the older professor who hired my student that he be considerate of my student's situation because he hadn't been given enough time to study. The professor immediately replied that he loved my student. I cried out in anger, instantly.

"You believe you love him. But how is it any different from the love you have for your dog? That is not love!"

At that time, I had not received tenure, and the elder professor had enough power to fire me. But I couldn't stand it. It was clearly racism, and it was working against my student.

When I joined the University of Georgia, African Americans cleaned the classrooms. Only one white man worked for the janitorial department, and he was the one who held the bundle of keys to unlock the classroom doors for the cleaners, who were always Black.

Despite the invisible racism at UGA, I tried to teach my students to the best of my ability. A professor usually teaches two or three subjects. However, I have taught US Government Theory, International Politics, Comparative Politics, Political Development, Asian Politics, Human Rights Policy, and Methodology of Political Science. By establishing the Institute for International Studies, I tried to do my best to nurture students 'international perspective.

American universities are integrated, as recommended by the government. Government policy also mandates that the military is run by a mix of Afro and Caucasian Americans. But in churches, voluntary associations, it is completely different. Black and white churches are completely separated, symbolizing the psychological distance that still exists between African Americans and Caucasian Americans.

There is an African American professor at Peabody College of Music that a friend of mine knows well. He is a famous pianist. One day, when he was late for class, he began to run down the street. A white police officer then chased him and arrested him in broad daylight, because the officer was suspicious of a Black person running on the street. The police officer only released him after taking him to the university and verifying his professorship.

I served as an exchange professor at Morehouse College for one year. Morehouse College is a Black men's college in Atlanta, famous for being Martin Luther King Jr's alma mater. I asked students there whether attitudes toward Black people in the United States had changed during Barack Obama's presidency. The students answered, "No, not at all." They said they couldn't even walk the streets alone at night because white people could always express hatred, start an argument over nothing, or even shoot them just because they're Black. Obama's mother was white. If Obama had campaigned for African American rights like King did, he would not have been elected president. In fact, Obama's mindset was similar to that of white people in his election campains.

Many American intellectuals argued that America entered a "post-racism" era with Barack Obama's election as President. However, I saw that such a claim was fundamentally just a theory and far from reality. Racism is still America's original sin. Unsurprisingly, Donald Trump, who ran for president after Barack Obama, was elected President despite blatantly advocating white supremacy. In fact, a large number of white people who were inwardly hostile to Barack Obama supported Donald Trump.

Indigenous Genocide, America's Second Original Sin

In addition to slavery, to understand the precise reason America is not free from the disease of war, we must explore America's Indigenous genocide. I believe slavery and conquest of indigenous people are the two pillars of America's original sin.

It is estimated that the original inhabitants of North America migrated from Asia in the 13th and 14th centuries to Central and South America, reaching 2 to 7 million by the 15th century. These indigenous people were scattered across the wilderness of the North American continent and lived peacefully. Each tribe had its own culture and language, and enough enthusiasm for education that they began schools. Some 18th-century European intellectuals, such as Jean-Jacques Rousseau, even idealized their way of life, calling them "noble savages" who lived in peace without law.

I have visited the Cherokee Reservation in northern Atlanta on several occasions and carefully observed their customs. At that time, I couldn't help but be very surprised. First of all, one can see at a glance that their facial features are similar to those of Koreans. Born and raised in Manchuria, I know very well what Chinese facial features are like. I have visited Japan often, so I have a pretty good knowledge of Japanese facial features as well. Unlike Koreans, the Chinese and Japanese do not have cheekbones protruding from their faces. However, the Cherokee faces have protruding cheekbones just like Koreans. They felt very familiar.

It wasn't only that. Before cooking, they winnowed the rice to remove the bran. They ground beans with a millstone, and make rice cakes by beating rice with a huge wooden mallet. Seeing these scenes made me feel like I was back in my childhood hometown. I also thought that there might be some affinity between the Cherokee and Korean ancestors. For a long time, I have wondered what it could be like for Korean civil society to work with the Cherokee community for the common good.

In 1492, when Christopher Columbus landed in North American, dark clouds began to fall on the peaceful life of indigenous people. In general, Columbus is remembered as a great explorer who discovered the new continent of North America by continuing his voyage westward in accordance with the belief that "the earth is round." However, the "discovery of the new continent of North America" is nothing more than a projection of a biased, Eurocentric mindset that does not regard indigenous people as human beings.

Columbus 'sea route opened the way for American colonization by many European countries. England, France, and Spain crossed over the Atlantic along Columbus 'route to North, Central, and South America from the 16th to 20th centuries. Colonization was, to summarize, a process of violence that ruthlessly and forcibly ravaged the lives of indigenous people. Needing force to protect their homes, weapons became the hottest commodity on the market.

The forbears of modern America used force to rob native people of their lands. This original sin was the start of American militarism. Indigenous American civilizations have almost completely been destroyed. In the modern United States, the indigenous people who remain live scattered across some 320 reservations. Although they are called "Indian Reservations," they are actually institutional devices to promote the extinction of indigenous peoples. According to the 1960 census, there were about 10 million people living in the reservation areas. That's about 2.4 percent of the US population. Today, there are roughly 5 million people living there. Many young people are finding ways to live off of the reservation. Indigenous Americans have a keen enough interest in education to establish and run the Navajo Institute of Technology, but many students attend universities off of the reservation to more easily find jobs after graduation.

Gambling is banned in white society, because it is considered a destructive custom that disturbs the morals of white society. However, the US government allows gambling (casinos) on "Indian Reservations." So, in order to shake off boredom, white people often go to reservations to gamble. Such money spent by white people is one of the major sources of revenue for indigenous people.

One of the things I particularly noticed when considering American militarism is the fact that the constitution guarantees that individuals can carry firearms, as stipulated in the Second Amendment of the Federal Constitution of 1791. Recalling the fact that the newly born nation's security capability was not sufficiently developed when the

Constitution was enacted, we can understand the reasoning behind the Second Amendment. However, it is difficult to understand why, well over 200 years later, it has yet to change.

The United States currently has the highest number of gun deaths in the world. Every time there is another mass shooting, more people believe carrying firearms should be banned, yet the 2nd amendment has not been repealed. The 2nd Amendment is well established and serves as the institutional foundation stabilizing the US arms market. The National Rifle Association (NRA) is currently the largest special interest group in the United States.

Why can't the US break away from militarism? Above all, we need to turn our attention to Christianity in the United States, because Christianity provides an ideological basis that strongly supports American militarism and racism. The United States is the country most influenced by Christianity on the planet. As Alexis de Tocqueville once said, "There is no other place in the world where Christianity has exerted a more powerful influence on the human soul than in the United States," and Harvard University's Perry Miller said, "You cannot understand America unless you have some understanding of Puritanism and its origins."

One of the most important Christian creeds in which the United States believes is the "the doctrine of election (elitism)," symbolized by the expression "City on a Hill." On March 21, 1630, aboard the *Arbella* during its voyage to the Massachusetts Bay Colony, John Winthrop, a Puritan lawyer from England, delivered a sermon entitled "A Model of Christian Charity." In that sermon, Winthrop urged his audience, upon their arrival to the colonies, to build a city on a hill, from where they could save the whole world by obedience to the will of God.

However, the good intention to be a city on a hill and spread the will of God to the world, in many cases, opened the gates of hell. Throughout its history, America has exemplified the saying, "The road to hell is paved with good intentions." To understand this unfortunate paradox, we need to examine the dominant American behavior derived from this idea of being a "city on a hill." Those behaviors include white supremacy, that only white people could carry out God's will, and a black-and-white logic that regarded American values as good and non-American values as evil. From the process of "spreading the word" to the world was derived a sense of calling to eliminate evil on earth, even by force, if necessary.

Accordingly, the more evil removed from the earth, the more "good works" in line with "God's will" could be achieved. Additionally, such achievement was regarded as indirect evidence guaranteeing God's salvation. Therefore, the United States, longing for God's salvation, felt compelled to use ruthless force to endlessly wage crusades to rid the world of evil. The military-industrial complex grew enormously in the US. This ultimately led to the widespread deep state activity centered in the military-industrial complex.

One of the reasons I came to the United States to study was because I expected the United States of America, as a Christian country, to love its enemies according to the teachings of Jesus. I realized over and over again that it was just an illusion. The US has labeled the forces that challenge its power as "evil," rather than enemies. It justified crusades to get rid of evil, based on Christian beliefs. This trend was especially exacerbated during the Cold War. The Korean War and the Vietnam War were carried out after the US labeled atheist communists as evil. After the 9/11 terrorist attacks, the so-called "war on terror" was waged by labeling terrorist forces in the Islamic world as evil.

In America's crusades against evil, any ethical considerations became superfluous. For example, the act of declaring war means that warring parties both adhere to the rules of war, but from America's point of view, adherence to such rules was nothing but coddling evil. It was no coincidence that Nobel Peace Prize winner Barack Obama assassinated Osama bin Laden without a declaration of war. America's view of war as crusades against evil gave birth to a demonic habit that overthrew all existing war ethics.

There is another matter of serious concern to me as I examine America's approach to war as crusades—the fact that the same view of war has rampantly been carried out on the Korean Peninsula since the Korean War. Before and during the War, America's massacre of more than 1 million civilians, under the pretext of "wiping out the reds," originated in the American view of war as a crusade. The American mindset that regards North Korea as a member of the "axis of evil," has entrenched the Cold War on the Korean Peninsula. Accordingly, the Korean Peninsula is bound to be divided forever, because the devilish DPRK is not considered a potential political partner, but an evil that someday must be eliminated by whatever means necessary.

American militarism is also a source of destruction to the health of the United States. One of the advantages of US-led capitalism is a market that operates on the principle of free competition. However, the military-industrial complex, fueled by American militarism, does not sell its weapons to individuals, but to the government. The government uses the taxes collected from its citizens to purchase said weapons. There can be no healthy capitalist competition in such a market, leading to rampant corruption. In this scenario, if the capitalist market collapses, it will take the middle class, protagonist of democracy, with it. These are not unrealistic assumptions, but the reality unfolding in the United States today.

America's ancestors wanted to build a city on a hill from which they could save the whole world. However, the United States has established itself instead as a hegemonic power that continually enforces their original sin, a combination of racism and militarism, on the world. At the end of the Cold War, the United States was the world's preeminent power. Thirty years later, however, the US is in decline. To find the cause of this decline, we must pay particular attention to the original sin of militarism. How could the US avoid exhausting its national power when it was constantly engaged in costly wars the world over?

To save its future, the United States needs to purge the original sins of militarism and racism. To put it in my own terms, the US must transform its intransigent "security paradigm" into a "peace paradigm." Instead of treating adversaries as evil and annihilating them, the

United States must create an ethic of life for peaceful coexistence. Doing so will change not only the future of America, but also the future of humankind. Wouldn't that make America the "city on the hill" of which America's ancestors dreamed?

Understanding Democracy through its *Idealtypus*

Ever since witnessing the violation of democracy in the April 19th Movement in 1960, I have asked myself a question. What is democracy? In Seoul National University classrooms, I learned that "American democracy" was the best example. Seeing such democracy being trampled upon by the tyranny of the Syngman Rhee regime, I had no choice but to take to the streets. Most of my friends had the same idea. After gathering *en masse*, we marched to Gyeongmudae, the former Blue House.

I've now lived in the United States for more than half a century since 1965, and I've been able to study the American democracy that I had so envied. During this period, I have observed ten Presidential administrations, from President Lyndon Johnson to President Donald Trump.[66] I observed American democracy from a certain distance, from a stranger's point of view. I also tried to understand it academically from the perspective of a professor of political science. Even so, I am still asking the question I first raised in the middle of the April 19th Movement. What is democracy?

---

[66] The original memoir was written before Joe Biden's administration; this translation was published after.

The democracy I observe here is unique to the United States, because it was born in a particular environment and historical moment. Therefore, it is by no means *the* democracy to be admired and followed in Korea, because democracy in Korea should prescribe solutions that fit the environment and particular problems that Korea faces.

Only upon discovering Max Weber did I begin to put an end to my long academic wanderings. I began to study Weber in earnest after attending lectures by Professor Don Martindale of the Department of Sociology at the University of Minnesota. Martindale was a German-American scholar who studied sociology directly from Weber. Studying Weber allowed me to explore almost anything I wanted. The reason I studied political science was because I wanted to diagnose the problems of the reality, where politics work, and provide a prescription if possible. Weber's scholarship provided a decisive opportunity to satisfy these needs. Weber's social science research tool, called "*idealtypus*,"[67] has been of great help to me in developing my own research methodology in the context of philosophy of science.

To understand democracy correctly, one must first construct the ideal type of democracy. To provide a simple illustration to help us understand *idealtypus*, think of a caricature of a character. The caricature exaggerates the character's best features and omits the rest. For example, if you look at the caricatures of Abraham Lincoln, the sideburns, thick eyebrows, and skinny face are particularly

---

[67] *Idealtypus* is a term coined by sociologist Max Weber, meaning "ideal type" or "pure type" in German.

emphasized. Therefore, although a caricature is inevitably an abstract composition that is far from reality, it has the advantage of clearly revealing the key aspects of a person's appearance.

Idealtypus can be constructed and used similarly to highlight the best features of a historical reality. It is worth noting that the "ideal" in *idealtypus* particularly means the "logical ideal," not the moral ideal.

If we construct the *idealtypus* of democracy, we can compare it to American or Korean democracy. Thus, it will be possible to critically evaluate the achievements of those particular democracies by analyzing how close they are to the ideal. One can also compare American and Korean democracies to get a clear picture of the problems each one faces.

Democracy was born in the Age of Enlightenment. As is well known, the Enlightenment emerged from the modern worldview created by the scientific revolution in the 17th century. The essence of the Enlightenment can be summarized into three main ideas—reason, science, and the individual. The scientific revolution, led by human reason, played a decisive role in replacing the Christian worldview of the middle ages. Humans were reborn as independent subjects who shape their destinies according to their own rational judgment. Before the Age of Enlightenment, humans only had to perform the duties imposed on them. Humans reborn in the Age of Enlightenment were subjective individuals who could assert their rights. With these attributes, the Enlightenment became the ground for the birth of various democratic thinkers.

The democratic ideal can be constructed by referencing the

democratic thinkers born in the Age of Enlightenment. There are five important perspectives, namely freedom, equality, separation of powers, consent, and persuasion.

The meaning of "freedom," which is essential in democracy, was established through the so-called "social contract theory" and has two main meanings—freedom from the medieval priesthood and freedom from the tyranny of the state. The Middle Ages was a time when religion dominated politics. But the Enlightenment separated politics from religion, based on scientific reason. The political freedom enjoyed in democracy also meant freedom from religion. This part deserves special attention, because if the principle of separation of church and state is not observed, the foundation of democracy, born during the Age of Enlightenment, will immediately collapse. The basic requirements of democracy were formed through social contract theory. The ruler is elected by contract with his subjects. Instead of ruling unilaterally, the ruler must exercise power according to the agreement established with the governed people. Thus, the people could enjoy certain freedom, within the terms of the contract.

There are certain things to keep in mind about the freedom enjoyed in democracy. Firstly, freedom never means self-indulgence. If freedom is permitted to be practiced as self-indulgence, democracy will soon shrink to anarchy. Liberal thinkers in the 18th Century consistently emphasized the difference between freedom and license. John Locke emphasized this point in his *Two Treatises of Government,* "...though this be a state of liberty, yet it is not a state of license... The state of nature has a law of nature to govern it, which obliges every one."

Secondly, freedom of democracy implies the right to resistance or revolution. When a ruler violates, rather than safeguard, the freedom promised by the social contract, the people have the right to resist or replace him. Thirdly, the freedom of democracy encompasses both passive and active freedoms. Negative freedom means freedom from something. This includes freedom from religion and freedom from the tyranny of the state. On the other hand, positive freedom means freedom of choice. For example, the freedom to participate in voting and choose a political party. Fourthly, I pay particular attention to freedom of the press, because the media plays the role of providing the necessary oxygen for a democracy to breathe. If freedom of the press is not guaranteed, the democracy will inevitably suffocate. John Milton also emphasized freedom of the press in his *Areopagitica,* "Give me the liberty to know, to utter, and to argue freely according to conscience, above all liberties."

However, we should not forget that if freedom of the press was practiced through license of the press, society would also immediately fall into anarchy.

Equality must be guaranteed for democracy to be materialize. Equality is usually understood as a socialist principle, but democracy also demands equality. John Locke emphasized in the *Two Treatises of Government* that, "Being all equal and independent, no one ought to harm another in his life, health, liberty, or possessions…"

Only when human equality is guaranteed can the principle of majority rule, the essence of democracy, be maintained. Additionally, requisite "submission" to the majority vote presupposes human equality. Democracy can only be maintained if the majority vote is accepted. Failure to submit to the decisions of the majority of equal human beings is to demand the privilege of rejecting human equality itself.

Democracy requires separation of powers. Power is an indispensable means of government, but history shows that when power is monopolized, it is almost invariably abused. If a ruler abuses power, the ruler's subjects cannot be guaranteed freedom. How can we solve the antinomian task of acknowledging the power necessary to govern while preventing its abuse? The classic solution to the problem is the separation of powers, proposed by Montesquieu. In Book 11 of *The Spirit of Laws*, "Of the laws which establish political liberty, with regard to the Constitution," Montesquieu proposed a plan to separate the legislative, judicial, and administrative bodies to achieve mutual checks and balances.

Democracy means politics by the consent of the people. The people's active political participation is necessary to achieve their wise consent. Therefore, the qualitative level of democracy inevitably depends on the people's political maturity. This is why political or civic education emerges as an important theme of democracy.

The role of the middle class is very important in understanding the democratic political participation, because the middle class is generally the class that pays closest attention to the country's peace and prosperity. The primary concern of the upper class is to maintain their vested interests, while, the lower class does not have enough time to think about the future of the country, because they are too busy living paycheck to paycheck. Therefore, a healthy middle class is essential for developing a democracy. A market culture with an active middle class has "selective affinity" with the culture of democracy, because the middle class 'act of selecting products based on rational calculations in the market is qualitatively similar to the act of selecting political candidates based on rational calculations during an election.

Politics by the consent of the people also means governing according to laws enacted with the people's consent. This is where the rule of law comes into play, namely, constitutionalism. When a government is governed by laws agreed upon by the people, the government secures legitimacy, which means support entailed by the feelings of the people. Democracy can only operate stably through legitimacy. When such legitimacy is not secured, and a government faces a crisis of legitimacy, that democracy is bound to collapse in an instant. Furthermore, constitutionalism requires the people to obey the law. If the people do not abide by the laws enacted with their consent, democracy is bound to degenerate into anarchy.

Finally, democracy requires reasonable persuasion. This means that rather than being pressured, by financial and political power, people reach decisions rationally, through a process of persuasion by reason.

American Democracy, Ideals and Reality

The eleven US Presidents I observed while living in the United States these more than fifty years have revealed the diversity of American democracy. During that time, the Democrats produced five Presidents, and the Republicans produced six. Johnson took responsibility for the Vietnam War and abandoned his re-election, while Nixon resigned shortly before impeachment due to the Watergate scandal. I also saw Obama step in as the first African American President in the United States, which I found bizarre since racism had not been resolved in the United States. Obama could be elected because American political culture had largely been reformed through Martin Luther King, Jr's civil rights movement. I also witnessed the particular limitation that not a single female President has been elected.

As one afflicted with a longing for peace, two Presidents I particularly noticed were Jimmy Carter and George W. Bush. America is a nation of war. All US Presidents, except Carter, have waged wars. There were no war dead during Carter's tenure. Carter is also a devout Christian, but he never reflected his faith in government policy. In other words, he strictly complied with the principle of separation of church and state, as set forth in the Constitution of the United States of America. For peace in the Middle East, he gave political recognition to not only Israel but also to the Islamic Palestinian Autonomous Region. This recognition birthed the Camp David Accords of 1978.

George W. Bush was the exact opposite of Jimmy Carter. After the September 11, 2001 terrorist attacks, he immediately started the "War on Terror." In particular, he declared that North Korea, Iraq, Iran, and Syria should be permanently removed from the earth, labeling them the "axis of evil." Like Carter, Bush is also a devout Christian, but unlike Carter, he resolutely reflected his Christian beliefs in his

▲ Beginning on September 5th, 1978, Egyptian President Sadat (left) and Israeli Prime Minister Begin (right) stayed together at Camp David for 13 days of negotiations organized by US President Carter (center), culminating with the historic "Camp David Accords" signed at the White House on September 17th. (Photo courtesy of Jimmy Carter Library)

policies. The concept of an "axis of evil" was itself a product of the Christian view of good and evil. Any member of this so-called "axis of evil," such as the DPRK, was not a partner for political negotiations, but merely an object to be thoroughly punished militarily.

Even Bush's term "war on terror" is a concept that cannot stand logical scrutiny. What they called a "war on terror" was not a war, but a kind of campaign aimed to gain the support of international public opinion. No matter how powerful the United States 'means of warfare, the campaign will never end. Therefore, the "war on terrorism" is bound to go on forever. If "war" continues like this, the US 'principles of democracy pursued will continuously and inevitably erode.

American democracy is not without its merits. Above all, American democracy was not a successor to an existing system, but a new creation. It was designed as a prescription to wisely respond to the various challenges posed by the particular circumstances of the United States. Such creative spirit was evident in Benjamin Franklin's speech at the convention of the Constitutional Congress on June 28, 1787:

> We have gone back to ancient history for models of government, and examined the different forms of those Republics which having been formed with the seeds of their own dissolution now no longer exist. And we have considered Modern States across Europe, but find none of their Constitutions suitable to our circumstances. In this situation of this Assembly groping as it were in the dark to find political truth...

In order to properly understand American democracy, we should consider a sociology of knowledge perspective, which regards environmental particularity as important. The challenges the United States had to face in the early days of its founding can be summarized into five points: firstly, after the Revolution, they had to create the political system of the Declaration of Independence to guarantee freedom, equality, and the pursuit of happiness; secondly, they had to create a means to ensure individual safety despite the limited national security capability; thirdly, they had to guarantee equal rights to the thirteen States; fourthly, after the Civil War, they had to guarantee equal rights to minorities, such as African and Indigenous Americans—making it necessary to create a political system that could realize social justice; and fifthly, since the United States is a country created by immigrants, they had to use that political system to resolve the problems raised by a multiracial society.

The United States has taken relatively effective countermeasures against these challenges. Let us evaluate it from the perspective of freedom established in the ideal type of democracy. In the first amendment to the Constitution, Congress systematically guaranteed the freedom, equality, and pursuit of happiness called for in the Declaration of Independence. The amendment, which is called the Bill of Rights, stipulated freedoms of religion, speech, press, petition, and assembly. In particular, it proclaimed a principle of freedom of religion, thoroughly separating politics from religion in accordance with the intellectual tradition of the Enlightenment. In addition, to ensure personal safety despite weak national security capability, the second amendment stipulated the right of individuals to carry firearms. The task of guaranteeing the rights of minorities, such as African and Indigenous Americans, was also solved through a difficult process.

Congress ratified the 15th Amendment to the Constitution in 1870, giving African Americans the right to vote, the 19th Amendment in 1920, giving women the right to vote, and the Snyder Act in 1924, recognizing the suffrage of Indigenous Americans.

The freedoms guaranteed by the US Constitution are relatively well implemented in real politics. For Americans, freedom means "freedom within the institution." There is a strong social consensus that freedom outside the system should be thoroughly sanctioned. This was the decisive reason why freedom in American society did not become "indulgent," as liberal 18th century thinkers feared.

The principle of thoroughly separating politics from religion is also relatively well observed, at least in US domestic politics. People tend to be completely turned off when certain religious groups openly support a particular candidate in an election campaign. The high level of civic education in the United States protects democracy.

What I pay most attention to is freedom of the press. I believe that guaranteeing freedom of the press is like giving democracy oxygen to breathe. This oxygen is supplied through objective reporting. The US media's role is intended to be limited to faithful, objective reporting. Accordingly, the media should not try to teach the people what is right and what is wrong, but only provide materials by which the people can judge situations for themselves. In particular, as a rule, the media in the US does not campaign in elections. In the United States, any media outlet that explicitly advocates for a particular politician or political party would not be able to survive, because the people would ignore it. The high standards of civic education in the United States protects freedom of the press.

On the other hand, editorial and column writers in the US media interpret and criticize media reports based on their own insight. This is one way the media performs a political education function. However, there is no case where a media company executive stepped forward as a writer.

I have also actively expressed my views through American and international media. For 14 years, I worked as a political critic on ABC, and then continued to work on CNN, among others. Even now, I continue to fill in as a political affairs commentator on the BBC in the UK, Al Jazeera in the Middle East, TRT in Turkey, and NHK in Japan.

◄ Broadcasting on CNN. (*Hankyoreh* file photo)

I was able to learn the norms of democratic debate through political criticism in the international media. For example, after I gave political commentary about North Korean issues on Al Jazeera, which has different political interests from the United States, American broadcasting companies often invited me for an interview on similar topics. They usually hire experts who have a different opinion than mine and get them to debate me. On Al Jazeera and American television, I have consistently expressed my views about North Korea, based on my research. The experts who disagree with me also express their views clearly. There has never been a case where an argument turns into a catastrophe, with each cast member blushing. Even if I do not agree with the other in debate, I take an attitude of understanding his point of view, and the other person does the same. The viewers horizon of understanding broadens while watching our debate. That process is a living example of political education.

Another important point that I have learned while participating in interviews with the American and international media is their dominant standard of "professionalism." "Professionalism" is a cultural phenomenon—wholly different from "expertise," meaning an individual's professional ability. Even a "generalist" who can talk about everything, but doesn't really know anything, can be professional in that context.

However, not all freedoms practiced in American democracy are good. From the point of view of freedom established by the ideal type of democracy, the constitutional right to carry personal firearms deserves criticism. The United States has the highest number of firearm-related deaths in the world. Carrying a gun to protect my freedom means a high risk of annihilating the freedom of others.

The United States created a federal system to ensure equal rights for the thirteen states. Congress adopted system of representation, in which each State, regardless of size, is allocated two Senators. The electoral college system was also created to reflect the autonomy of each State in the Presidential elections. However, these institutions are not problem-free, from the point of view of equality established by the ideal type of democracy. In the Enlightenment, equality meant individual equality, not group equality. The US Senate and the Electoral College are premised on equality of groups called "States." As a result, there continue to be undemocratic contradictions, such as Al Gore and Hillary Clinton failing to be elected President despite gaining the majority of the American people's support.

Of course, American democracy is not without merits when evaluating it in terms of equality. The first strength is a "culture of acceptance." No matter how fiercely the presidential candidates fight during the election campaign, when the election results are announced, the loser is expected to surrender without delay and gives the winner a congratulatory call. Because I believe that this American-made standard of accepting the will of the people is one indicator symbolizing the health of American democracy. A majority vote system presupposes individual equality. Failure to submit to the majority vote means violating individual equality, in which case, democracy itself will inevitably collapse.

The United States 'Articles of Confederation were prepared in 1776 and adopted by the Continental Congress 'when all of the colonies ratified them in March 1781. However, because there was little power conferred upon the Confederation, the nation created through the Articles of Confederation was weak in its capacity for political coordination. To solve this problem, in 1787, the Constitutional Convention created the federal government. The federal government created the office of the President, which was entrusted with executive political power. However, fearing that the President could abuse power and violate the people's freedom, the Convention adopted a system of separation of powers. To prevent corruption of power, the legislative, judiciary, and executive branches maintain checks and balances between each other. However, the Presidential power has expanded, especially during the Cold War. The President could start a war by executive order, even without congressional approval. Additionally, the President can appoint all nine Supreme Court judges and can even exercise amnesty, all of which threaten the basis of the separation of powers.

Another strength of American democracy is the "jury system," which I think is the most dramatic implementation of consent by the people. A jury of twelve members is randomly selected, irrespective of educational background or social status. The selected jury makes its decision through democratic debate. I, too, have been selected to serve on a jury several times and took a leading role in the democratic debates. Each time, I was able to experience a living embodiment of the consent of "We the People," for which the American democracy stands.

Finally, American democracy can be said to be a system operated by rational persuasion. Democratic customs are so firmly rooted that any persuasion based on kinship, academic ties, regionalism, money, or power is generally unacceptable.

South Korean Democracy, Ideals and Reality

Visiting South Korea, meeting acquaintances, and chatting about democracy has often left me thinking. I notice, as I listen to them talking, that the United States 'democracy is usually presupposed to be the gold-standard for democracy. I always feel uncomfortable leaving conversations where America's "advanced" democracy is presumed the example for criticizing the ROK's "backward" democracy.

How can American democracy be regarded as the standard for the ROK to follow? Wasn't American democracy a particular form designed to respond to the challenges unique to the United States? If such characteristics of its democracy were properly understood, shouldn't the ROK's democracy also be made "Korean," in that it is designed to effectively meet the challenges posed by South Korea's unique context?

I summarize the historical legacies posing challenges to Korean democracy in five points. First is the legacy of monarchy. The Three Kingdoms period, the Goryeo period, and the Joseon period were all ruled by monarchs. Under monarchy, there was no concept of individual freedom and equality. In particular, the Joseon Dynasty brought about qualitative changes in political culture by establishing Neo-Confucianism as the state religion. Korean historians focused on ignoring or positively interpreting party strife and flunkyism under the excuse of overcoming so-called "colonial history." Such attempts only contributed to preserving a legacy of party strife and flunkyism. The uncompromising political struggle so clearly seen in the ROK's current political environment and the mentality so biased toward the United States—to the extent that people wave American flags at rallies—cannot be explained without the Joseon Dynasty's legacy of party strife and flunkyism.

Second is the legacy of Japanese colonial rule. The Japanese imperialists tried to annihilate Korean national identity through policies like the Name Changing Program. In the meantime, the pro-Japanese faction gained momentum, and those who participated in the independence movement suffered unspeakable hardships. This absurd legacy still exists today. The saying, "Those who fought for independence will perish for three generations" is an expression that directly exposes a harsh reality.

Third, there is the legacy of division. When the Korean peninsula was physically divided by foreign powers, the Korean people's way of thinking also became deeply divided. Thus, it was impossible to develop an independent political consciousness that could promise the common prosperity of the Korean people.

Fourth is the legacy of the Korean War. Millions of people died in the War, not to mention the Yeo-Sun Incident, Jeju April 3rd Incident, Korean Territorial Army Incident, and National Guidance Alliance

Incident, among others. In the films *Red Tomb* and *Haewon* (meaning "relieving grievances") which director Koo Ja-hwan produced after 10 years of visiting sites of civilian massacres, it is clear that the entire land of Korea was a killing field. My father was also one of those who had to suffer his whole life being stigmatized "a red." I, too, was regarded as a pro-North Korean scholar, another name for "a red," and lived my whole life with many restrictions on my academic research and social activities. Hostility against "the reds," that arouses an almost instinctive curse, still dominates the mental world of Koreans. In Korea, branding people as reds is used as indulgence to justify all kinds of violence.

Fifth is the legacy of the Cold War. The Cold War solidified the division and legacy of the Korean War. It cemented the distrust, fear, and force of a security paradigm on the Korean Peninsula, accelerated the war of legitimacy between the two Koreas, and normalized military tensions on the Korean Peninsula. Meanwhile, the ROK and DPRK both became military powers. South Korea has a military-industrial complex modeled after the US military-industrial complex, and conducts annual ROK-US military exercises. Threatened and backed into a corner, North Korea became a nuclear-armed state.

South Korean democracy was unable to face these challenges posed by Korean history, because its democracy was not created independently by Korean people but was transplanted from the United States. As a result, the ROK's democracy reflexively focused more on solving the agenda set by the US global strategy instead of solving national problems. For this reason, the pro-Japanese faction in Korea transformed itself into a pro-American faction and was able to lead Korean democracy. Although the current South Korean democracy is considered an example of successful acceptance of American democracy, severe conflicts and all sorts of irregularities persist, mostly due to the clash between the system imported from the United States and the challenges posed by Korea's historical legacy.

Let's analyze the reality of the problems inherent in South Korean democracy using the ideal type of democracy as the standard. The most important value in democracy is individual freedom. However, individual freedom has been incessantly violated throughout the history of South Korean democracy. Consider the case of the Special Investigation Committee of Anti-National Activities that was led by the pro-Japanese police, the case of the Fraction in the National Assembly led by the Japanese imperialist prosecutor, the case of Jo Bong-am who was framed and killed as a Communist spy, the case of East Berlin which was the biggest fabricated espionage case since the Liberation, the case of the Inhyuk Party, the May 18 Gwangju Massacre, and that of Park Jong-cheol's torture resulting in death, among others. Even now, the National Assembly has not passed the Liquidation of the Past History Act, as solicited by the Korean War-Bereaved Association.

Liberal thinkers in the 18th Century consistently emphasized the fact that liberty and license are two completely different things. Freedom necessarily requires discipline to comply with laws and norms, the foundation of social order. When freedom lacks discipline, it soon turns into indulgence. In my view, the freedom asserted in Korean democracy is often very close to indulgence. For example, under the Park Geun-hye administration, a human rights group joined by North Korean defectors was defending the act of sending "propaganda leaflet balloons" to North Korea in the name of freedom of expression. In the world of international politics, war is always possible. If a war breaks out due to the act of sending those balloons, could anyone defend it in the name of freedom of expression? In fact, the DPRK had warned several times that it would fire at South Korea if it continued to send the balloons. Ignorance to a degree of taking freedom as license to indulgence could lead to a catastrophe on the Korean Peninsula.

Liberty, which is highly valued in democracy, is basically a value born out of the philosophy of the Enlightenment. One of the major focuses in Enlightenment ideology is the separation of politics and religion. The political and religious freedoms permitted by democracy must be completely separated. Such separation was achieved so that religion's intrusion into the public realm of politics was prohibited, limiting religion to the private realm of the individual.

Nevertheless, in Korea, there is a pattern of close ties between powerful Presidents and certain religions. We should not forget that the most horrific catastrophes experienced in human history stemmed mostly from religious wars in which politics and religion collided. Look at the Middle East, where religious wars are rampant and continue endlessly. A political struggle based on negotiation and compromise is completely different qualitatively from a religious struggle in which negotiation and compromise are impossible. When politics and religion collide, negotiation and compromise become virtually impossible, and politics itself disappears.

The important democratic value of equality that is the theoretical basis of majority rule. Since the majority vote presupposes equality, it must always be accepted. It is a privileged claim that denies equality by refusing to agree to a majority vote. In my view, Korean democracy is very weak in the culture of acceptance of diversity.

It is common sense that separation of powers, not concentration of powers, is the basis of democracy. That common sense did not work properly in the history of democracy in Korea. As is well known, during the military dictatorship, the President illegally exercised enormous power and violated human rights of the people countless times. The phenomenon of understanding the President, who wielded such mighty power, as the nation's Father, or his wife, as the nation's Mother, proves that Korean society has not yet cast off the legacy of monarchy.

As Korean democratization progressed after the June Uprising in 1987, a consensus was formed that it was necessary to weaken the power of the President. The ideology of liberal democracy in Europe significantly influenced that consensus. In liberal democracy, it is desirable to weaken the power of the ruler to achieve a minimal government. However, it is important to note that modern democracy is not realized by weakening the power of the rulers. A government with a weak ruler is a politically incompetent government. A politically incompetent government is likely to provide an excuse for dictatorship by failing to resolve social chaos. It was no coincidence that the politically incompetent Chang Myon government provided this excuse for General Park Chung-hee's *coup d'etat*.

Democracy means legitimate exercise of power. The purpose of checking the power of the President through separation of powers in democracy is to prevent illegal exercise of power. However, that does not mean a weakening of power. If we weaken the power, the key means of governing, the government will not be able to perform its original function. The State requires a great deal of power to pursue public goods such as security, economic growth, distributional justice, and resolution of environmental problems in particular.

Democracy is essentially a political system operated on the consent of the people. As I said earlier, the key to the people's consent is the support of the middle class. In reality, the interests of the upper class is to maintain its vested interests, and the interests of the lower class is focused on economic survival, while the middle class can pay attention to the public values of the country and future problems with some economic leeway. In Korea, it was not easy to foster the middle class because the national economic development strategy was centered on large enterprises. Moreover, as globalization progresses in Korea, wealth polarization is deepening, which means that the decline of the middle class is accelerating. When the middle class collapses, democracy inevitably faces a crisis.

Democracy is also a political system operated by rational persuasion. The culture of rational persuasion in Korean democracy is very weak. Violent protests are staged in the National Assembly and the hall of democracy, and lawmakers are often witnessed fighting outside of court. In particular, if we carefully observe the pattern of life-and-death struggle between the ruling and opposition parties, we cannot help but admit that it is the same dead split of the party strife from the Joseon Dynasty. How can we expect a future for democracy in Korea without making efforts to create a climate for rational persuasion?

One task of Korean democracy, which is clearly revealed through Korea's historical legacy and cannot be found in the ideal type of Western democracy, is the peaceful unification of the Korean Peninsula. In other words, peaceful unification of the Korean Peninsula is a particular task imposed only on Korean democracy. Without peaceful unification, there is no lasting guarantee of peace and stability on the Korean Peninsula.

Nevertheless, research papers and textbooks on Korean democracy circulated in Korea commonly miss the task of peaceful unification of the Korean Peninsula. I believe this serious limitation is derived from the fact that Korean democracy has mainly tried to follow the instructions of democracy books published in the United States. As a result, the importance of peace and unification on the Korean Peninsula has inevitably faded in Korea's "climate of public opinion." Even among Korean intellectuals, opinions such as "Our wish is not unification" and "Peace should be prioritized over unification" are spreading. Intellectuals, who should lead the "climate of public opinion," tend to ignore the existential challenge of the nation due to their non-historical, anti-intellectual, and non-subjective mentality. Have the intellectuals of the country they adore, America, turned away from the challenges America faced?

Democracy in Korea must become a "Korean" democracy that solves the existential problems facing the nation of Korea. The *raison d'être* of Korean intellectuals must be found in their dedication to such solutions.

Part 3:
The Path to
Understanding North Korea

When I first visited the DPRK, I often felt perplexed, particularly when
hearing slogans such as "Nothing to envy in the world," "I love my
country the most," and "People's paradise"... A high-ranking North
Korean official once told me, "There are countless countries in the world.
However, the DPRK is set far apart from those countries, standing alone.
As a country, we could say it is like Dokdo Island."

Understanding Socialism through its *Idealtypus*

Thinking Beyond the Line is a book that presents a proposal to overcome anti-DPRK prejudice by crossing various "lines" that strangle our thinking. I couldn't help but be surprised to hear that the first 15,000 copies sold in six months. I never expected the book would receive such a great response because it was just a narrated summary of some problems about which I had long felt sorry—in an interview format no less! Perhaps that response is evidence that Korean readers long to move past their anti-DPRK prejudice. Could it be that such a longing could drive open the way for peace and unification on the Korean Peninsula, fulfilling my lifelong desire?

The DPRK is a socialist state. Therefore, to truly understand it, one must first understand socialism. However, North Korea has not achieved the abstract concept of socialism at face value, because socialism in Korea was formed in response to the historical challenges on the peninsula. Therefore, we should first examine the *idealtypus* of socialism, as we examined the *idealtypus* of democracy.

The socialist ideal can encompass concepts from Marx's theory of socialism, Lenin's Soviet socialism, and Mao's Chinese socialism. The DPRK's socialism was created by careful selection of various aspects of all three—Marxist, Leninist, and Maoist socialism.

Marx was born in 1818 and died in 1883. The contemporary 19th century was a time when democracy and capitalism, which emerged against the backdrop of the Enlightenment, took root in European society. The basis for democracy is individual freedom, while individual ownership is the basis for capitalism. As an inevitable result of the individualized values, as democracy and capitalism developed, the gap between the rich and the poor increased. In this system, those with a means of production were tended to become the bourgeoisie class, while those without a means of production tended to become the proletariat class. Class conflict intensifies in unequal societies.

Marx tried to suggest an alternative to overcome the inherent contradictions of capitalism. He viewed private ownership as the source of inequality in capitalist society. Therefore, in his judgment, achieving an egalitarian society requires abolishing private property. He thought that so-called "just distribution" could be achieved if private ownership and distribution were replaced by collective ownership and distributed on the basis of need rather than desire. He was convinced that necessity-based distribution was just.

However, it was not an easy task to abolish private property and establish an egalitarian society in a society where capitalism had already taken root. Faced with the reality of those challenges, Marx advocated the so-called "dictatorship of the proletariat," through which the proletariat defeats the bourgeoisie and ascends to political power through struggle against capitalist society. Marx was convinced that the proletariat could inevitably physically subdue the bourgeoisie by virtue of numerical superiority. Convinced of their victory, Marx imagined a society in which a proletariat dictatorship abolished private property. Without private property, he predicted society would be classless and free of class struggle. Marx imagined such a society would be a utopia where all men would be equal.

Marx believed that socialism should be implemented globally, rather than capitalism. For this reason, at the end of the Manifesto of the Communist Party, which he co-authored with Engels, Marx emphasized, "Workers of the world, unite!" This is where we find the internationalist character of Marx's socialist revolution.

In the preface to the *Critique of Hegel's Philosophy of Right,* Marx famously argued that "religion is the opium of the people." In his view, humanity makes religion, not vice versa. He did not believed humans were souls that existed outside of the physical world. For Marx, who valued the secular world, religion was nothing more than an illusion that inverted physical reality. Therefore, he emphasized the critique of religion as the premise of all critique.

Marx's critique of religion stems from his historical materialism. Put simply, historical materialism is economic determinism. He decided that the economy, constituting the substructure of society, determines the politics, law, and human consciousness which comprise the superstructure of society. Therefore, he predicted that by transforming the proprietary relations of the substructure, it would also be possible to transform the entire superstructure. However, Marx thought that by paralyzing human consciousness, religion could be the most powerful factor in hindering transformation. Therefore, he could never tolerate religion functioning as an impediment to social development.

However, most of Marx's theories have not materialized in reality, because the predicted fierce struggle between the bourgeoisie and the proletariat did not occur in European capitalist society in the first place. The reason the class struggle did not occur in European society was the emergence of the middle class. In capitalist society, the proletariat established itself as a so-called "pillar of industry" by becoming skilled laborers. The bourgeoisie could not easily discharge such members of even the low class. The proletariat was empowered to collectively resist the bourgeoisie by forming trade unions. Therefore, the bourgeoisie was forced to choose a strategy to increase the productivity of the factories while raising the wages of the proletariat. As wages rose, the proletariat entered the middle class. The middle class now had enough income to become market consumers. The goods the middle class purchased were those produced in bourgeoisie factories. In short, as capitalism developed, rather than an overt class war, the bourgeoisie and proletariat's relationship evolved symbiotically.

Another important moment in my opinion is the emergence of the machine gun. Marx foresaw that the proletariat, outnumbering the bourgeoisie, would secure victory in a straight fight. However, the advent of automatic weapons during World War I precluded the inevitability of the masses overcoming the few. The few bourgeoisie with machine guns could easily overpower the majority of the proletariat.

Although Marx's theory was not fulfilled in Europe, Lenin took note of it in Russia. He decided that Marx's theory could not be applied directly to Russia as it was born in the context of the growing contradictions of European capitalism. However, Russia was not capitalist, but a rural society made up mainly of impoverished peasants. Therefore, capitalism could not drive the struggle between the bourgeoisie and the proletariat, and without a class struggle, one could not expect a dictatorship of the proletariat. Therefore, Lenin concluded that the state should be the protagonist of the socialist revolution. So he undertook an innovation that replaced the private ownership of capitalism with state ownership. Rather than collective ownership, which Marx suggested as an alternative to private ownership, Lenin transformed the concept into state ownership across rural Russia. Lenin himself took over as head of state, ruling all of Russia. Stalin further expanded and deepened Lenin's totalitarianism when Russian leadership passed to him.

Socialism in China was established by Mao Zedong. Because of the great differences between Russia and China, Mao decided that Russian socialism could not be directly transplanted into China's context. He first paid attention to the reality of the impoverished rural areas in China. (Pearl Buck's novel *The Good Earth* provides a clear depiction of China's poverty at that time.) In addition, Mao paid special attention to what he called the "Century of National Humiliation,"[68] the reality that, for over a century since the Opium Wars, China had been ravaged by Western powers.

---

[68] Mao used the term "百年國恥" to describe the "Century of National Humiliation."

Mao Zedong created Chinese socialism to wisely respond to the challenges posed by its historical legacy. He proposed a two-staged revolution to liquidate the legacy of the Century of Humiliation. The first step was to overthrow the foreign powers, and the second one was to carry out a revolution within China. To realize this two-staged revolution, Mao's socialism had have a very nationalistic character that was not found in Marx's theory.

Mao Zedong also coined the term "the people."[69] He defined all people of Chinese nationality as "the people." Therefore, capitalists, the lower classes, peasants, and minorities all belonged to the people. That was why he named the country the People's Republic of China. Even the name reflects Mao's strong will to guarantee a free life for the people by completely eradicating the legacy of 100 years of shame and completing a political revolution within China.

During Mao Zedong's lifetime, without question, most of China's population were peasants suffering from severe poverty. Because Marx's class struggle between the bourgeoisie and the proletariat originated in the context of mature capitalism, the class struggle or dictatorship of the proletariat that Marx predicted could not be expected to occur in China. However, Mao wanted to reorganize the unequal structure of rural areas dominated by a small number of landowners into an equal one. Only then could the lives of the majority of peasants struggling in destitution be saved. Marx's argument that equality should be established by abolishing private property was very attractive to Mao. However, unlike Lenin, who chose state ownership,

---

[69] "The people" is pronounced "rénmín" and written "人民" in Chinese.

Mao chose collective ownership in which the people would play the leading role. It was for this reason that socialism in China has been implemented through "people's communes" of various sizes.

"People's communes" developed in two stages. At first, they began as collective farms, consisting of about 250 farming families. Afterwards, as the "Great Leap Forward" campaign (Second Five Year Plan) started in 1958, the people's communes were scaled up to entire urban areas. An individual commune often consisted of thousands of households of city workers. The people's commune system became the motor of China's socialist revolution machine.

The communes were operated in a two-headed system. One of the two leaders was elected by the commune, a skilled man with expertise. Another was sent by the Communist Party, a person with strong party loyalty. Of the two leaders, the real political power was held by a person dispatched by the Communist Party. Even so, he could not control everything. If he exercised his power arbitrarily, members of the commune could communicate their grievances to the Communist Party through their elected leader. Considering that, we can say that Chinese socialism has the characteristics of "people's socialism." The Russian socialist system only had leaders dispatched by the Communist Party, without leaders elected by the people.

North Korean Socialism, Ideals and Reality

I think that socialism in the DPRK should be examined in the same way we earlier considered democracy in the ROK. Having considering the *idealtypus* of socialism, I will examine the aspects of universal socialism that materialized in North Korea, then focus on how it resolved its own historical legacy in a socialist way to achieve certain particularities only found in the DPRK. By examining the universality and particularity of North Korean socialism, at the same time, I would like to propose a three-dimensional way of understanding it.

In the light of socialist *idealtypus*, the historical legacy borne by North Koreas was the same as that borne by South Koreans. Like its neighbor to the south, the DPRK had to overcome the legacy of monarchy, Japanese colonial rule, division, the Korean War, and the Cold War. However, unlike South Korea, the DPRK had to further struggle to resolve international political tensions caused by the Sino-Soviet conflict, security threats imposed by US forces on the peninsula and the ROK-US alliance, and systemic competition between the two Koreas. In the process of responding to this series of challenges, the DPRK ended up with a form of socialism unique to itself. As the universal ideology of socialism was filtered through the parameters of its particular environment, a unique socialism emerged that is only found in the DPRK.

The DPRK sought to establish equality by abolishing private property and adopting collective ownership, as advocated in Marxist theory. They put this collective ownership into practice in the form of cooperative farms, implemented with reference to people's communes in China.

Because there is no private ownership, it is impossible to accumulate wealth in North Korea, and income is relatively evenly distributed. When I visited universities, hospitals, and government institutions there to do firsthand research on the income differential within society, the gap between the top and bottom classes did not exceed double. Although I have visited quite a few socialist countries, I have not come across a case in which income was as evenly distributed as it is in North Korea.

In the DPRK, even when selling apartments, it is strictly necessary to sell "to each according to his needs." Apartments with many rooms are sold to large families, and apartments with fewer rooms are sold to those with fewer members. Social status is not considered to prevent selling large apartments to high-status people and small apartments to low-status people.

Marx predicted that abolishing private property would bring an end to class struggle and a peaceful utopia thereafter. Marx's utopian ideas were passed down to North Korea, whose ultimate goal became building a "paradise on earth" where class struggle is finished.

We could say that the DPRK adopted the concept of "the people" from Chinese socialism. Just as Mao Zedong tried to guarantee freedom for the people by removing historical shame from imperialist oppression and completing an internal political revolution, so Kim Il Sung also tried to guarantee the freedom of the people liberated from Japanese colonialism and American imperialism. We can also see Kim Il Sung's will evident in North Korea's official name, the Democratic People's Republic of Korea.

Following the example of the Chinese Communist Party, the DPRK organized the Workers' Party of Korea (WPK). There are hammers, brushes, and sickles drawn on the WPK's flag, symbolizing workers, intellectuals, and peasants, respectively, who are all members of the people. The flag emphasizes that the Workers' Party, the Mecca of North Korean politics, belongs not only to party members but to all the people of the DPRK.

South Koreans often ask me, "Who is the real ruler of North Korea?"

Every time I hear this question, I struggle to answer. In my view, there is no specific individual who can be regarded as the real power in the DPRK. Important decisions are made through collective discussions within the Workers' Party. Many say that Kim Jong Un makes decisions on his own, but that would not make any sense if they knew the nature of the Workers' Party.

Socialism in the DPRK includes unique features that cannot be found in the *idealtypus* of socialism, such as the *Juche* ideology, the leader theory, strong nationalism, the North Korean nuclear program, and the theory of reunification. All of these unique features stemmed directly from their special circumstances.

Juche ideology can be said to be the *Lebensführung* (principle for the conduct of life) that governs the social behavior of North Korean people. There is a vast repository of *Juche* ideology, steadily evolving along with the circumstances in the DPRK.

To put it simply, North Korean history is defined by its responses to the challenges of international politics. Throughout history, they have responded to many existential threats, including, but not limited to, those posed by Japanese colonial rule, national division, the Korean War, the Cold War, Sino-Soviet split, US hegemony, and systemic competition between the South and the North. They have developed strong nationalism while walking through the history of harsh international political struggles. In particular, North Korean nationalism inherited the "Martial Spirit" [70] characteristic of Goguryeo and Goryeo dynasties and is characterized by completely dismantling the legacy of the Joseon Dynasty's flunkyism and party strife. Kim Il Sung emphasized this in his memoir *With the Century*:

> Historically, corrupt and incompetent feudal rulers, who practiced flunkyism, fought within their own factions under the control of foreign powers, even when the fate of our country was at stake. As a result, if the pro-Japanese faction prevailed today, the Japanese army guarded the palace; if the pro-Russian faction prevailed tomorrow, the Russian army would escort the king; if the pro-Qing faction prevailed the day after tomorrow, the Qing army would guard the palace... If even the royal

---

[70] "Martial Spirit" can be written 상무정신 or 尙武精神 in Korean and Hanja/Chinese, respectively.

palace guard was entrusted to foreign armies, who will protect and take care of this country?

When I visited Pyongyang in the mid-1990s, television was not yet widely available there, and I could always hear *With the Century* being read on the radio. They read all eight volumes of *With the Century* throughout the year. Through such broadcast education, the DPRK instilled the people with a national consciousness.

North Korean nationalism was conceived in the form of anti-Japanese ideology through Kim Il Sung's anti-Japanese partisan movement. You can feel the the anti-Japanese ideology when you watch the famous North Korean movie *Sea of Blood*. I once met with Oh Jin-woo, Kim Il Sung's right-hand man who served as the head of the Korean People's Army and the chairman of the Party's Military Commission, to discuss current issues in North Korean society. Oh Jin-woo, a five-star general who was involved in anti-Japanese operations with Kim Il Sung, was two years older than him.

I asked Oh Jin-woo, "I feel that anti-Japanese sentiment is very strong in the DPRK. Wouldn't excessive anti-Japanese sentiment be a hindrance to pursuing your national interests?"

He answered, "Professor Park, you say that because you never experienced Japanese occupation firsthand. My sisters were taken as 'comfort women' for the Japanese military and suffered horrible slavery. It was not just my sisters. There are so many people in our nation who experienced similar suffering. I will never forgive the Japs."

I later confirmed that his words aligned with the Workers' Party position toward Japan.

North Korean nationalism, which inherited the national spirit of Goguryeo and Goryeo, was also practiced in foreign policy. The DPRK conducted equidistant diplomacy to maximize national interests in the midst of Sino-Soviet conflicts. The equidistance diplomacy skillfully used by the Joseon Dynasty inherited Goryeo's traditional "diplomacy of indecision."[71] Goryeo Dynasty carried out equidistant diplomacy between the Song and Khitans and between the Khitan and the Jurchen, to maximize their national interests.

That's not all. Many scholars call the DPRK's method of negotiating with the US "brinkmanship diplomacy." This, too, can be seen as what they learned from the brinkmanship diplomacy that Goryeo carried out against the Yuan Dynasty, the world's most powerful country at the time. Goryeo consolidated its national power by creating the Tripitaka Koreana, while repeatedly negotiating with the Yuan dynasty on one hand and resisting it on the other to protect the country to the end. Goguryeo also fought a decisive battle against the strongest powers, Sui and Tang, which could be understood in the same context. Can't we feel a sense of *déjà vu* in the nationalistic way that the DPRK conducts diplomacy on the brink against the world's most powerful nation, the United States?

I did feel the national spirit that was handed down from Goguryeo and Goryeo even in the various historical sites I visited. If you go to the Joseon History Museum, you can see at a glance that the artifacts

---

[71] "Diplomacy of Indecision" has been used here to connote the equidistant foreign relations to balance the national interest, and is written 양단외교 or 兩端外交 in Korean and Hanja/Chinese, respectively.

on display empirically and primarily demonstrate the national pride of Goguryeo and Goryeo. I saw the huge mausoleum of King Taejo Wang Geon[72] when I visited Kaesong, the capital city of Goryeo. The royal tomb of King Dongmyeongseong, the founder of Goguryeo, located near Pyongyang, was even bigger.

There is another point that must be noted when trying to understand North Korean nationalism. The DPRK places the origin of its legitimacy in the *Dangun Joseon* dynasty.[73] Unlike the *Gija Joseon* dynasty,[74] which King Wu sealed as a vassal state, *Dangun Joseon*

▲ Located at the foot of Mansusan Mountain in Kaesong city, Gaepung-gun, Haeseon-ri, the tomb of King Taejo of the Goryeo Dynasty is a national treasure of the Joseon Dynasty and was designated as a UNESCO World Heritage Site in 2004. Photo taken by Jin Chun-kyu, CEO of Unification TV, around November 2017.

---

[72] King Taejo Wang Geon is written 태조 왕건 and 太祖 王建 in Korean and Chinese/Hanja, respectively.

[73] *Dangun Joseon* is written 단군조선 and 檀君朝鮮 in Korean and Chinese/Hanja, respectively.

[74] *Gija Joseon* is written 기자조선 and 箕子朝鮮 in Korean and Chinese/Hanja, respectively.

was an independent state, established outside of the feudal order of the Zhou Dynasty. The tomb of Dangun is in North Korea, built to dramatic scale, symbolizing the spirit of the emancipated nation. I have visited the site twice, before and after the tomb was built. I was even able to see the massive appearance of the tomb from the window of the place where I stayed. When I was invited to a large-scale academic conference held after the DPRK completed the tomb, I could feel the people's passionate, national pride.

Without understanding North Korean nationalism, we cannot explain their development of nuclear weapons. The DPRK has been exposed to the threat of nuclear bombing by the United States for about 70 years since the Korean War. The stronger the threat from foreign powers, the   stronger the resistance of their nationalism. We can easily understand this by recalling the Martial Spirit of Goguryeo which directly translates into modern, North Korean nationalism.

Kim Il Sung decided to develop nuclear weapons when he saw how the Japanese imperialist power, against which he fought in do-or-die spirit, collapsed in an instant under American atomic bombs. He further cemented his resolve to develop nuclear weapons after confirming that nearly 40 percent of the atomic bombs victims were Korean forced laborers, working in the military industry in Hiroshima. Kim Jong Il brought the nuclear weapons program that Kim Il Sung envisioned into its maturity, by adopting military-first policies. Kim Jong Un inherited the legacy of his predecessors and completed it. The purpose of North Korea's nuclear weapon development was, in a word, "deterrence" against the threat of nuclear bombing by the United

States. The United States has demanded that North Korea give up its nuclear weapons completely, which is beyond the realm of reason in international politics. Nuclear weapons only exist in the world of international politics for the purpose of mutual deterrence.

Still, Trump says he believes in Kim Jong Un's willingness to give up his nuclear weapons. Considering that North Korea is a collective decision-making system of the Workers' Party, not Kim Jong Un's one-man dictatorship, Trump's comments are absurd. Although the DPRK has said that they could relinquish their nuclear weapons, they have never said that they would give them up "unconditionally." Unless the DPRK's national security is assured through measures including reversing the US' hostile policy toward North Korea, officially ending the war with a peace treaty, and establishing diplomatic ties between the DPRK and the US, North Korea will not even consider partially abandoning their nuclear program.

The DPRK's strong nationalism makes unification more of a necessity than an option. Unlike in South Korea, whenever major school or government events are held in North Korea, they sing together the song entitled, "Our Wish is Unification," which was written and composed in South Korea. Everyone there knows this song. As was established in the June 15th Declaration, North Korea's official reunification plan is unification by federation. The concept of "federation" presupposes peace. Therefore, the DPRK pursues federal unification and rejects unification by force.

However, North Korea had to pay a great price to build the unique DPRK-style socialism we discussed above. The price was international isolation and economic privation. At the "5th Plenary Meeting of the 7th Central Committee of the Workers' Party of Korea," held December 28-31, 2109, North Korea declared its plan to overcome isolation and economic privation head-on. I think there is only one path at this moment for them to choose.

People Live Here, Too!

To recover from the longing for peace which afflicted me since childhood, I have to understand North Korea as accurately as possible. That seemed, to me, the first step toward finding a path to peace and reunification between the two Koreas.

However, neither in South Korea nor in the United States could I find a way to understand North Korea clearly. It was impossible to approach the reality of the DPRK with the American social sciences, so dominated by behavioralism, and it was very difficult to understand the DPRK fairly in the climate of public opinion where all kinds of anti-North Korean prejudice are endlessly propagated, even labeling them part of an "axis of evil."

After much deliberation, I came to the conclusion that I had no choice but to visit North Korea and observe the reality for myself. I had no intention of visiting to write a travel essay. I wanted to study the DPRK academically to write academic articles that accurately reveal the nature of the nation.

Because the United States and North Korea do not have diplomatic relations, visiting was not easy. When I was unsure how to proceed, the opportunity to visit the DPRK arose from a completely unexpected place. In 1981, North Korea opened its doors and started a project to invite foreign scholars. At the invitation of Chairman Huh Jeong-suk of the Overseas Compatriots Association,[75] Korean scholars working in the United States were able to visit North Korea in July 1981, and I was lucky to be part of the trip. There were six scholars—B.C. Koh from the University of Illinois, Gil Young-hwan from Iowa State University, Kim Jong-ik from West Michigan University, Yang Sung-chul from Kentucky University, Chae-jin Lee from California State University, and me from University of Georgia.

I still vividly remember the moment I set foot on the ground in North Korea, which I had longed to do for so long. There were people just like us living there! Just like us, they invited the neighbors over to celebrate if their children did well in school; just like us, they held

▲ In July 1981, a group of Korean-American scholars, visiting the DPRK for the first time at the invitation of the Overseas Compatriots' Association, visited Kim Il Sung University in Pyongyang, Daeseong-gu, Yongnam-dong, talked with professors, and took a commemorative photo in front of the library. Back row from right: Yang Sung-chul (2nd), Han Shik Park (5th), Kim Jong-ik (6th), Gil Yeong-hwan (9th); front row: B.C. Koh (middle), Chae-jin Lee (far right). (Photo courtesy of Han Shik Park)

---

[75] The Overseas Compatriots' Association is called 해외동포원호회 in Korean.

wedding parties at home; and just like us, the young men and women enjoyed themselves at night by the Daedong riverside! Living in South Korea and the US for decades, I had been immersed in the demonization of North Korean people. I had been taught that they were completely different from us. They were literally dehumanized. The moment I witnessed people's daily lives in North Korea, I could clearly sense the delusions that had brainwashed me were crumbling.

The Overseas Compatriots Association welcomed our group with great respect. Our group was provided with a Mercedes-Benz. Bruce Cummings, who visited the same time as us by a different route, was given a Volvo. When I asked Huh Jeong-suk the reason for the car choice, she responded, "Korean people are particularly special, so we have to treat them differently from other peoples."

Her answer was completely opposite to the one I had encountered in the south. I went to Seoul after finishing my visit to the DPRK, and stayed at the Plaza Hotel located in front of City Hall. When I asked if I could have a room with a view of the city, the hotel receptionist answered, "We leave the rooms with a city view for our foreign guests. Why don't you just use this room?"

I can't forget the time I had at the Potonggang Hotel in North Korea. The restaurant at the hotel took food order 24 hours in advance. When I asked what the menu was, I was told to order "anything." I got playful and asked, "Do you serve raw fish?"

The answer came right away, "Of course we do!"

The next day, a large carp, that they must have caught in the Daedong River, was on my plate at the table in one piece. It was still opening and closing its mouth. I was surprised. *Are they trying to make fun of me?* I wondered. It turned out that they had filleted the carp very carefully and then covered it again with its skin. I was surprised once again. I have never enjoyed a raw fish dish like that in any restaurant in the world. I was so amazed the whole time as I ate the freshest, softest carp.

After my visit to North Korea, I had an opportunity to give a lecture at the Committee for the Five Northern Korean Provinces when I came to Seoul. Minister of Unification, Hong Seong-cheol, arranged that lecture. After telling the audience of over 300 people the interesting things I had seen and felt in the DPRK, I made a suggestion, "Let's not try to see only bad things but to see also good things in North Korea, and create a culture of mutual admiration."

One of the audience immediately raised his hand and shot a question, "Are you sure there is something good about North Korea? Tell me just one thing, if you can!"

"Why not?" I answered right away, "You can catch fish in the Daedong River and eat it on the spot. Would that be possible from the polluted Han River?"

I had the impression that the DPRK was a "country of slogans." If you walk through the streets of North Korea, you easily come across slogans such as "Nothing to envy," "Paradise on earth," "Single Hearted Unity," and "A match for a hundred." The interesting thing is, I also noticed a lot of slogans hanging all over the place in Seoul when I was there. Why is that? I still mull this question over in my mind.

After visiting the DPRK, my party and I returned to the United States. We published *A Journey to North Korea: Personal Perceptions* in 1983. This book was translated into Korean and published in 1986 under the title *Joseon Travelogue*.[76] The book was a collection of the papers that each of us wrote based on our experiences. Instead of writing a travelogue, I wrote a paper on the *Juche* idea, which had fascinated me for some time.

In fact, I had expected the 1981 visit to the DPRK to be an academic tour. However, we followed the arrangements of our host, the Overseas Compatriots Association. In North Korea, this "arrangement" referred to the itinerary prepared by the hosting organization. I was unable to meet with the scholars I had personally wanted to meet. What comforted me during that tightly arranged schedule was my first visit to Kim Il Sung University. I was able to have some academic conversations with the professors there, with whom I also had the chance to take a commemorative photo. I had a close look at the books in the university library, one location I had particularly wanted to see. What surprised me was that I was unable to find a copy of Marx's *Das Kapital* and that there were fewer books related to the *Juche* idea than I expected.

At the time, it more than 30 years since the DPRK had been founded in 1948. If North Korean intellectuals no longer read Marx's main work, this indicated we needed to radically change the way we

---

[76] The book's title is 북한기행 in Korean.

understood socialism in North Korea. I realized that the historical context unique to the DPRK, which is not captured by the socialist *idealtypus* previously mentioned, must have been decisively important in shaping DPRK-style socialism.

▲ *Journey to North Korea*, published in the US in 1983 by the six scholars who visited the DPRK. (Photo courtesy of Han Shik Park)

The fact that there were not many books on the *Juche* idea at the Kim Il Sung University library in 1981 also gave me an inkling. The Library was overflowing with "Laborious Work" (Kim Il Sung's sayings) that could be used as primary source for learning *Juche* ideology, but it was not easy to find books that systematically analyzed and studied the *Juche* idea. The fact that there were not many such studies on the *Juche* idea did not mean that the reality of *Juche* was absent, however. North Korea was already a country of *Juche*. In other words, the ideology that governed North Korean society as a whole was the *Juche* idea.

North Korean politics operated as "*Juche* politics" with independence as the main element. North Korean economy operated as a "*Juche* economy" with self-reliance as the main element. There is also "*Juche* architecture" that is typified in the Okryu-gwan restaurant or the People's Grand Study House. *Juche* architecture is characterized by a tiled roof and Western interior design and functions.

There is also "*Juche* music" performed with a fusion of foreign and traditional instruments; "*Juche* hairstyle" limited to a few styles; and "*Juche* dance" that mainly moves the upper body with little to no movement of the lower body.

In 1981, the research of the *Juche* idea was still in its infancy, because it did not meet the requirements for political ideologies or religious beliefs. In my view, there must be a systematic theory on the justice of distribution in order to meet the requirements for political ideologies, and a systematic theory on the afterlife in order to meet the requirements for religious beliefs. *Juche* ideology had neither of them. As I witnessed the great gap between where the theoretical study of the *Juche* idea was situated and the reality of self-reliance that *Juche*[77] represented, I predicted that *Juche* studies would continuously increase in the DPRK in the future, to close the gap.

Back in the United States, I still wanted to research *Juche* ideology. I thought that understanding North Korea accurately would only be possible by conceptually grasping the ideology that governed their society. At that time, the foremost researcher of the *Juche* idea of whom I was aware was Hwang Jang-yop, the director of the Juche Idea Research Institute. I wanted to communicate with him, but there simply was no way to contact him directly from the United States. One day, after repeatedly wracking my brain for solutions to this challenge, I thought of China. Having been born in Manchuria, I had some friends living in China. My relatives were in Manchuria. Perhaps I could deliver a letter to the DPRK through my friends in China? Since

---

[77] *Juche* literally means" main subject" or "principal agent"

China and the DPRK had diplomatic ties, wouldn't it be possible to send and receive correspondence with North Korea through my acquaintances in China?

I wrote a letter and sent it to a friend in China. My friend put my letter in a new envelope and sent it to Hwang Jang-yop. After all that work, I waited with great anticipation, but no reply came. I wrote another letter and sent it. Still, there was no reply. Time flew by as I continued writing echo-less letters.

1987 was a notable year for me for two reasons. One was that the Juche Academy of Sciences was established under the Juche Idea Research Institute in the DPRK, and the other was that the North Korean nuclear crisis began. After hearing that the Juche Academy of Sciences had opened, I concluded that North Korean scholars had finally begun systematically studying the *Juche* idea. But, my interest rapidly turned from the study of *Juche* ideology to preventing war on the Korean Peninsula. I attentively monitored the atmosphere in which the North Korean nuclear crisis was developing. The whole thing reminded me of the Korean War nightmare I had lived through as a child. I became impatient. My desire to return to the DPRK intensified.

In 1990, the long-awaited news finally arrived. The Korea Asia-Pacific Peace Committee (KAPPC) issued me an invitation to North Korea. KAPPC is a non-governmental organization established in the DPRK to deal with countries that do not have diplomatic relations with them, such as South Korea, the United States, and Japan. From that time, I began visiting frequently. Between 1990 and 2015, I visited twice a year. I met with high-ranking officials in the KAPPC, mainly discussing ways to prevent war.

One of the fruits of that effort was the birth of "Track II" diplomacy. I invited opinion leaders from North Korea, the United States, and South Korea to the University of Georgia where we discussed ways to achieve peace on the Korean Peninsula and to create a consultative body dedicated to policy recommendations. By visiting the Juche Academy of Sciences and participating in or observing their study, I deepened my own research on the subject.

▲ A view of the Juche Institute of Science, part of the Juche Idea Research Institute, which was established in Mangyongdae District, Pyongyang in 1987. It is understood to have been closed after its founder, Hwang Jang-yop, defected in 1997. (Photo courtesy of the Institute for Peace Studies)

Examining *Juche* Through the Lens of Empathy

Many argue that North Korea should give up its nuclear program. However, North Korea has not given up its nuclear weapons throughout many cycles of intimidation and conciliation. People say they do not understand North Korea, make all kinds of accusations against it, and call for stricter sanctions. Nevertheless, the DPRK shows no signs of giving up its nuclear weapons despite the cost. Why is that?

◀ Professor Han Shik Park (left) had a long association with Hwang Jang-yop (right), former secretary of the Labor Party and theorist of the DPRK's Juche idea, beginning in 1990 and continuing until 1997, after his exile to South Korea. The picture shows them together in the reception room of the president of the Juche Institute of Science in Pyongyang when the author visited North Korea in 1993. (Photo courtesy of Han Shik Park)

Many argue that capitalist reform and openness are necessary for North Korea to overcome its economic difficulties. However, despite their splendid logic, the DPRK has not engaged in capitalist reform or opening up their economy. While many claim they do not understand North Korea, at the same time, they strongly condemn the DPRK's leadership for neglecting the economic welfare of its people. Despite all this condemnation, the DPRK shows no signs of embarking on capitalist reform and liberalization. Why could that be?

I call the act of using theories, concepts, and language familiar to ourselves to research or condemn North Korea at will "epistemic imperialism." You cannot portray the DPRK beneficently through epistemic imperialism. In order to understand it accurately, we must abandon epistemic imperialism and approach the very ideology to which the DPRK adheres. As mentioned in title of this section, I call the attitude of trying to understand the behavior of North Korea from North Korea's point of view "empathy."

There are some who criticize me, referring to me as pro-North or a North Korea-collaborator. I only say that we need empathy. Please keep in mind that just because I understand the DPRK does not mean I agree with it. During all these years, the policies which have been devised toward North Korea without accurately understanding it have turned out to be unsuccessful. We have borne all the burden and costs of that failure.

If we look at the DPRK through the lens of empathy, we can gradually assess the motives that govern their actions. The more you pay attention to the motive, the more clearly the "*Juche* idea" emerges.

The reason North Korea does not give up its nuclear weapons, despite all kinds of criticism from the world, is because of a guiding principle of the *Juche* idea, "self-defense in national defense." The reason for its reluctance to reform and open up to capitalism despite economic difficulties is also found in the *Juche* ideology.

There was once discussion about how China would build a special economic zone in the DPRK to stimulate its economy. If economic exchanges between North Korea and China were revitalized by constructing special economic zones there, the DPRK's economy could develop dramatically. The leaders I met inside were well aware of that fact. However, they were also very concerned about the possibility of North Korea becoming an economic colony of China. They adhered to a guiding principle of the *Juche* ideology, "self-reliance in the economy."

The *Juche* idea is also reflected in the DPRK's reunification policy. Article 1 of the South-North Joint Declaration from the first inter-Korean summit, held on June 15, 2000, reads as follows:

"The South and the North have agreed to resolve the question of reunification independently and through the joint efforts of the Korean people, who are the masters of the country."

This sentence is a typical description of a guiding principle of the *Juche* idea, "independence in politics." As confirmed in several cases like this, the *Juche* ideology is a living ideology that governs the overall way of life in North Korea. In a single sentence, the DPRK can be said to be a "country of *Juche* ideology." I have no hesitation in saying that if you do not know what the *Juche* idea is, you cannot understand the DPRK. It is a socialist country, of course. However, I would like to emphasize that it is difficult to accurately understand the reality of North Korea when approaching it only from a socialist perspective.

Nevertheless, there are many scholars who study the *Juche* ideology and say that the *Juche* ideology died at the end of the Cold War. They point out that in North Korea, discussions about the *Juche* idea are not as active as they were in the past. However, they overlook the fact that the *Juche* idea has completely infused into the lived reality of North Korean society.

Koreans return to our hometowns to visit our parents on *Chuseok*[78] or on *Seollal*.[79] On the morning of *Chuseok* or *Seollal*, we hold ancestral rites. Homecomings and ancestral rites can be said to be a practice of filial piety and ancestor worship, which are important in Confucianism. However, no one extensively studies Confucian scriptures about filial piety and ancestor worship in advance, whether on the journey to their ancestral home or before performing ancestral rites. Homecoming and ancestral rites are an established custom in Korean society. Likewise, the reason why the *Juche* ideology is not discussed as actively as in the past is not because its life has come to an end, but because it has become custom—integrated into North Korean society.

The *Juche* idea is also the conceptual framing of Kim Il Sung's life, as delineated by researchers. Kim Jong Il began this conceptualization.

---

[78] *Chuseok,* the Korean harvest festival, is celebrated on August 15th in the lunar calendar.
[79] *Seollal* is lunar New Year's Day and one of the biggest Korean holidays of the year, along with *Chuseok.*

Therefore, we can say that Kim Il Sung created the *Juche* idea and Kim Jong Il implemented it.

However, in South Korea, the story that has been generally understood and circulated is that Hwang Jang-yop theoretically constructed the *Juche* idea and even revised it into its current form. I met Hwang Jang-yop inside North Korea repeatedly over the course of 8 years, and we mainly discussed *Juche* ideology. Hwang Jang-yop came to Seoul in 1997. After that, I met him in Seoul several times, and we have had many conversations. I have read most of what he has written or spoken publicly. At this point, looking back on those meetings, I must say that the Hwang Jang-yop I met in the DPRK was not the same person in Seoul. The Hwang Jang-yop whom I met in North Korea and the Hwang Jang-yop whom I met in Seoul are vastly different.

The meaning of Kim Il Sung's life is summarized in his memoir *With the Century*, and the *Juche* idea is incorporated into it. However, Hwang Jang-yop argued that the book was a forgery because Kim Il Sung did not write his own memoir. He disregarded the fact that memoirs are often written by someone else or even ghost writers. There are countless writers who specialize in memoirs in the United States as well. Hwang's claim that *With the Century* was a forgery was the claim of the Hwang I met in Seoul, not the Hwang I knew in the DPRK.

The theme that carries through the entire memoir is the collapse of the Joseon Dynasty and the construction of an independent state. Kim Il Sung identified the ultimate cause of the Joseon Dynasty's ruination as party conflict and flunkyism. Kim Il Sung had insight into the fact that even those who fought for independence were not able to break away from their legacy. Kim Il Sung recalled the actual circumstances by borrowing the words of his father:

> ... my father spoke of the factional strife which continued from the period of the Ri dynasty, and he deplored the fact that even when the country was lost due to the factional struggle, the people who called themselves champions of the independence movement still did not come to their senses, continually splitting into small groups and squabbling in factions. Without doing away with the factional strife, he went on to say, it would be impossible to either achieve national independence or to bring about civilization and enlightenment. Factional strife causes a decline in national strength and attracts foreign forces. When foreign forces come in, the country falls to ruin. During your generation it is imperative to root out the factional strife, achieve unity and rouse the masses.[80]

In the midst of the anti-Japanese movement, Kim Il Sung decided that it was necessary to have talented and qualified people in order to build an independent state. Those people had to be those who had completely dispelled the legacy of factional strife and flunkyism of the Joseon Dynasty. Looking around him, Kim Il Sung discovered it was not easy to find such people. He came up with the idea of nurturing such individuals to independently carry out the construction of an independent state. In other words, this is how he began to conceive the *Juche* idea. Kim Il Sung recalled the situation at that time as follows:

---

[80] From Volume 1: April 1912 - May 1930, *With the Century*

[After liberation] Stationing the Soviet and US armies on the peninsula might have turned our country into an arena of confrontation between socialism and capitalism. Our national force was liable to be split into left and right, patriots and traitors to the nation. If factional strife prevailed and any faction conspired with foreign forces it would end in the ruin of the country.

In these circumstances, we had to strengthen the capacity of our revolution in every way in order to defend the independence of our nation and speed up construction of a new country.

The people themselves are the subject of our revolution. Since the first day we set out on this road, we made every effort to educate, organize and mobilize the people who were to undertake the anti-Japanese revolution.[81]

The *Juche* idea conceived by Kim Il Sung during the anti-Japanese struggle is embodied in the speeches he gave in the 1950s. For example, in 1955, Kim Il Sung delivered a speech on how to overcome flunkyism and dogmatism, and establish *Juche*, which was transcribed later into a document, "On eliminating dogmatism and formalism and establishing *Juche* in ideological work."

In 1982, Kim Jong Il comprehensively systematized Kim Il Sung's work on the *Juche* idea and published a treatise *On the Juche Idea*. In 1983, Ri Sang-geol published *On Dear Leader Comrade Kim Jong Il's Thesis on the Juche Idea*. In 1985, all 10 volumes of *Collection of the Great Juche Idea* were published. *On the Juche Idea* is a general theory of the *Juche* idea, while the *Collection of the Great Juche Idea* is a detailed exegesis of the *Juche* idea. The subject of each volume of

---

[81] From Volume 8: April 1940 - August 1945, *With the Century*

the *Collection of the Great Juche Idea* is as follows:

Volume 1 The Philosophical Principle of the Juche Idea
Volume 2 The Social and Historical Principle of the Juche Idea
Volume 3 The Guiding Principle of the Juche Idea
Volume 4 The Theory of Anti-imperialist, Semi-feudal Democratic Revolution and Socialist Revolution
Volume 5 The Theory of Socialist·Communist Construction
Volume 6 The Theory of Human Reconstruction
Volume 7 The Theory of Socialist Economic Construction
Volume 8 The Theory of Socialist Cultural Construction
Volume 9 Leadership System
Volume 10 Leading Art

In 1987, under the leadership of Hwang Jang-yop, the Juche Academy of Sciences was established in a U-shaped building near Mt. Yongak. Hwang Jang-yop had the ambition to spread the *Juche* idea to the world. The Juche Academy of Sciences was a large-scale research institute with about 300 experts in the *Juche* ideology. The fields of specialization of these experts covered almost all fields of study, because the purpose pursued by the academy was to explore the universal applicability of the *Juche* idea.

From 1990 to 2015, three years after the academy was founded, I visited North Korea twice a year on average. At that time, research on the *Juche* idea was booming around the academy, so my visits were of great help for my research on the *Juche* idea. I met with experts from various fields and raised countless questions, discussing with them day and night. When I was asked to reveal my thoughts on the *Juche* idea, I made several presentations and gave lectures in front of those experts. The scholars with whom I was particularly close, such as Ri Ji-soo, Park Seung-deok, and Jeong Gi-poong, are key to unforgettable memories in my life.

▲ Ri Ji Su (left), director of the Juche Institute of Science; Park Seung Deok (middle), director of the Juche Idea Research Institute (주체사상연구소) at the Juche Institute of Science (주체과학원); and Ki Gi Pung (right), former director of the Institute for National Unification and current professor at Kim Chol Ju University of Education in 1990. (Photo courtesy of *Encyclopedia of Joseon Folklore*)

The Socio-Political Life
of Kim Il Sung

Most of the existing studies on the DPRK were conducted in such a way that concepts mobilized from outside—such as democracy, socialism, and communism—have been forced on the DPRK. It was impossible for me to rationally understand North Korea in that way. Over a decade of my research on the *Juche* idea was summarized in *North Korea: The Politics of Unconventional Wisdom*, published in 2002.

As already explained, Kim Il Sung conceived the *Juche* idea while critically reflecting on the anti-Japanese national liberation movement and the communist movement developed in the 1920s. The anti-Japanese national liberation movement and the communist movement can be summed up as independence movements. Above all, Kim Il Sung saw the need for a new type of people who broke away from flunkyism and factionalism, to become the kind of independent human being capable of achieving an independent nation-state.

Kim Il Sung emphasized that the *Juche* ideology is a people-centered ideology and specifically defined people as social beings with autonomy, creativity, and ideological consciousness. Autonomy refers to the necessary attributes of sleocial human beings who want to live and develop independently, as masters of the world and their own destiny. Creativity refers to the property of a social being who purposefully remodels the world for that purpose. Ideological consciousness refers to a social human attribute that regulates all activities to both understand and change the world and oneself.

In particular, Kim Il Sung paid attention to human autonomy. In an interview with the *Mainichi Simbun* on September 17, 1972, Kim Il Sung defined a "socio-political living being" as follows:

> For man, autonomy is life. When a person loses his social autonomy, he cannot be said to be a man; he is no different from an animal. It can be said that the socio-political life is more precious than physical life to man as a social being. If a man is socially abandoned and his political independence is lost, then, as a social human being, he is as good as dead, even though he has breath.

◀ The front page of *Mainichi Shimbun* on September 19th, 1972 featured an article about interviewing Kim Il Sung.

Put simply, a "socio-political living being" can be described as an alternative type of human who has cast off flunkyism and factionalism. Whereas a human being who is caught up in flunkyism and factional strife is an individualist—pursuing individual desire, freedom, and interests—a socio-political living being is an evolved human, whose existence is dedicated to the values pursued by the group. In the DPRK, socio-political living beings are nurtured through *Juche* education. There is no place for individualism in North Korea, where socio-political living beings are idealized. Therefore, there may be competition between groups to which individuals belong, but competition between individuals does not exist. The most perfect socio-political living being imaginable in the DPRK is said to be Kim Il Sung himself. Only socio-political living beings are entitled to become members of the Workers' Party.

In Kim Il Sung's conception, socio-political living beings become the protagonists in the struggle to build an independent nation-state. Kim Il Sung suggested a "leadership of the Party and the Leader toward the masses," which Kim Jong Il's laborious work On the Juche Idea explained as follows:

> In order for the masses to occupy their position as subjects of history and fulfill their roles, the leadership and the masses must be combined. The popular masses are the creators of history, but only under the right guidance can they take their place as the subjects of social and historical development and fulfill their roles... In the revolutionary movement and the communist movement, the leadership is the leadership of the party and the Leader over the popular masses. The working class party is the headquarters of the revolution, and the Leader of the working class is the supreme leader of the revolution.

In North Korea, the Party's leadership, the Leader, and the masses are often described with the term "trinity." Not only Hwang Jang-yop but many other North Korean scholars used this term. However, it should be noted that the Party's leadership, the Leader, and the masses are technical terms used in Kim Jong Il's work and other writings, whereas "trinity" is a non-technical term adopted to help ordinary people understand. Therefore, although scholars often use the term "trinity" in daily conversations, they rarely use it in books that describe the core of the *Juche* idea.

Many South Korean scholars studying the *Juche* ideology grasp the core of the proposition of the Party's leadership, the Leader, and the masses and interpret it analogously with the Christian Trinity. All interpretations made through such analogies only lead to serious misunderstandings of the *Juche* idea because the masses of the people, the Party, and the Leader, who make up the Trinity of *Juche* ideology, occupy a completely different position ontologically from the Father, the Son, and the Holy Spirit making up the Christian Trinity. For example, the Christian "Father" is a transcendent being that exists outside the world. However, the "Leader" of the *Juche* idea is a secular entity that exists within the world. Therefore, there is a difference between the Christian Trinity that corresponds to a religious ideology, and the trinity in the *Juche* ideology that corresponds to a political ideology.

The leadership of the Party and the Leader represent a kind of political leadership. Since its foundation, the DPRK has lived in a state of quasi-war, constantly exposed to military threats from the United States and South Korea. Such a reality is said to require the political leadership of the Party and the Leader over the popular masses. Political thinkers such as Sun Tzu,[82] Mao Zedong, Clausewitz, and Machiavelli emphasized the importance of political leadership during wartime. The leadership of the Party and the Leader over the masses as emphasized in the *Juche* ideology is nothing unique to North Korea, but a proposition universally accepted in human political ideology.

In an interview with various media outlets in the international community after Kim Il Sung's death in 1994, whenever I was asked "Who is the real ruler in North Korea?" I would answer "Kim Il Sung."

The person inevitably tilted his head and asked again, "Who is the real ruler of North Korea?" They did not understand my reply that although Kim Il Sung had already died, Kim Il Sung was still in power. I would proceed to explain North Korea's unique "politics of last instructions."

In order for the DPRK to survive the state of semi-war or overt war, it must maintain the political leadership of the Party and the Leader. During Kim Il Sung's lifetime, such political leadership was relatively easy to maintain because of Kim Il Sung's charisma. However, in order for the DPRK to survive politically after his death, his political leadership—as exerted during his lifetime—had to be maintained. North Korea has managed to maintain his leadership through the politics of last instructions, even after his death, by preserving the charisma he exerted during his lifetime.

Juche ideology does not simply exist theoretically, or in the abstract,

---

[82] Sun Tzu (Sūnzǐ, 孙子) was the Chinese philosopher and military strategist who authored *The Art of War*.

but has established itself as a practical ethic dominating the lifestyle of North Korea's entire society through ongoing *Juche* education. Ethical practices are called the guiding principles of the *Juche* idea. For example, *Juche's* self-reliance is realized through four guiding principles: ideological self-determinism, political independence, economic self-reliance, and national self-defense. *Juche* principles in ideology play the role of leading *Juche* in the other fields of politics, economy, and national defense.

Juche principled ideology is first realized as political independence in politics. Economic self-reliance and national self-defense are guaranteed only when political independence has first been achieved. In particular, political independence is only realized by exercising complete national sovereignty and sharing equal rights in international relations. This principle of political independence has always guided North Korea—through the anti-Japanese movement in the early 20th century, independent diplomacy during the Sino-Soviet split, and the anti-imperialist movement against the United States.

Economic self-reliance is the guiding principle for the national economy. Unlike a capitalist economy that pursues profit itself, the self-reliant economy aims to meet the needs of the country and the people. In particular, the self-reliant economy opposes the economic domination of and subordination by other countries.

National self-defense is a guiding principle that one must defend one's own country with one's own strength. To carry out national self-defense, the nation must have its own armed forces, for only then can the country's political and economic independence be guaranteed.

The DPRK developed nuclear weapons despite condemnation from all over the world, in practice of their guiding principle of national self-defense.

The *Juche* idea is widely embodied in North Korean daily life. I briefly mentioned *Juche* music earlier. It is a fusion of Western and traditional Korean instruments. In February 2018, during the Pyeongchang Winter Olympics, North Korea's Samjiyon Orchestra performed in Gangneung and Seoul. If you watch the performance closely, you can see that both Western instruments and traditional Korean instruments are being used, a perfect example of *Juche* music.

In the DPRK, Yun Yi-sang's music is highly acclaimed *Juche* music—because it created the form—deeply fusing the emotions of Korean people with Western modern music. North Korea founded the Yun Yi-sang Symphony Orchestra and the Yun Yi-sang Music Hall to continuously perform *Juche* music. Because I am a music lover and have a long relationship with Yun, I wanted to introduce his music to the United States. In 1994, as the president of the North American Congress of Christians, I proposed that the ROK and DPRK hold the "Yun Yi-sang Music Festival" in New York. When they agreed, we even announced the festival for January 1995. However, unexpected saboteurs thwarted the plan. It was only after Yun's death that the International Yun Yi-sang Association in Berlin, Germany and the Korean Symphony Orchestra in New York were able to hold the "World Master of Contemporary Music – Yun Yi-sang Contemporary Music Concert" in November 1996 at the Lincoln Center in New York. There, my eldest daughter, Clara Park (Joo-young), a music professor and pianist, premiered Yun Yi-sang's "Sonata for Violin and Piano" trio in the United States.

There is even a *Juche* hairstyle. In the recent, popular Korean TV drama, *Crash Landing on You*, there is a scene where the heroine visits a North Korean beauty salon. Upon entering the beauty salon, she notices several hairstyles displayed a poster. These are *Juche* hairstyles. Customers have to choose one of them. Of course, the types of *Juche* hairstyles change over time. There is also a *Juche* dance. *Juche* dancing is characterized by centering movements in the upper body while refraining from lower body movement, because excessive lower body movement is considered offensive. There is also a form of *Juche* architecture. The Grand People's Study House's roof is elaborately decorated with tiles, while the interior features modern facilities. In short, one can say the *Juche* idea is the soul that constantly drives North Korean social life.

The Familial State of the Fatherly Leader

The *Juche* idea first came to my attention during my master's studies at the College of Political Science at American University. I entered in 1965, and had to work several part-time jobs due to financial difficulties. One of my jobs was translating editorials of a North Korean newspaper called the *Rodong Sinmun*[83] into English. I was able to participate in the US Department of Commerce's translation project quite by coincidence.

The Department of Commerce gave me permission to read limited, classified information. I used to go to the Library of Congress, read

◀ In 1998, the DPRK established 1912–the year of Kim Il Sung's birth–as the first year of the Juche era, and April 15th–Kim Il Sung's birthday–as the "National Day of the Sun." On April 15th, 2012, on the 100th anniversary of Kim Il-sung's birth, the *Rodong Sinmun* published an editorial on the front page entitled "The History of Juche's Sun will Flow for 10 Million Years."

---

[83] *Rodong Sinmun* (로동신문, 勞動新聞) is the DPRK's Workers' Party Newspaper.

the *Rodong Sinmun*, make copies, and translate relevant articles. I did this throughout my master's program, so I read the *Rodong Sinmun* carefully for about two years.

During that time, I came to two very important conclusions. One was that I had to have an accurate understand of the *Juche* idea in order to properly understand North Korea, and the other was that it was impossible to properly understand North Korea only by reading publications like the *Rodong Sinmun*.

Above all, the more I read the *Rodong Sinmun*, the more I encountered the terms "*Juche*" and "*Juche* ideology." It seemed odd if the newspaper did not use those terms, but, I could not clearly grasp their meaning. Nevertheless, those two terms seemed vitally important.

I entered the Department of Political Science at Seoul National University in 1959 and studied political ideology with special interest. I also majored in political philosophy during my master's studies at American University. I wrote my thesis in this arena. Because of that political propensity, my desire to understand the *Juche* idea only grew stronger with time. That is why, after being appointed professor at the University of Georgia in 1971, I started sending letters to Hwang Jang-yop, the DPRK's foremost scholar on *Juche* ideology.

Also, while translating the *Rodong Sinmun*, I had a completely unexpected experience. I began to gain a reputation as a North Korea expert, increasingly fielding questions about the DPRK from various parts of American society. In 1974, the US State Department even appointed me a "scholar diplomat," consulting me about the DPRK from time to time. In actuality, whenever I was asked such questions,

I couldn't help but feel embarrassed. *Why on earth are they asking me? I wondered. Americans must have terrible general knowledge about Korea!* Although Americans may have considered me a North Korea expert, the more I grew accustomed to the *Rodong Sinmun*, the more I realized that I did not have an accurate understanding of the DPRK. That thought has not changed to this day.

One day, when I translated an editorial requested by the Department of Commerce and submitted it to the person in charge, he looked me in the eye and asked, "Why is this the same as the editorial you translated yesterday?" The implication was that I had loafed around instead of working; I had not. The contents of the two editorials I translated were very similar. Of course, that just doesn't make sense to most people, particularly the Department of Commerce. However, the DPRK is a country that exists outside the realm of our "common sense." *Rodong Sinmun* editorials are always prepared according to *Juche* principles. And this meant that the contents were occasionally repetitive.

Even the DPRK-related books published in the United States did not help me understand North Korea. We could even say that those books obstructed my accurate understanding, because they were written not for the purpose of understanding North Korea, but for the purpose of condemning it. Moreover, since the outside world hardly had access to the DPRK, no matter how many errors those scholars made in their research, there was no way to check the accuracy. Practical verification had to be postponed indefinitely.

To this day, that situation has not changed much. The prevailing public opinion in the United States regards North Korea as an awful place. Didn't George W. Bush brand it part of the "axis of evil"? Whether you hate North Korea or not, you must understand it accurately in order to deal with it. Our understanding cannot expand, however narrowly, until we stop demonizing the DPRK. To properly qualify as a scholar who understands North Korea, one must have both intellectual ability and the academic spirit to transcend its demonization.

After my long and winding journey to visit North Korea, I was still unable to understand it to my expectations because their academic system was completely different from that of South Korea or the United States. It was not easy to find bookstores in the DPRK. There are no huge book sellers like Seoul's Kyobo Bookstore. For example, scholars studying the Korean War can visit the US Library of Congress, or other research repositories, to look up and photocopy material. Such services are not provided anywhere in North Korea. If you go to the library of a South Korean or American university, you can easily access books and papers distributed around the world. However, university libraries in the DPRK mainly stock books officially published by the state.

I wondered, What can I do if the door to understanding North Korea does not open naturally—even when I visit?

I realized my initial visit to North Korea was no different than a tour—like an uncertified, pseudo-doctor visiting a patient, equipped only with a stethoscope. I was frustrated.

After many trials and errors on my journey to research the DPRK, I came to the conclusion that I had no choice but to open up this new path to research the DPRK by myself. First of all, mobilizing all my academic abilities, I prepared research questions and constructed various theoretical propositions accordingly. From then on, my visits to North Korea were structured with a series of processes to raise prepared questions and test my corresponding propositions. There, I had political conversations with politicians, academic conversations with scholars, and conversations about daily life with the people. Using the questions I prepared as my guides, I tested my theories by visiting various institutions, historic sites, villages, and marketplaces. During my visits, I also leveraged my relationships with the people I met to access the books I wanted.

It is not hard to understand how so much misinformation about North Korea proliferates, particularly considering the difficulties of conducting research on the DPRK. However, I believe such misunderstandings must be discouraged and ended. If our nations ever hope to peacefully coexist, we cannot afford to ignore—much less embrace inaccurate understanding of North Korea.

Based on my research to this point, I would like to discuss some myths related to the *Juche* idea. First of all, there seems to be a lot of misunderstanding about the relationship between *Juche* ideology and *Songun* policy. For example, there is a misunderstanding that the *Juche* ideology is an old idea which has been replaced with a new, military-first ideology—or that military-first implies that the military should lead the people's lives.

I would like to emphasize that *Songun* is not a subject that can be easily understood outside of the DPRK. Even within North Korea, there are no booklets or papers which systematically organize this idea. Every time I visited, I asked the politicians, soldiers, and scholars I met about this ideology. However, I was unable to understand it academically by simply listening to their responses. Their stories were one form of raw data, which could inform an understanding of the *Songun* idea.

I processed that raw data academically, to the best of my ability. Through that process, I wrote two papers related to this thought: "Military-First Politics 'Songun:' Understanding Kim Jong Il's North Korea" in 2007 and "Military-First 'Songun' Politics: Implications for External Policies" in 2010. As the first papers to introduce the Songun idea in English, they received a lot of attention from the international community.

First, *Songun* must be understood as an extension of *Juche* ideology. *Songun* did not replace *Juche*, but rather expanded and deepened it. *Songun* existed even during the Kim Il Sung period. Remember, during the Kim Il Sung era, an established principle guiding *Juche* ideology was "national self-defense." National self-defense requires the people to faithfully serve in the military.

The meaning of *Songun* expanded during the Kim Jong Il period. Kim Jong Il successfully completed a nuclear weapon test in 2006. This allowed North Korea to secure some leeway through its military power. Kim Jong Il leveraged this new military power toward the practice of economic self-reliance, another one of the guiding principles of *Juche* ideology. In order to practice the principle of national self-defense, the people must faithfully serve in the military. And, as the military serves the people through their work, to implement the principle of economic self-reliance. That explains why, during the busy farming season, we often see military servicemen working alongside farmers in the North Korean countryside.

Another misconception is that the Juche idea can be interpreted in the context of the Joseon Dynasty's Neo-Confucianism.[84] Some argue it is possible to understand the Juche concept of "parental leadership" in the context of Neo-Confucianist teachings on filial piety and loyalty. However, Juche ideology does not accept such an understanding. Juche ideology was initially presented as an alternative ideology to break the Joseon Dynasty's legacy of factional strife and flunkyism. In that time and context, Neo-Confucianism was the dominant ideology and the ultimate source of factional strife. It seems self-evident to me that the Joseon Dynasty's commitment to Neo-Confucianism was related to the very things *Juche* ideology was intended to displace.

Neo-Confucianism prioritized filial piety over other kinds of loyalty. In other words, the logic of self-cultivation[85] was prioritized over the logic of national governance.[86] For example, the reason King Injo was given the throne in the midst of the transition from the Ming to Qing Dynasties was the Neo-Confucianist belief that prioritized filial piety over loyalty to a leader. Although King Gwanghaegun was good at

---

[84] Neo-Confucianism, or Zhuzi studies (朱子), are the teachings of Chinese philosopher Zhu Xi (朱熹).

[85] Self-cultivation, or *xiūshēn* (수신제가, 修身齊家), is a neo-Confucian value in which one cultivates one's mind and body according to the expectations of one's elders and with the good of the family in mind.

[86] National governance (치국평천하, 治國平天下) refers to working for the good of the nation.

diplomacy and tried to prevent the ravages of war, the Restoration forces thought it was more important to deal with the King's deposal of his step-mother, Queen Inmok, and killing of his younger step-brother, Grand Prince Yeongchang.[87] In *Juche* ideology, filial piety and loyalty converge, giving qualifications for both to the nation's "Fatherly Leader." Under *Juche* ideology, it would be unimaginable to abolish loyalty to the Leader on the basis of filial piety.

If one wants to find a reference that illuminates *Juche's* concept of "parental leadership" in relation to traditional Eastern thought, one should examine the "rule by means of filial piety" implemented during Emperor Wu's rule during the Han Dynasty.[88] Emperor Wu practiced filial piety by referring to the *Classic of Filial Piety,* which emphasized the use of filial piety as the rule of the empire. The *Classic of Filial Piety* emphasizes the convergence of filial piety and loyalty to leadership, as can be seen in the expression, "As they serve their fathers, so they serve their rulers, and they reverence them equally."

This Confucian treatise *Classic of Filial Piety* is actually a teaching legalistic enough to be called the "Book of Loyalty."

Because the DPRK considers itself a country ruled by a parental leader where filial piety and loyalty converge, the nation is a huge extended family of 25 million members.

---

[87] Despite King Gwanghaegun (光海君, 광해군) being a great diplomat during a turbulent period in northeast Asian history, he was the son of a concubine to the former king, and his younger step-brother (Grand Prince Yeongchang, 영창대군, 永昌大君) was widely considered to be a more appropriate heir to the throne. His eventual fratricide served as pretext for a political coup (인조반정, 仁祖反正), installing King Injo in place of King Gwanghaegun.

[88] Emperor Wu (孝武皇帝) ruled the Han Dynasty in China from 141-87 B.C.

Juche, the Ideology that Sustains North Korea

After arriving in the DPRK, I returned the hotel where I usually stayed in Pyongyang. The familiar furnishings were the same as my last visit—TV, radio, and calendar. I felt the familiar fatigue that comes after a long flight halfway around the globe from the United States. When I lay down on the bed, there was absolute silence. The TV broadcast did not begin until 6 pm, so I had to endure the quiet until then.

If you opened the drawer next to the bed, you would find a daily calendar. If you turned its pages, you would see instructions from Kim Il Sung for every single day. For example, during the busy farming season, there are verses to guide farming. In North Korea, this calendar is like holy scripture.

Right at 6 pm, as if in anticipation, I turned on the TV. A familiar song started playing as the screen lit up with splendid images— embodying lyrics that praised the "Fatherly Leader," retold the last instructions of Kim Il Sung, and emphasized the *Juche* idea—all set to a powerfully, mournful melody. I turned on the radio and heard a similar song.

If I listened to the music uncritically, it would feel like a hymn at church. Repeatedly revisiting Kim Il Sung's last instructions on television, radio, and a daily calendar would feel like listening to a pastor's sermon. If I, who only visits the DPRK occasionally, get this feeling, how must the North Korean people feel, who listen to them on a daily basis? After thinking about these things for some time, I came to the conclusion that the *Juche* idea has a religious quality.

The religiosity of the *Juche* idea can be clearly seen in the "theory of Eternal Life," which emerged after Kim Il Sung's death in 1994. If you visit the DPRK, you will see "Towers of Eternal Life" emblazoned with the slogan, "The great Comrade Kim Il Sung is with us forever." Kim Jong Il's name was also added to the slogan after his death in 2011. North Korea uses a unique, *Juche* calendar, with year 1 being the year 1912, when Kim Il Sung was born—just as we begin the modern era (dividing BC from AD) with Jesus' birth.

There are papers and booklets that compare and interpret the character of *Juche* ideology in relation to Christianity. However, it bears repeating that the religiosity of *Juche* ideology has a completely different character from that of Christianity. Christianity is a religion that fundamentally denies the present world and aims for the future. Therefore, there is an afterlife unique to Christianity. However, unlike Christianity, *Juche* has no conception of an afterlife because it religiously affirms the present world. The "eternal life" emphasized in *Juche* ideology means that the people in this world will live forever with the soul of Kim Il Sung.

As I emphasized earlier, the ultimate reason for the religious nature of *Juche* ideology was to preserve the charismatic nature of Kim Il

Sung's life even after his death, to maintain uninterrupted political leadership. If the *Juche* ideology were comparable to Christianity, North Korea, constantly exposed to military threats from the United States and South Korea, would give up its own political survival to seek eternity in an afterlife. That is obviously not the case.

There is another issue that cannot be ignored in relation to the religious character of the Juche idea. Currently, many people, including scholars, journalists, and politicians, interpret the essence of *Juche* ideology as idolizing Kim Il Sung. They understand the DPRK as the "Kim Il Sung Republic." In other words, they believe the *Juche* idea is solely mobilized to make Kim Il Sung into a godlike figure. Most outside observers firmly believe this, and that fundamental belief underlies the assumption that North Korea would collapse if Kim Il Sung was removed.

Kim Il Sung died on July 8, 1994. Subsequently, on October 21st, the North Korea-US Agreement (Geneva Agreed Framework) to end the first North Korean nuclear crisis was signed. The agreement called upon Pyongyang to freeze its operation and construction of nuclear reactors, suspected of being part of a covert nuclear weapons program, in exchange for the US providing North Korea with two 100 megawatt light water reactors and 500,000 tons of heavy oil for industrial use. Why did the US suddenly sign an agreement three and a half months after Kim Il Sung's death? According to my understanding from Americans who participated in the negotiations at the time, the Clinton administration was convinced that without Kim Il Sung, North Korea would collapse within three months. Therefore, the US believed they would not be held responsible for any agreements they signed. The DPRK was bound to collapse soon anyway.

However, the DPRK did not collapse. The expected North Korean demise, of which the Clinton administration was so convinced, turned out to be a miscalculation. Nevertheless, Americans did not abandon that belief. In October 2015, Obama and Park Geun-hye drafted the "2015 Operation Plan" to decapitate North Korean leader Kim Jong Un and top officials in the case of war. This plan was also based on the belief that the DPRK is a system ruled arbitrarily by Kim Jong Un. But did Iraq collapse after the US eliminated Saddam Hussein? We must realize that these illusions about North Korea are constantly producing destructive policies for the Korean Peninsula.

The notion of understanding North Korea as a "Republic of Kim Il Sung" directly conflicts with basic principles of politics, as described in political science textbooks. A state basically means a relationship of domination over people. Rulers rule by means of power. For a state to exist, subjects must obey their rulers. Why would they obey? They obey because, in their minds, the ruler is justified in exercising power. In political science, such a recognition is called "legitimacy." When the ruler's exercise of power is not recognized as legitimate in the minds of the subjects, a "legitimacy crisis" occurs. The idea is that when the legitimacy of the state is shaken, it leads to collapse.

The fact that the DPRK has existed from 1948 until now tells us that North Korean people have granted legitimacy to their rulers. In other words, the basic theory of political science reveals that the DPRK is not a republic of Kim Il Sung, but a "people's republic" with the people's support.

There are many clues pointing to the fact that the DPRK is a people's republic. I spent my childhood in Manchuria, when Kim Il Sung devoted himself to the anti-Japanese movement there. My father was born in 1912, the same year as Kim Il Sung. Although my father did not know him, many of his friends did. I used to ask them what kind of person Kim Il Sung was. They told me that he often said, "It is much more important to have one of 'the people' for a friend than a hundred soldiers."

In the 1930s, Kim Il Sung engaged in guerrilla warfare in The Northeast Anti-Japanese Allied Army along with Kim Chaek, Choi Yong-gun, and Choi Hyun. The warfare they waged based its strategy on Mao Zedong's unique concept of "the people." Mao Zedong used

▲ In the late 1930s, Kim Il Sung was active in the Northeast Anti-Japanese Alliance, a combined Korean and Chinese unit. The photo shows military leaders from the Northeast Anti-Japanese Union Army at the 1949 ceremony for the production of the   first Korean submachine gun. From left, Choi Yong-gon, Kim Chaek, Kim Il, Kim Il Sung, and Kang Kon. (*Hankyoreh* file photo)

247

to say that if the people were the water, then the guerrillas were the fish; swimming among the people like a fish in the sea. Mao Zedong was able to defeat Chiang Kai-shek and establish the People's Republic of China by launching, not a class struggle, but a "people's war," based on his concept of the people.

Kim Il Sung recreated Mao's concept of the people. In *On the Juche Idea*, Kim Jong Il explained that concept of "the people" as follows:

> The communists and nationalists, who said they were working for the national liberation movement in Korea in the 1920s, did not intend to enter into the masses. They did not educate -and organize them, neither did they provoke them into a revolutionary struggle. They were alienated from the masses and only after leadership battles and bickering, divided the masses into factions instead of uniting them. From the first period of the revolutionary struggle, the Leader saw through their mistakes and behaved differently, walking a path of true revolution which meant entering into the masses of the people to fight for their cause alongside them. He revealed the truth that the people are the masters of the revolution and that the revolution is won only by educating and mobilizing the people. This is one of the points upon which Juche ideology is predicated.

Juche's spirit of valuing the people is also confirmed in the DPRK's view of history, which depicts the people as history's protagonists. The foreword of *Joseon Tongsa*[89] reveals it was written according to

---

[89] *Joseon Tongsa*, The Synoptic History of Joseon, is entitled 조선통사 and 朝鮮通事 in Korean and Chinese/Hanja, respectively.

the following teachings of Kim Il Sung:

> When we want to learn history, we do not want to know the history of kings or feudal rulers, but rather the history of the struggles and creation of our people. Only when we are well acquainted with the people can we possess feelings of love for our country, as well as national and revolutionary pride.

In fact, when you look at the table of contents of *Joseon Tongsa*, you can see the perception that the people play the lead in all wars. For example, expressions that catch the eye are those related to the people, such as "the Goguryeo people's struggle against the Sui and Tang invaders," "the Goryeo people's struggle to defeat the Khitan invaders," and "the people's struggle to defeat the Mongolian invaders in the 13th century." The part where General Eulji Mundeok defeated the Sui invasion is described as follows:

> Facing an invading army ten times their size, the patriotic soldiers and people of Goguryeo defended Liaohe watershed and Liaodong Fortress, under the command of Eulji Mundeok. Through inducement and ambushes, they decisively won a big battle that played an important role in the ultimate victory in this war.

Without the *Juche* idea, I do not think the DPRK's political survival would have been possible. Their foundational secret to surmounting all kinds of international political challenges and economic difficulties was the *Juche* idea. For example, to understand America, we need to understand Christianity. If we use the same logic, to understand North Korea, we need to understand *Juche*.

At this point, I would like to look back on the time I spent in North Korea with Hwang Jang-yop. Every time we had conversations there, over the course of eight years, Hwang talked a lot about Ludwig Feuerbach. Feuerbach was a materialist who believed in human reason. According to Feuerbach, there are many doctrines in Christianity that cannot be explained rationally, such as the resurrection, salvation, and the Holy Spirit. Feuerbach determined that Christianity's existence would be shaken if such doctrinal issues could not be rationally explained. So he tried to explain them rationally, without success.

Hwang Jang-yop argued that the problems which Feuerbach could not solve could be solved through the *Juche* idea. I had a long discussion with Hwang Jang-yop to understand his argument. However, Hwang and I were unable to close the gap between our thoughts. From my point of view, Hwang was a rationalist armed with reason like Feuerbach. On the other hand, I understood that metaphysical thinking, beyond the limits of reason, was necessary to understand religious doctrines.

Hwang Jang-yop published several books after coming to South Korea in 1997. In 1999, his first memoir, *I Saw the Truth of History*,[90] caught my attention. The moment I saw the title, I assumed that Hwang Jang-yop had solved the problem that Feuerbach could not. But the book contained something completely different.

---

[90] *I Saw the Truth of History* was published in Korean entitled 나는 역사의 진리를 보았다.

The Special Relationship between North Korea and China

"*Juche* ideology plagiarizes Mao Zedong ideology," is an argument one often encounters in the literature on *Juche* ideology circulating in the United States. There are even doctoral dissertations written on this argument. Whenever I encountered it, I was thrown into confusion, becoming lost in deep contemplation.

I personally rate Mao Zedong the greatest politician in human history, because he managed to feed 60 million hungry Chinese people. Mao Zedong said, "There are three big problems in this world. The first problem is to feed the people, the second problem is to feed the people, and the third problem is to feed the people."

Furthermore, Mao Zedong rescued 20 million Chinese who had been addicted to opium.

In my view, Mao Zedong wore four hats—that of a revolutionary leader, a politician, a scholar, and a guerrilla commander. Playing such a variety of roles, Mao Zedong managed to build an independent state that guaranteed the material conditions and spiritual freedom of the Chinese people. So I always kept a picture of Mao Zedong hanging in my office at the University of Georgia. I also taught graduate level seminars on Mao Zedong thought for several years.

For me, when comparing Mao Zedong's thought, which I have studied as a professor, with *Juche* ideology, which I researched traveling to and from North Korea, I cannot accept the claim that the latter is a plagiarism of the former. Of course, I admit that there are similarities between the two ideas. However, most of these similarities stem from the fact that the existential life conditions of Mao Zedong and Kim Il Sung were substantially similar. After all, both of them devoted their lives to building an independent state while fighting foreign powers.

◀ Kim Il Sung (left) and Mao Zedong (right) stand side by side to observe the military parade held at Beijing Square on October 1st, 1954, the 5th anniversary of the founding of the People's Republic of China. (Photo courtesy of *Gyeonghwa Times*)

Still, aren't the political and social realities of China and Korea completely different? If *Juche* ideology had copied Mao Zedong thought, it could not be successfully implemented in the political and social reality of the DPRK, which was vastly different from that of China. Mao Zedong thought is an ideology that matured in the political and social reality of China, whereas the *Juche* idea inevitably came of its own in Korea. The fact that the DPRK, having chosen the *Juche* idea as its regime's ideology, has survived for more than 70 years means that *Juche* ideology has been successfully rooted in a political and social reality unique to North Korea.

As is well known, Mao Zedong carried out a popular revolution by inheriting the ideas of Li Dazhao[91] who modified Marx's theory of revolution to fit the reality of China. Li could not apply the revolutionary theory that Marx proposed, about the class struggle between the bourgeoisie and proletariat derived from industrialization of a society, at face value to the realities of China. This is because China was still a rural society without the division between the bourgeoisie and the proletariat. According to Li Dazhao's perspective, related to China, the Chinese peasants being invaded by imperialist powers were in a similar situation to the proletariat that Marx noted. Therefore, Li Dazhao emphasized a type of People's Revolution in which the Chinese peasants were the main players. That People's Revolution was realized through Mao Zedong, leading the way to a modern China. This was why, in 1982, Peking University graduates raised a donation and erected a statue of Li Dazhao on the campus.

Like Li Dazhao and Mao Zedong, Kim Il Sung had an accurate view of how dangerous ideas could be when separated from reality. Kim Il Sung's way of thinking was embodied in a spirit consistent with the entire *Juche* idea. For example, Kim Jong Il's *On the Juche Idea* emphasizes, "In revolution and construction, there cannot be a prescription that is suitable for every era and every country. Therefore, we must always start from reality and solve all problems creatively, responsive to the actual situation."

After examining the similarities Mao Zedong and Kim Il Sung faced

---

[91] Li Dazhao (李大釗) was an intellectual who co-founded the Chinese Communist Party in 1921.

in more detail, I will examine the differences between Mao Zedong thought and *Juche* ideology. Born in 1893, Mao Zedong was forced to live in the midst of China's "Century of Humiliation" that began in 1840 with the Opium War. The Chinese military was fractured by wrangling warlords, and the people were in a state of chaos.

Mao Zedong saw two conflicts in China. One was the conflict from outside, against foreign aggression, and the other was the conflict inside, problems caused by the wealth gap, regional sentiments, and minority issues. Mao Zedong adopted the theory of a two-stage revolution as a means of overcoming these two conflicts. In Mao's view, external conflict could not be resolved peacefully, but only through war. In addition, he thoroughly eradicated traitors, pro-American and pro-Japanese sects in China that welcomed foreign powers. On the other hand, he judged that internal conflict could be resolved peacefully. Mao Zedong, therefore, adopted a policy of educating and leading a revolutionary vanguard, land reform, and preferential policies for minorities.

Kim Il Sung also faced the double task of defeating foreign powers and resolving the gap between the rich and the poor. Kim Il Sung nurtured the people, the subjects of the revolution, through *Juche* education capable of eradicating flunkyism and partisanship, to lead them through the anti-Japanese war in Manchuria, the Korean War (known in the DPRK as the "Fatherland Liberation War"), and other conflicts. He eradicated the internal pro-Japanese and pro-American sects, and also tried to narrow the wealth gap between the rich and the poor by implementing land reform and other policies.

▲ October 5th, 1943: Kim Il Sung was a member of the 88th Independent Sniper Brigade (International Brigade) and served as the 1st Warrant Officer of the Korean Army. Front, from Left to Right: N.S. Batalin (Soviet Union), Li Jo-rin (李兆麟, China), Wang Il-ji (王一知, wife of Ju Bao-zhong), Brigadier Ju Bao-zhong (周保中, China), and Kim Il Sung. (Photo courtesy of Jilin Province Library, China)

Mao Zedong and Kim Il Sung's similar life experiences can be especially seen in their guerrilla activities. Mao Zedong and Kim Il Sung had no choice but to engage in guerrilla warfare in situations where the available equipment and manpower was insufficient to the task. Mao Zedong's Chinese Civil War and the Great March, and Kim Il Sung's Manchurian guerrilla activities are good examples.

The guerrillas activities of Mao Zedong and Kim Il Sung have great political significance. Having passed through life and death experiences together, colleagues who engaged in guerrilla activities with Mao Zedong and Kim Il Sung shared close comradeship. Their bonds were so strong that they could not break under any circumstances. The spirit of the guerrillas thus became the founding spirit in Mao Zedong's China and in Kim Il Sung's Korea. As is well known, Khrushchev, who became the general secretary of the Communist Party of the Soviet Union after Stalin's death, launched a campaign to downgrade Stalin. However, Deng Xiaoping, elected chairman of the Central Military Commission of the People's Republic of China in 1983, never launched a campaign to downgrade Mao Zedong because Deng Xiaoping participated in the guerrilla campaign with Mao Zedong. Even after Deng Xiaoping, the picture of Mao Zedong in Tiananmen Square has not been removed.

Similarly, in the North Korea, those of Kim Il Sung's colleagues who engaged in guerrilla activities with him became leading figures in nation's founding. For this reason, the DPRK can be called a guerrilla country. In 2012, my wife and I attended an event in Kim Il Sung Square to commemorate Kim Il Sung's 100th birthday. Many soldiers paraded, but soldiers in guerrilla uniforms led the march. I felt that the spirit of their guerrilla fighters was still alive

To solve China's problem of extreme poverty, Mao Zedong decided it was necessary to share the scarce food evenly. So, instead of capitalism, which competitively pursues human desires, he adopted socialism as an alternative that pursues equal distribution of needs essential for human survival. Kim Il Sung adopted socialism for the same reason. Currently, the DPRK implements the principle of socialist equality far more thoroughly than China, which has adopted a capitalist market economy. From my point of view, North Korea is the most egalitarian country on the planet.

It is true that they struggle economically, but that does not undermine the principle of equality in socialism. As I mentioned before, between the highest paying wage and the lowest, the wage gap in North Korea was not wider than double. Additionally, their nation

◄ The special alliance between the DPRK and China continued after Mao Zedong's death in 1976 into the era of Deng Xiaoping. Deng Xiaoping (left), who took power in 1981, visited Pyongyang in April of the following year and is pictured at a welcome ceremony with Kim Il Sung (right). (*Hankyoreh* file photo)

reflects not only economic equality but also social equality. An important norm governing North Korean society is the collectivist spirit of "one for all, all for one." Therefore, there is no such thing as bullying. Also, since they adopted a form of socialism that seeks to share the means of production, class itself, determined by owning a means of production, cannot exist. Without class, there is no class consciousness and it is hard to imagine one person arrogantly dominating another. During the so-called "Arduous March," everyone went hungry regardless of their social status. Even people in leadership, such as party cadres, starved to death.

▲ The audience at a military parade in Pyongyang, commemorating the 100th birthday of Kim Il Sung on April 15, 2012. Han Shik Park and his wife are pictured in the middle of the fourth row from bottom. (Photo courtesy of Han Shik Park)

When trying to differentiate between Mao Zedong thought and *Juche* ideology, we should pay attention to their respective concepts of "the people." China's official name is the People's Republic of China, and Korea's official name is the Democratic People's Republic of Korea. "The People" is such an important concept that they are used as keywords in the official names of both countries. However, the meaning of the people in the two countries reveals a big difference.

In China, "the people" is the concept of the "members of the nation," encompassing the Han Chinese as well as 54 ethnic minority groups. In North Korea, however, "the people" refers to the concept of a single ethnic group and is based on blood ties. Therefore, Chinese nationalism is inclusive, whereas North Korea's concept is exclusive.

Also, while Mao Zedong thought has a thoroughly political character, *Juche* ideology adds to that a religious character.

The similarities and differences between Mao Zedong thought and the *Juche* idea contributed decisively to the formation of a special relationship between China and the DPRK. In international politics, a "special relationship" refers to a close political, diplomatic, military, economic, historical, and/or cultural alliance, such as the special bond maintained between the United Kingdom and the United States. It would behoove us to remember that the DPRK and China's relationship is no less special than that of the US and the UK.

The special relationship between China and North Korea is easy to understand if we consider the combat experience that Mao Zedong and Kim Il Sung shared in Manchuria as anti-Japanese guerrillas. On February 27, 1936, Kim Il Sung reported as follows at the Namhodu Congress:[92]

> As you all know, Korea People's Revolutionary Army units are the main forces within the Korean-Chinese anti-Japanese militias operational in Manchuria. Not only that, but many Korean communists play a key role as political and military officials in the Chinese army. Under such circumstances, if the Korean-Chinese anti-Japanese armed forces were divided into Korean units and Chinese units, the capacity of the anti-Japanese fraternal Chinese struggle would be weakened, and eventually, the development of the Korean people's anti-Japanese armed struggle would be at a loss... Until some future when we lay a solid foundation for the armed struggle in our own

---

[92] The Namhodu Congress was called 남호두회의 and 南湖頭會議 in Korean and Chinese, respectively.

land, we must continue to conduct military and political activities in southeast Manchuria's large forests and advantageous terrain. Under these conditions, the Korean People's Units and the Chinese People's Units should jointly organize and develop as Anti-Japanese Allied Forces, rather than forming separate units to carry out their respective activities.

Mao Zedong's military victories in Manchuria allowed him to take military control of all of China. The Korean-Chinese Anti-Japanese Armed Forces were the main players who provided a foothold for Mao Zedong. The photos and names of all those who died in Manchurian battles are on display at the Northeast Martyrs Memorial in Harbin, China. I visited there and counted the Korean people, record each of their names in a notebook. There are approximately 230 people memorialized there; nearly 100 of them are Koreans.

On October 12, 1962, in Pyongyang, Zhou Enlai[93] and Kim Il Sung signed the "North Korean-Chinese Border Treaty,"[94] a treaty between the two countries on either side of Mt. Baekdu. Zhou Enlai agreed to sign a treaty with very favorable terms for the DPRK. North Korea received 54.5 percent of Lake Cheonji, on Mount Baekdu, along with 264 of the islands and sandbars in the Yalu and Tumen Rivers. China was only granted 45.5 percent of Lake Cheonji and 187 islands and sandbars.

---

[93] Zhōu Ēnlái (周恩来) worked closely with Mao Zedong and succeeded him as Chairman in 1954.

[94] The North Korean-Chinese Border Treaty is called 조중변계조약 and 中朝边界条约 in Korean and Chinese.

◀ President Kim Il Sung (left) and Prime Minister Zhou Enlai (right) signed the North Korea-China Friendship Treaty in Beijing, China in July 1961. Deng Xiaoping stands right behind Zhou Enlai.

Zhou Enlai died in 1976. In April 1975, while on an official visit to China, Kim Il Sung visited the hospital where Zhou Enlai was hospitalized to see him. Zhou Enlai got up from his sick bed, put on a suit, and greeted Kim Il Sung. Deng Xiaoping[95] was also there. Zhou Enlai told Kim Il Sung, "If anything happens in the DPRK in the future, please come see Deng Xiaoping." In May 1979, Kim Il Sung erected a statue of Zhou Enlai inside the Heungnam Fertilizer Factory. He personally took part in the unveiling ceremony.

---

[95] Deng Xiaoping (鄧小平) succeeded Zhou Enlai.

North Korean Standard of Happiness

In English, we talk about comparing "apples to oranges." Because apples and oranges are qualitatively different, this phrase implies one should not directly compare two different things. The phrase, "they are apples and oranges" implies that two things are as different as heaven and earth.

When I hear people talking about North Korea's economy, I always think of the idiom "apples to oranges." They see South Korea's economy as a big, fresh apple, then compare and evaluate North Korea's economy based on that apple. In such comparison, the North's economy is bound to appear a small, worm-eaten apple. This is the process by which the general consensus about North Korea's economy has arisen.

However, the DPRK operates the most unique socialist economy on the planet. Therefore, those who try to draw direct comparisons between the North Korean economy and that of another nation, inevitably make the mistake of comparing "apples to oranges."

When I first visited the DPRK, I often felt perplexed, particularly when hearing slogans such as "Nothing to envy in the world," "I love my country the most," and "People's paradise." During one of my visits to North Korea in 2012, North Korea's GDP was just one-third that of South Korea's. So how could they conceivably unfurl such slogans?

As I came to understand North Korea better, my doubts were gradually resolved. The North Korean standard of happiness was completely different from the standard we understand. North Korean people said, "Our ancestors told us that happiness is eating rice, living in a home with a tile roof, and educating our children well. Now we have achieved all these goals."

Looking back at their slogans based on these standards, I was able to understand them to some extent.

There are several criteria by which the North Korean economy can be evaluated. While there are quantitative evaluation criteria such as gross domestic product(GDP), there are also qualitative evaluation criteria such as the "Quality of Life Index." If we only looked at GDP, the DPRK's economy would inevitably be undervalued. However, when analyzed based on "quality of life" indices such as life expectancy, equality of economic distribution, and educational environment, we come to a completely different conclusion. Before the Arduous March, the DPRK had a relatively high life expectancy. Equal economic distribution and 12 free years of education is the standard. There are no illiterate people in North Korea, nor violence or "bullying" at school. Also, as a collectively-run society, the suicide rate is close to zero.

A high-ranking North Korean official once told me, "There are countless countries in the world. However, the DPRK is set far apart from those countries, existing alone. As a country, we could say it is like Dokdo Island."

As my visits increased, my understanding gradually deepened and as a result, I could see why he said that.

If the DPRK were a unique country on the planet, it would be impossible to understand its economy based on economic theories widely circulated elsewhere. I tried to understand its economy by directly observing it through field surveys and interviewing people working there, organizing these experiences in light of the social scientific concepts I prepared in advance. I visited the house of a "doctor professor" of economics and had a theoretical discussion about the North Korean economy. (In the DPRK, scholars who attain the highest level of academic ability and achievement are given the title "doctor professor," even if they do not have doctoral degrees.)

The first thing to notice when looking at the North Korean economy is that its internal and external economies operate in qualitatively different ways. The domestic economy focuses on just distribution, according to socialism. This means emphasizing equality rather than freedom; cost of living rather than consumption; and common property rather than private property.

On the other hand, the external economy focuses on responding to the world's capitalist order. For example, the DPRK exports abundant underground resources, following the logic of capitalism. Zinc, magnesium, uranium, and other minerals produced in the DPRK are known in the international market for their excellent quality. Coal, an abundant resource, is also an important North Korean export.

In addition, the DPRK plans to build its economy by developing rich crude oil reserves in the West and East Korean Seas. Although the DPRK does not currently produce any oil, it has a government ministry dedicated to the crude oil industry. They have already tested crude oil samples after drilling in eight places in the West Sea and the East Sea through oil companies from five European countries, including Britain, France, and Italy. The results showed that the oil deposits in the West Sea are normal quality, while the East Sea's deposits are very good quality. When these results were released to the world, Dick Cheney, former Vice President under President Bush, Junior, reached out to me through his attorney. Dick Cheney is well known as the CEO of Halliburton from 1995 to 2000, one of the world's largest oil companies. The lawyer said that they would like to participate in an oil development project in North Korea, and asked me how they could have a chance. Since the DPRK had no intention of welcoming American companies, I conveyed that message, as it was. The DPRK has abundant economic potential, but is unable to utilize it at present due to harsh sanctions imposed against them by the United States and the United Nations.

In the DPRK, rather than receiving a monthly salary according to the price of individual labor, people receive "living expenses." These living expenses are broadly distributed in two ways—according to needs, such as is required for people's livelihood, and according to "social contribution." Because living expenses are distributed according to need, there is not much difference between households. Also, the cost of living for a kindergarten teacher may be higher than the cost of living for a university professor, because the social contribution of kindergarten teachers could be considered greater than that of university professors. Since North Korea is in a state of quasi-war with the United States, they highly value the military's social contribution. Therefore, military servicemen are favored economically. In particular, those injured while serving in the military are regarded as social heroes, and even their descendants receive preferential treatment. Young women consider it an honor to marry a man who was injured while serving in the army.

I was particularly interested in the Kaesong Industrial Complex. The DPRK closed the Kaesong Industrial Complex from May to September 2013 because of "radical remarks" from Kim Kwan-jin, then South Korea's Minster of Defense. I met several high-ranking policy makers in North Korea, including Ri Jong-hyeok and Won Dong-yeon, to discuss various options for reopening the Kaesong Industrial Complex. Fortunately, the discussion paid off. The DPRK reopened the facility.

For the reopening of the Kaesong Industrial Complex, I met and had many conversations with the leaders of the two Koreas. In the process, I confirmed in great detail how differently their economic systems operate. For example, South Koreans ask about the wages for North Korean workers working at the Kaesong Industrial Complex. Considering the ROK's economic system, that is a very natural question. However, South Korean business owners working in the Kaesong Industrial Complex do not pay wages directly to North Korean workers. Rather, they pay the total wages to the head of the Kaesong Industrial Complex, who represents the DPRK government.

The person in charge then distributes it to the workers according to their own standards.

North Korean workers at the Kaesong Industrial Complex follow the direction of their government, not the Korean employer who hired them. They are doing what their government needs. But because they were so productive and made good quality products, most South Korean business owners were quite satisfied.

We can understand the significance of Kaesong Industrial Complex's unique wage payment method if we refer to China's special economic zones (SEZs). Local workers in China's SEZs receive their wages directly from the foreign business owners there. They are paid a much higher wage than workers outside the SEZs. This created a large wage gap between those working within and outside the special economic zones. The wage gap that SEZs created between the rich and the poor became a social problem. Furthermore, workers in SEZs became more loyal to the foreign business owners who paid them directly than to their Chinese government, which became a very serious problem for the Chinese government.

So, North Korea adopted a different wage payment method in the Kaesong Industrial Complex, having learned lessons from the case of China's special economic zones. In this way, they were able to prevent creating a wealth gap between the rich and the poor in their society, as well as preventing the conflict in loyalty for the workers in the Kaesong Industrial Complex.

North Korean individuals do not choose their own jobs, but are assigned work by the state. Therefore, there are no general procedures for individuals to get jobs, such as submitting applications to the company, having job interviews, and getting hired. Even graduates of Kim Il Sung University, one of the most prestigious universities in North Korea, are assigned jobs by the state. This is how the employment rate reaches 100 percent.

I once asked a young graduate from Kim Il Sung University who was now working, "Isn't it a little sad to live so far from your hometown?"

He replied, "No, not at all."

He said that it was quite natural for him to work for his country, since he had been fed, nurtured, and even educated by the state his whole life. "It is an honor to work," he said. As I listened to his answer, I could see clearly how the *Juche* principle "one for all, all for one" is implemented even in an individual's job selection.

Because there is no private property in the DPRK, it may be the only place on earth where you can live without money. Without being able to own private property, there is no such thing as real estate speculation. Also, there is no accumulation of income through interest by saving in the bank. Most income is directly used for living.

Because the nation operates its military as an independent for-profit system, it is not a drain on the economy. Their largest source of foreign income comes from arms exports. Weapons are sold for cash. North Korean short-range ballistic missiles, guns, and tanks are know for their good quality in the international arms market. In fact, 40 percent of the scud missiles Iran used in the Iran-Iraq war were imported from the DPRK.

As stated earlier, the international community's suspicion that the North Korean military extorts all food aid sent to the DPRK is based in a huge misunderstanding. As there are no privately owned cars, army trucks transport food donations. Military trucks are the most common means of transport in North Korea. Moreover, if the economically prosperous army took food aid from the people, that would directly oppose the "Military-First" policy. Since developing nuclear weapons, the DPRK has had a surplus in military power. The purpose of the Military-First policy is that the army will serve the people with their surplus.

Many people see the revitalization of the marketplaces in North Korea and then determine the nation is transitioning to a capitalist market economy. Capitalism, as we all know, operates on the basis of private ownership. However, because everyone belongs to a "work unit," even the people who sell things in the market do so as part of a greater collective. Moreover, the items sold in the market are mainly daily necessities; there are few luxury items. To talk about the capitalization of the North Korean economy, using the *jangmadang*[96] as an example, is to make the mistake of forcing the capitalist perspective, with which we are familiar, onto their economy.

---

[96] *Jangmadang* (장마당) is the DPRK term for informal markets. Many North Korea watchers interpreted the increase of these markets as an indicator that the DPRK economy's was shifting toward capitalism.

Family Reunited after 35 Years

I come from a separated family. Our family's history of separation goes back to the year 1906. At the time of Korea's deep sorrow at the loss of their sovereignty to the Japanese colonial administration, my grandfather and grandmother immigrated to Heilongjiang Province in northern Manchuria. About 90 percent of the immigrants who settled in Heilongjiang were from our home province, Gyeongsang. The people of Pyeongan Province had settled first around the Yalu River, and the people of Hamgyeong Province around the Tumen River and in the Yanbian region. The people from Gyeongsang Province had to go further north, finally settling in Heilongjiang. My father was born in Heilongjiang in 1912, and I was born there in 1939.

Most of the Korean people who immigrated to Manchuria cultivated rice in the traditional way. In Manchuria, rice paddies were called "watery fields."[97] At that time, Chinese people did not eat rice grown in paddies, but Manchuria was overflowing with rice harvested from watery fields by Korean people. Therefore, most Korean people sent their rice harvest back to their hometowns.

After having settled and begun his own rice farm in Heilongjiang Province, my grandfather started a rice mill, which my father later

---

[97] The Chinese word was written 수전 or 水田 in Korean and Hanja/Chinese, respectively.

inherited. We always had plenty of rice in our house. One day, shortly after liberation in 1945, we received a report that Chiang Kai-shek's National Army would attack our mill. During the Chinese Civil War, mills stocked with rice were a target for looting. Feeling our lives were in danger, we fled in the middle of the night. Although we escaped, our grandfather, grandmother, and numerous relatives remained in Heilongjiang. That was the beginning of our lives as a separated family.

After Liberation and the Korean War, we found ourselves in the Cold War era. China was covered as if with a great "bamboo curtain," and it was impossible to meet Grandfather and Grandmother. What is worse, we did not even know if they were alive. My father started performing ancestral rites for Grandfather and Grandmother in 1959, the year I started my studies at Seoul National University.

As I said earlier, one day in 1975, while I was absorbed in a lecture at UGA, news came from Korea that my father was in critical condition. I hurriedly returned home and rushed to the hospital. My father, lying on the bed, held my hand and smiled warmly. I sat by his bedside and we had long conversations. He was so relieved by my presence that his condition temporarily improved. At one point in the conversation, my father looked me in the eyes and asked me to do two things. First, he told me, "Don't come back to Korea. Remain in the United States and concentrate on the Korean Unification movement. It is not easy to do that in Korea."

And secondly, he said, "Make sure to find your Grandfather, Grandmother, and separated relatives in Heilongjiang."

I promised him that I would. That promise became an essential task to fulfill in my lifetime.

I had no idea how to keep that promise I made to my father. Where in the vast and expansive land of China—so isolated and hidden from the rest of the world—would I ever be able to find Grandfather, Grandmother, and our other relatives, with whom we had parted more than three decades before? But as the old Korean saying goes, "Even if the sky falls, there always is a hole through which you can rise."

Jimmy Carter, who was elected President of the United States in 1976, declared that from then on, Americans could travel anywhere in the world. This meant Americans could visit countries such as Cuba, Vietnam, North Korea, and Albania, which until then, they had not been able to visit. Carter also opened the way for Americans to visit China by establishing diplomatic ties with China in January 1979.

As I was by then also a US citizen, I couldn't help but be excited. I was so anxious that I couldn't sleep at night. I visited the Chinese embassy in Washington D.C. and asked Deputy Ambassador Ji Qiaozhou to help me locate my grandparents and relatives in Heilongjiang. Although he said his field of work was diplomacy and he did not know much about domestic issues in China, he offered to check into it. I waited in anticipation. But I received no word from him for a long time.

After a season of disappointment, I heard a priceless piece of news. Deng Xiaoping would visit the United States from January 28th to February 6, 1979 to hold talks with President Carter. What was even more exciting, President Carter, a native Georgian, had even arranged for Deng Xiaoping to visit Georgia's state capital, Atlanta. Because it was very close to the university where I taught, my heart was pounding. I was determined to seize this opportunity somehow, so I made my request to the Carter administration and obtained an invitation to attend Deng Xiaoping's reception ceremony in Atlanta.

I still cannot forget the very first time I saw Deng Xiaoping. President Carter introduced him to the audience, and he started his speech. "My name is Deng Xiaoping. I am from China. China is so poor. China wants to learn a lot about economics, science and technology from the United States. The purpose of my visit to the United States this time is to learn. Please give me lots of help."

I was amazed. Despite his small stature, the moment I heard his remarks he suddenly seemed like a giant. Perhaps his speech that day marked the starting point of China's remarkable economic development to the level we see today. Using the slogan "Great Leap Outward," Deng Xiaoping aggressively promoted economic reform and liberalization policies. He decentralized the economy into 22 autonomous provinces and 5 autonomous regions, laying a solid foundation for China's economic development.

As soon as Deng Xiaoping's speech was over, I went to his interpreter, the Deputy Ambassador Ji Qiaozhou, who looked a bit apologetic when he saw me. It must have been because he had not succeeded in my previous request to locate my relatives. I asked him to tell Deng Xiaoping about my situation. Then, hearing our conversation, Deng turned to us to ask what was going on. Ji Qiaozhou immediately told him my story. Deng Xiaoping asked me where my relatives were. When I replied that they may still live in Heilongjiang, he asked if I knew their names. I wrote the Chinese names of seven relatives I could remember on a napkin at the table. There were more than 30 relatives I wanted to find, but I couldn't list them all in such a short time. Deng Xiaoping looked delighted and said I was very good at writing Chinese characters. He nodded his head and said he would investigate. With gratitude, I asked to shake his hand. Very politely, he got up from his seat and took my hand.

A couple weeks after I met Deng Xiaoping, I received a call from Ji Qiaozhou. He said they found all of my relatives and encouraged me to go and meet them. Tears covered my face.

During summer vacation in 1980, I took two large bags and boarded a flight to Beijing. Upon arrival, people from Deng Xiaoping's office greeted me and even kindly showed me the way. After about 20 hours by train, I arrived in Harbin, the capital of Heilongjiang Province. Two soldiers boarded the train to carry my luggage. As we disembarked, a military band welcomed us with loud fanfare. There to greet me warmly were 30 waving relatives. There was even a banner which read, "Welcome Home Professor Han Shik Park."

That moment embodied the phrase "a glorious return." It really felt like a dream.

I was proceeding from there to my aunt's house when a Chinese official approached me and invited me not to just leave but to take a rest at the International Hotel in Harbin, for a few days if I would like. Ji Qiaozhuo made an international phone call to confirm whether or not I had found my relatives. I could not ignore their consideration, so

I stayed overnight at the hotel. My 30 relatives joined me there. As you can imagine, the hotel became crowded and hectic as we all entered together. For those who had lived in poverty in China, the hotel was a great spectacle.

The next day, we headed straight to my aunt's house. On the way, I couldn't help but be surprised again. I learned that the long road from the hotel to my aunt's house had recently been cleaned up. Deng Xiaoping came to mind again. None of this would have been possible without his consideration. Throughout the ride, I felt deep gratitude.

◀ A glorious reunion after 35 years. The author with his aunt (right) by the Songhua River near his hometown during the July 1981 visit. (Photo courtesy of Han Shik Park)

I was able to meet all the relatives living in Heilongjiang Province. Finally, I kept the promise I had made to my father. While talking through the night with my relatives, I heard so many stories filled with *han.* I also learned that my grandfather and grandmother managed to outlive my father. My grandmother passed away in 1976. Since my father began to hold ancestral rites for the two of them in 1959, we held ancestral rites for my living grandmother for 17 years.

I realized that the *han* harbored by separated families could only be resolved when they met each other in person. I found that almost all

▲ Dean Rusk (middle) served as a law professor at the University of Georgia beginning in 1970 and helped to organize Uniting Families, Inc. He was the person who proposed the division of the Korean Peninsula along the 38th parallel in August 1945, when he was an intelligence officer. (Photo courtesy of Han Shik Park)

of the Korean-Chinese whom I met in Heilongjiang Province were part of separated families, just like myself. They were all living in bitter *han* and utter poverty. They looked to me, and because I had once lived like them, I couldn't turn my back.

As soon as I returned to the United States, I went to visit Dean Rusk with whom I had worked closely as a fellow professor at UGA. As previously mentioned, he was a professor of law there after serving as Secretary of State for nine years under the administrations of John F. Kennedy and Lyndon Johnson. He was also one of the personnel to draw the 38th parallel division line across on the Korean Peninsula in August 1945, as a desk officer for the National Strategic Policy Group under the War Department's Office of Operations.

Hearing my stories of the reality of separated families, Rusk seemed to feel guilty. He asked what he could do for unification of the Korean Peninsula. I replied that it would be good to create something like an association for separated families. I told him I wanted to form such an organization, but it was difficult on an assistant professor's salary. Rusk went straight ahead and formed a 501c3 tax-exempt, non-profit organization with the US federal government. Although forming an organization like that is not easy, he mobilized all his personal connections to help. He named the organization, "Uniting Families Inc." or UFI.

Every vacation after that, I visited Heilongjiang Province with the help of UFI. Many separated families would gather and wait to meet me. I interviewed them one by one. What are the names of the family members you are seeking? Where is your hometown? How did your family become separated? They responded to my questions, showing me large pieces of paper with the names of their relatives, their home addresses, and so on. We video recorded all of the interviews.

There were many elderly people who could not come meet me, so I traveled all over Heilongjiang Province to meet them myself. It was not easy to walk long distances on a dirt road, carrying heavy equipment. Sometimes, I hitched rides on the back of manure collection carts, easing my journey through the countryside with the fragrance of dung.

One day, during an interview, a smart young man caught my eye. I talked to him about the difficulties of this reunification work I had undertaken, and when I asked if he could help me, he offered without hesitation. I traveled a long way with him and met with countless compatriots. I later learned that young man went to Japan to study and became a professor.

I sent the videos I recorded to KBS, a public broadcaster in Korea. The video I sent was aired on programs about finding separated families, such as "Let's meet in PRC" and "Find separated families."

This is how we were able to locate roughly 200 people from separated families. On June 19, 1989, I even appeared in one of those programs, "See you at 11 O'clock," where I told the painful story of how many separated families lived in China. KBS President Lee Ki-hong later presented me a plaque of appreciation, so highly did he regard my efforts to unite separated families.

Love and *Han*

Could there possibly be people on this planet who live with more piercing *han*[98] in their hearts than Korean separated families? When talking about the characteristics of our people, we often say we have a lot of *han*, or that our *han* is deeply held, inherent in us. Although it is not easy to define what *han* means, it becomes possible to understand *han* if we make even a cursory look at the heartrending lives of separated families. I have been living in the United States for more than 50 years, but I have yet to discover a word in English that corresponds with the Korean concept of *han*.

Our nation's agonizing history, marked by the collapse of the Joseon Dynasty, the US-Soviet Cold War, and the ongoing Division, has driven countless families to harrowing separation. The *han* that has come to be rooted in people's hearts because they cannot see their own loving families, their natural blood ties, is a problem that touches human dignity and human rights. In order for humans to evolve beyond biological existence to live as social beings, above else, they must possess a right to give and receive love. I would like to call the "right to love," the most basic human right. It breaks my heart when I think of the pain of separated families, deprived of happiness and the

---

[98] *Han* (한, 恨) is a concept of bitter sadness or grief that is often associated with Korean modern history.

right to cry or laugh while sharing a warm meal with loved ones.

Most separated Korean families were parted in one of two historical contexts. The first of our nation's diaspora (displaced people) formed in the late 19th and early 20th centuries, and the second came through forced separation according to the Division and as a result of the Korean War. In order to survive, many Koreans migrated to one of China's three northeastern provinces, including the Gando region[99] and Primorsky Krai[100] in Russia. There were many peasants who migrated to make a living, and there were also many fighters who devoted themselves to the anti-Japanese independence movement. Also, many Koreans were taken for forced labor by the Japanese imperialists and never returned to their hometowns after Liberation. Our compatriots abandoned in Sakhalin[101] are one typical example.

The news of Japan's defeat and the Liberation brought exuberant joy to Koreans living outside our borders. It awakened a hope that they could return to their homeland. However, the road back home was as bumpy and backbreaking as their difficult life abroad. Most Koreans who decided to return home did not want the whole family to come back at once, but rather chose a way that the head of the family could go first, prepare a plan and shelter for his family, and then bring the family home. It was not easy to make a living and find shelter for any family in the chaotic period after Liberation. During those days, the

---

[99] Gando (間島, Jiandao in Chinese) is part of China, north of the Tumen river, bordering modern DPRK.

[100] Primorsky Krai (Приморский край, 沿海州) is part of Russia, bordering modern DPRK.

[101] Sakhalin is an island in the Primorsky Krai region, where the Japanese forced Korean people to work during colonization. After Japan's defeat in WWII, tens of thousands of Koreans remained in Sakhalin as stateless people.

38th parallel was drawn across our peninsula, and the Cold War began in earnest, with bamboo and iron curtains pulled shut between nations.

The people who had already returned to the Korean Peninsula and their families still outside the borders were now unable to travel. Families who had no choice but to be separated found themselves trapped in that situation for a long time. In the case of my family, we left Grandfather, Grandmother, and all the rest of our relatives in China. Had we only foreseen the impending separation, our whole family would have returned together to Korea at any cost.

Since my return visit in 1980, almost every year, I have visited the Heilongjiang Province, Changchun, and Yanbian areas in China. I carried the heavy Betamax camera, traveled across mountains and rivers to remote areas where our compatriots lived, and conducted interviews with members of separated families. My only reason was to help them find their family and alleviate even a little of the painful *han* of separation in their hearts. I believe we are bound to experience *han*, but that *han* must be relieved. The grievances of separated families cannot be resolved simply with the passing of time. They are healed only when the separated ones meet each other. When I met separated families, I was never calm and collected while filming their interviews. I always shed tears, feeling with them.

Although 40 years have passed, I would like to introduce two separated families that I still remember vividly. The first was an elderly man who lived alone, miles outside of Harbin. All of his other family members had passed away, and this old man wanted to find his family scattered to the south. When I visited him with my camera, I found a frail, white-haired man in his nineties, lying in the dark basement of a hut, unable to move.

After helping him sit and lean against the wall, I asked the old man, "Who are you looking for?"

"I am looking for my father."

I blurted out, "If I heard you right, you said you were looking for your father, but he may have died of old age."

"I want to find him, regardless if he's living or dead. If he has died, I must see his grave with my eyes to confirm that he is dead. Then I can relieve this bitter *han* that I carry."

I was deeply moved. The old man's words resonated in my heart. I have no way of knowing what happened after the filmed interview was sent to KBS, but I sincerely hope that the old man poured a glass of wine in front of his father's grave, made a deep bow, wept bitterly, and relieved his *han*.

The second is a story of an old woman, who came to find me at my aunt's house after she heard I was taking pictures and videos of separated families. The woman said she was looking for her husband, from whom she had been separated for over 40 years. She came to me with her daughter and her son-in-law, who were both in their forties. Her husband left for Korea while her daughter was still in her womb. Once the Division was drawn across the 38th parallel, she had to remain where she was. She was unable to move or even find out whether he and his family were okay. Every single day, she filled a bowl with purified water as a prayer for her husband's health and the reunion of her family. This old woman's story was so heart-wrenching that I took elaborate photos and videos of her and provided them to KBS.

The old woman's story aired on TV, and I returned to the States. There, I received an unexpected phone call from Canada. The caller was the very husband whom the old woman had been so desperately seeking. He told me he worked as a university professor in Korea, retired, and immigrated to Canada. He told me how he left his pregnant wife behind in Heilongjiang Province and traveled to Korea in his 20s. After the Division, he gave up on all hope to meet them again. He lived in despair, until he met a good woman and started a new family. After speaking with me on the phone several times, he asked me for advice, "What should I do?"

I replied, "It's all up to you," and sent him the old woman's address and contact information.

The following year, when I returned to Heilongjiang, this grandmother came to see me with her daughter and son-in-law once more. It seemed to me that her husband had not contacted her. Unable to tell her the news about her husband directly, I called her son-in-law outside and told him what I knew. The son-in-law said he would think about what to do, and we said our farewells. The next year, when I visited my aunt again, the old woman's daughter and son-in-law came to visit me. The woman was nowhere in sight. When she learned the news of her husband from her son-in-law, she was so heartbroken that she gave up eating and drinking. Eventually, she fell ill, became bed-ridden, and passed away. To this day, whenever I think of the old woman who longed for her husband her entire life, who looked forward to the day of their reunion, whose life ended fraught with *han*, tears well up my eyes.

I would like to add one final thing about the lives of separated families; their pain continued even after they settled in the South. While it is sad and lonely to live apart from one's family, they also suffered from tremendous political persecution. The communist label was affixed to them like a scarlet letter all their lives because they came from communist countries, or because they had a family in a communist country or in North Korea. My father settled in South Korea at a relatively young age, yet throughout his entire life, he was subjected to background checks and was considered unemployable due to the shackles of being labeled a "red." In this matter, the North was just like the South. In the DPRK, one's origin is particularly important. Coming from the ROK or having family living in the South is a huge obstacle in life. This terrible situation means that separated families live with the pain of separation and of political persecution in both South and North Korea.

After ROK-Soviet diplomatic ties were established in 1990 and ROK-China diplomatic relations in 1992, the situation for separated families living in South Korea and the former Soviet bloc (including Koreans who were forcibly displaced to Central Asia in the 1930s) improved significantly. Travel become relatively easy, so unlike before, you could reunite with your loved ones if you wished. However, the issue of separated families between the two Koreas remains unresolved to this day. The top priority for both South and

North Korean governments now should be to relieve the sorrow and pain of separated families from both Koreas—the *han* of those who voluntarily scattered or were forcibly separated during the Division and the Korean War.

It is not that there were no efforts to sympathize and relieve the human pain of separated families. At the 1971 Inter-Korean Red Cross Summit, both South and North Korea agreed that the tragedy of separated families between the two Koreas is symbolic of the tragedy of mankind in the 20th century and agreed to reunite separated families as soon as possible. However, the first reunion was not held until September 1985. It was called a "Hometown Visiting Group of Dispersed Families." Then, inter-Korean family reunifications were paused for a time, resuming after the first inter-Korean summit in August 2000. Since then, there have been a total of 21 family reunions and seven video reunions.

It seems to me that separated family reunions are nothing more than a political show. I question whether North and South Koreans leaders have genuine sympathy and consideration for separated families. The current system for reunions of separated families only increases the *han* of separated families further. I would like to point out three problems and make one recommendation for a better policy.

First, let's look at the most recent example of family reunions, held in August 2018. Out of roughly 57,000 applicants for the reunion, only 100 were selected, by computer lottery. The competitive ratio was 570 denials to 1 acceptance. Separated family reunions are not lottery tickets or college entrance exams. How can "competition" have anything to do with families who have longed to meet after more than 70 years of separation? I read one news article that makes me more angry than sad. It tells the story of an elderly man who applied for a family reunion. The 95-year-old man said, "My older and younger siblings remain in the North... My sister would be 93 if she is still alive. My wish is to hear from her about the last hours of my parents' life before their death."

This man was eliminated from the lottery. Hearing the news, tears filled his eyes. He said, "I'm finished," and turned around.

Secondly, those rare reunions which have been held since 2000 have only lasted 3 to 5 days. Family members were only permitted to meet face to face at a specific location for three or four hours, under the "supervision" of North and South Korean officials. Those short hours must disappear like a dream. Can these highly controlled meetings relieve the pain and sorrow of families separated for more than 70 years? How can we understand their *han* so poorly as to make them say goodbye without any promise of when, or even if, they could ever see each other alive again?

Thirdly, reunions of separated families should never be politicized. When political conflict arises between the Koreas or between North Korea and the United States, scheduled reunions have often been canceled. Separated families are a humanitarian concern in the realm of human rights, universally valued. Therefore, reunions should not be one-time, political events. Above all, we should not have to beg for separated families to be reunited, and neither Korea should treat reunions as if they were special political favors to separated families.

For a more fundamental solution, we should reject the selective, one-time, politicized method of holding reunions in favor of a new policy that allows separated families to meet freely, at any time, and without any conditions. We have run out of time. All first-generation separated family members are now over 80 years old. I believe that separated family policy should be carried out as a part of unification policy.

I propose the establishment of a "reunion district" for separated families in Kaesong. Hundreds of apartments should be built so separated families can meet and stay together at all times. It should not matter if they meet for a week or a month. If they want to, governments must allow separated families to live there together for the rest of their lives to relieve their han. I have no doubt that a separated family reunion district in Kaesong will play an important role in fostering a culture of unification, becoming a shortcut and touchstone to the unification of which we dream.

Part 4:
Our Peace, Our Unification

The first generation separated from their hometown, before the division,
were independence activists.

That was the spirit of the times. Both the independence fighters, who
actively participated in independence activities, and the common people
wished for the independence of their country and worked hard to realize
that aspiration... Liberation was achieved due to the dedication of so many
independence activists who died without their names being memorialized.

The spirit of the times in our contemporary era is reunification.

Unmasking US Demonization of North Korea

The current situation on the Korean Peninsula is not much different from that of the 1950s. Confrontation between the North and South still exists. The DPRK has already become a de facto nuclear state, and the US military is stationed in South Korea. Harsh words are constantly exchanged between North Korea and the US. Despite President Moon Jae-in's efforts and two DPRK-US summits, the Armistice Agreement is still in effect, and even an end of war declaration—let alone a Peace Agreement—is far away. Why are inter-Korean and North Korea-US relations seemingly on an endless loop for the past 70 years?

The problem lies with the United States. The root cause lies in their persistent demonization of North Korea. The Christian ideology of being a "chosen people" and the dichotomous behavioral pattern of judging good and evil according to their own values is how America justifies labeling North Korea an evil to be expunged from this earth. In the American mindset, evil is something to vanquish, not something with which one may dialogue and compromise. Killing demons can be justified by any means or method, and requires no morality or rules of war.

American society has been strongly indoctrinated with the belief that North Korea is evil. Educated and uneducated Americans alike freely express their disdain for the DPRK. While traveling to and from North Korea, I worked hard to improve North Korea-US dialogue and relations. Consequently, I received significant attention from the American media. I was interviewed numerous times by local media as well as national broadcasts such as ABC and CNN. As I became more well known through such broadcasts, I encountered unexpected persecution. Several times a year, I suffered criticism and intimidation from people I had never met for having "taken sides,'" "praised North Korea," and acted "against the national interest of the United States." I received specific threats that I should watch out on the road at night, after which my family refrained from going out in the evening for several days. Because anyone can own a gun in American society, I was always worried about my safety and that of my family.

While working as a professor at the University of Georgia, I once received a call from the university president. The university had received a formal protest letter from the most preeminent lawyer from the largest law firm in Atlanta, pressuring them to immediately fire Professor Han Shik Park and never give him a platform again. In the letter, the lawyer said he could not let his children study under someone like me because I represented and advocated for the DPRK's demonic regime. He went one step further, threatening to suspend his law firm's annual contribution to the University of Georgia were his request unmet. Fortunately, because the president respected academic diversity and was well aware of my passion for peace and academic endeavors, I managed to escape harm. Although I have worked for peace on the Korean Peninsula all my life, I still have mixed feelings when I think about how I was labeled either "a red" or a "North Korea collaborator," both in the US and in South Korea.

Recognizing that overthrowing North Korea by force was virtually impossible, the United States turned to the strategy of economic sanctions and political isolation. Of course, it is also clear that this strategy will not overthrow North Korea. Following the 1990s, the US began to demonize even more earnestly, defining them as an enemy nation whose very existence signals a military threat. By American standards, North Korea is the perfect candidate for demonization. It has a different political system from that of the United States, is non-democratic, lacks freedom of religion, violates human rights, commonly oppresses its people and accepts political prisoners as necessary. It is the country that killed the young American Otto Warmbier. If you look at the countries demonized by the United States—North Korea, China, Iran, Iraq, etc.—the US' demonization shares a common denominator, that is, a sense of racial superiority.

Demonizing the DPRK is designed to achieve the United States' political and economic goals and is motivated by three factors. The first has to do with countering China's expansion. The United States Forces Korea's (USFK) role in effectively deterring China's rise is more important than ever. By demonizing North Korea, the United States intends to reinforce the presence of US forces in Korea, while actually trying to contain China's expansion and increasing military power. This is clear if you consider the controversy over deploying the THAAD high-altitude missile defense system. The US claims

THAAD is intended to deter North Korea, but everyone knows that its real purpose is to deter China. The second motivation is to further legitimize the presence of US troops in Korea. Protecting the South from the evil North is the pretense by which the US justifies and makes "sacred" the US' military presence. In my opinion, the third motivation is economic. Demonizing North Korea and positioning it as South Korea's main enemy was the pretext for the United States to persuade and coerce South Korea into purchasing US-made weapons. The annual South Korea-US joint military exercises are a veritable weapons fair, showcasing state-of-the-art US weapons.

In order to sell arms, the military-industrial complex instigates military conflicts and tensions in every corner of the globe, often by deliberately demonizing other nations. But in the absence of information, it is difficult to decide where to foment military conflict and who to demonize. In other words, the military-industrial complex uses information to justify its actions. This is why we say most of the information pouring out about North Korea is either false or manipulated or distorted. There are also many cases of exaggerating small nonsensical facts. Intelligence agencies creates fake information that suits the taste of the military-industrial complex, and the media plays the role of a trumpeter by propagating it without verification. It is really frustrating to see US media reports that North Korea is making an intercontinental ballistic missile able to be equipped with a nuclear warhead *to attack the US*. As far as I know, the DPRK has no plan—or intention—to attack the United States. Even they are well aware that would be suicidal.

The United States has not only demonized the North Korean regime, but also the good-hearted, common people. The civilian massacre in Sinchon, Hwanghae Province during the Korean War is one example. The Sinchon Museum was built to soothe the souls of these people and to be used as a place for anti-American pilgrimage. During my frequent travels to and from the DPRK in the 1990s, I visited the Sinchon Museum several times, praying for the peace of the innocent people who were demonized and victimized. I think the term "memorial hall" would be more appropriate, but North Korea uses the museum as a place to educate people about the brutality and cruelty of the United States. For 52 days, beginning on October 17, 1950, the US Military brutally massacred 35,383 civilians, including children, women and the elderly. Could such a massacre have been possible without first demonizing the innocent?

I took note of every single comment and explanation the museum guide made. As the DPRK explains it, the massacre was carried out under the leadership of Army Major General Harrison D. Madden, an officer of the imperialist US invasion force. The museum exhibit contains several documents confirming Harrison's identity, along with his photograph. Later, when I returned to the United States and tried to confirm Harrison D. Madden's existence through ABC, the broadcasting company to whom I provided North Korea commentary, the U.S. Department of Defense replied simply that there was no record of such a person's military service. It seemed clear to me that America wanted to hide Harrison D. Madden's existence.

Although there were no photos taken of the 1950 massacre, the museum was filled with paintings based on living testimonies. The paintings were so vivid and terrifying that I had to look away. There were household tools, shoes, eyeglasses, and other personal items used by the civilian victims on display. One particular exhibit drew attention to the victims' physical remains, including their ashes and hair.

Whenever I visited the Sinchon Museum, I was reminded of Dachau concentration camp memorial in Munich, Germany. I could not stop thinking that the Nazis' atrocious massacre of Jews in Dachau and the massacre of civilians in Sinchon were very similar.

US military massacres of civilians were not confined to the North. As many now know, in July 1950 in No Gun Ri, Chungcheong Province, South Korea, the US military also carried out a horrific and criminal civilian massacre. They slaughtered innocent civilians for the absurd reason that there were one or two North Korean soldiers in the refugee procession. Would such atrocities have been possible if they had not demonized innocent civilians and seen our people as insignificant and inferior?

Crafting fake news about North Korea is malicious, but misinformation can also be rooted in ignorance. I do not believe we have even scratched the surface of knowing the DPRK. How many people in the United States and South Korea even know the fundamental driving forces and factors that determine the DPRK's actions and policies? Let's consider an example. The relentless economic sanctions imposed on North Korea stemmed from one hypothesis—that once the people could no longer endure suffering under sanctions, their dissatisfaction would morph into resistance against the regime, starting a revolution like the Arab Spring. Do you think such a scenario is likely? If you believe that, it is the product of ignorance. I don't believe that will ever happen.

Whether in a democratic or communist country, the state's legitimacy is the basis of maintaining the system. There is only one source of legitimacy, the consent and support of the people. When a political system loses the people's support, it loses legitimacy and the system collapses. North Korea's system is not one that seeks legitimacy by filling the people's pockets with money to satisfy their economic needs. It is impossible to understand and explain this without looking directly at *Juche* ideology, its ruling ideology. Rather than delegitimizing the government, the economic sanctions that interrupt the lives of the people are serving to unite North Korea and making it even more nationalistic.

I witnessed this firsthand through conversations with officials and ordinary residents on dozens of trips. For example, an American spy ship, the *USS Pueblo*, is on display there as a trophy and symbol of victory over the US. It was captured by North Korea during secret reconnaissance in the East Sea in 1968, moved from Wonsan to the Daedong River, and then moved again to the Pothong River for display under the Kim Jong-eun regime.

All North Koreans go see the *Pueblo* at least once, particularly students. I never miss going when I visit Pyongyang. Inside the ship, one can view videos of the entire investigation process, confessions, and repentance of the 82 American crew members. Most of the North

Korean residents I met and talked to them thought that the *Pueblo* was a symbol of a glorious victory—to the point of obtaining the US' surrender. The *Pueblo* is a place of anti-American education and a historical site that inspires North Korean nationalism. Whenever there is a diplomatic battle between the DPRK and the United States, the Pueblo gets particularly crowded.

The illusion that America bears a moral responsibility and God-given mission to eliminate North Korean evil—by any means possible, including force—has long guided American policy toward the DPRK. Additionally, in pursuit of the common good and to rid mankind of its evil, the United States promotes the logic that other countries should cooperate with their mission. South Korea has sympathized with US demonization of North Korea, blindly subordinating inter-Korean relations to relations between North Korea and the US.

Although demonization will not lead to North Korean collapse, that does not stop the United States. In these circumstances, what breakthrough will change the current situation on the Korean Peninsula? The answer is outlined clearly in joint declarations from the last three inter-Korean Summits. The June 15, 2000 Inter-Korean Joint Declaration, the October 4, 2007 Inter-Korean Summit Agreement, and the April 27, 2018 Panmunjom Declaration all use a common expression in Article 1—the "principle of national independence."

South Korea needs more flexible autonomy to formulate and promote policies in line with its own national interests as an independent, sovereign state. It must urgently explain the peculiarities of inter-Korean relations to the United States—and the international community—to persuade them diplomatically that inter-Korean exchanges, cooperation, and reunification are beneficial, rather than harmful, to the United States' national interest as well as global coprosperity.

Linking Two Countries to Release Two Journalists

On March 17, 2009, reporters Laura Ling and Euna Lee, of the American cable channel Current TV, were arrested by North Korean authorities. The reporters claimed they were arrested by Army guards who suddenly appeared while they were covering the North Korean defector issue in the North Korean-Chinese border region near the Tumen River. They protested that they had done no criminal activity and were engaged in legitimate reporting activities.

However, the investigation and announcement by the North Korean authorities concluded differently. The two reporters crossed the Tumen River in violation of the national border. Because they were filming the locations of military facilities, guard posts, and guard movements, they were captured and arrested in accordance with due process. The DPRK also claimed that the videographer who accompanied them fled to China, carrying photos and videos taken during the arrest, which contained sensitive military information that could seriously harm their national security. Because there are heavy charges for border trespassing and anti-state espionage, North Korea signaled through their international media outlets that the investigations and trial would be conducted according to due process.

On June 8th, the two reporters were found guilty of "hostility to the Korean people" and "illegal border-crossing." They were sentenced to 12 years of reform through labor.

Although they had committed a crime and been convicted, I thought it would be undesirable from a humanitarian standpoint for two American journalists to spend 12 years in prison in North Korea. The newly launched Obama administration was then seeking to improve relations with North Korea, and North Korea was also expecting the Obama administration to change its North Korea policy. I was concerned that this abrupt variable may adversely affect North Korea-US relations, because any deterioration of North Korea-US relations is a problem directly related to peace on the Korean Peninsula.

Being familiar with North Korea and the United States and understanding both countries' behaviors, my intuition told me I had some work to do as a "peace mediator" for the release of the two reporters. The 140 days of the reporters' detention in North Korea was a tense and difficult time for me as well. More than a decade has passed, but my memories are still vivid, as if it were yesterday.

I traveled back and forth between the United States and North Korea twice in March and July of that year, struggling to mediate between North Korea and the United States for their release. During a meeting with high-ranking Korean officials, I prepared a negotiation proposal for the reporters' release, and delivered the negotiation proposal to the US' side. I stayed in contact with the two reporters' families, as well the US State Department and intelligence officials, to inform them of their current situation and provide advice throughout the release negotiations. I tried to do my best to promote dialogue between North Korea and the United States and to promote mutual understanding.

When I heard the news of their arrest, I thought that the matter was serious and urgent, so I immediately set out and visited Pyongyang from March 24 to 28. Even though I have visited more than 50 times, each visit is a challenge. First of all, I must receive an invitation from the North Korean authorities and present the invitation to their embassy in Beijing to obtain a visa before I can book a ticket to Pyongyang. I generally travel by air—from Atlanta to Beijing and then on to Pyongyang. Because there are not daily flights, it is common to waste a day or two waiting in Beijing. And, it is not cheap—one trip costs $10,000—although, the salary of an American university professor is actually quite low. Because I traveled there so regularly, I befriended an increasing number of people. It was impossible to go empty-handed, so I would usually take along simple gifts.

As soon as I arrived in Pyongyang on March 24, 2009, I did my best to learn where the two reporters were, how they were doing, and whether there was anything wrong with their health and safety. I was told that an investigation into "criminal allegations" was underway somewhere in Pyongyang and that they were being treated well. That evening, I met with North Korean officials to find out more about the situation. They were usually close friends, and they were high-ranking figures who could even directly report to Chairman Kim Jong Il. Although their names cannot be disclosed here, they were mainly persons who held positions in the United Front Department and the

Korean Asia-Pacific Peace Committee.

At the drinking party after dinner, the tense atmosphere gradually softened. We talked about people's lives and also exchanged opinions on pending issues in North Korea-US and inter-Korean relations. Sharing a glass of wine in both South and North Korea has a similar effect in easing tension and allowing people to share more openly. I was able to naturally bring up the two reporters, which of course, the North Korean officials expected. As the conversation unfolded, it seemed to increasingly reveal how North Korean authorities would handle the matter of releasing the two reporters.

▲ The author chats with Ri Jong Hyok (right), vice chairman of the Asia-Pacific Peace Committee, who led the DPRK's delegation to the track II diologue hosted by the University of Georgia in October 2011. (Photo courtesy of Han Shik Park)

I felt strongly that the authorities had no intention of holding the reporters for long and that they would release them in a way that North Korea could save face. Looking at North Korea-US relations and the political situation in the United States in March 2009, it was easy to understand North Korea's intentions. It was only two months after the Bush administration, which had defined North Korea as part of the axis of evil, resigned and the Obama administration took office. The DPRK, which was seeking to improve relations with the United States, wanted to offer an "olive branch" to the Obama administration, which seemed young, fresh, and enterprising. Releasing the two reporters seemed to be viewed as a vehicle for improving relations with the United States. But they said an immediate release, as the United States would like, would be difficult. They explained that the two reporters definitely violated North Korean laws, were arrested on the spot, and could not be released without investigation and trial. In other words, once the authorities completed the investigation and confirmed a guilty verdict, they told me those foreigners could be released through deportation.

Returning to the United States, I reassured the reporters' families and the US government that they were safe and being treated well, not in a detention center or prison. However, I advised them it would be better to take a little time to approach the situation calmly, as it would be difficult for North Korea to release the reporters until they were found guilty at trial. In late April, we received news that the DPRK was beginning the formal trial against the two reporters. Less than two months later, on June 8th, the Central Court sentenced each of the reporters to 12 years of reform through labor on charges of "hostility to the Korean people" and "illegal border-crossing." Secretary of State Hillary Clinton immediately responded to the sentence as I expected, claiming North Korea's conviction was unfounded and urging the immediate, unconditional release of the two reporters on humanitarian grounds.

Given the seriousness of the matter and the US government's attitude, I did not think that the release of the two reporters would be easy. On July 4th, I visited North Korea again to earnestly negotiate for their release. I met once more with the high-ranking officials whom I had interviewed during the visit in March. We had candid conversations over the course of five days.

I tried to learn what the North Korean authorities wanted in exchange for the reporters' release, and their answer was surprisingly simple and clear. If the U.S. government would admit that the two reporters illegally crossed the border in an act hostile to Korea, made an official apology, and then asked for amnesty, the reporters would be released. They proposed this so-called "3A condition." High-ranking officials directly emphasized three words—Admission, Apology, Amnesty—and asked me to deliver them to the United States. Particular emphasis was placed on the word "apology." In other words, the condition was that the US government should not use the word "regret" but must express their "apology." In the negotiation process, each word was of decisive importance. They also added that the only way to release someone who has been convicted of a crime in the DPRK is by the pardon of the Supreme Leader, so the US government must politely request a pardon to enable the convicts' release.

Another condition related to amnesty was that a person of proper rank and grade from the United States come to North Korea to directly request amnesty from Chairman Kim Jong Il. This was similar to how, if a student got in trouble at elementary school, the parents may apologize to the administration and take the student home, promising to prevent any future recurrence of the problem behavior. In this case, who might have the right stature to come as a special envoy? When officials asked me for advice on what kind of person was appropriate, I immediately thought of Al Gore. He had served as vice president for eight years and ran for the Democratic presidential nomination. Also, as the founder and chairman of Current TV, where the two reporters worked, I thought he might be the most suitable person. But they were astonished at my suggestion and shouted, "No!" to Al Gore. They told me if he came, he would also be arrested and questioned—due to their suspicion that Al Gore had instigated and manipulated the two reporters from behind the scenes—making the situation even worse.

The DPRK officials and I thought it would be best if Secretary of State Hillary Clinton came, but we agreed that it was too great a political burden for an incumbent official to come in person. I mentioned several former Secretaries of State, but they did not think them a good fit and excluded them from the list of candidates. Former President Jimmy Carter, who visited North Korea in 1994 to resolve the North Korean nuclear issue and bring about an agreement to hold an inter-Korean summit, was also mentioned, but North Koreans were not fond of that idea either because he seemed too old-fashioned. I later realized that the DPRK seemed to have one person in mind from the beginning—former President Bill Clinton. He had served as President of the United States for eight years, and as an elder statesman for the Democrats, he was still politically influential in the Obama administration—not to mention that he was also the husband of incumbent Secretary of State, Hillary Clinton. There was no one better in terms of dignity, stature, and symbolism.

In fact, in October 2000, there had even been coordination between

North Korea and the United States to arrange a visit to North Korea for incumbent President Bill Clinton. On October 23rd of that year, Secretary of State Albright had visited North Korea to discuss the schedule for President Clinton's visit to North Korea with the North Korean side. I was in North Korea at the time, and knew high-ranking officials had already accepted President Clinton's plans to visit North Korea. However, Clinton's visit was ultimately canceled due to the domestic political climate in the United States and the perception that such a visit could adversely affect Democrat Al Gore's candidacy for president.

Despite the intervening nine years, the DPRK still wanted former President Clinton to visit. The officials insistently emphasized Bill Clinton's past hopes to visit North Korea and requested that I persuade the United States. On the condition that I would deliver their request, I made a counter proposal to the North Korean authorities that the two reporters should never be sent to a prison or labor camp, not even for a single day. I asked them to keep the reporters at the invitation station, as a signal to the United States that North Korea was willing to release the two reporters and that preparations for their release were already complete. I managed to convince them.

On the other hand, I realized that the United States may struggle to accept such conditions, as they had still not normalized relations with North Korea during 70 years of hostilities. The United States believed that the DPRK had illegally abducted and detained the two reporters, and so issuing an apology and requesting a pardon would implicitly legitimize North Korea's laws and systems. On the other hand, I believed it was not an unreasonable condition for the US to accept in exchange for the reporters' release. Because the DPRK was already preparing to hand over the two reporters, the most important thing was to convincingly deliver their proposal to the US government.

As soon as I left Pyongyang and arrived in Beijing, I phoned the US government to notify them of the DPRK's conditions of release. It was so urgent that it couldn't wait until my return to the States. After arriving in the US, I delivered the terms of the negotiations to the administration in greater detail, emphasizing the importance of an official apology and former President Clinton's visit to North Korea. I also explained in detail how to communicate with North Korea.

Less than a day later, on July 10th, at a State Department meeting, Secretary of State Hillary Clinton said that the two reporters and their families deeply regretted the incident and that she thought everyone was very sorry that it had happened, showing a completely different attitude from her criticism of the DPRK in June. She also suggested that the two reporters had committed offenses with expressions of remorse and regret, although she did not use the word "apology," as North Korea had demanded. She also responded to the North's request by stating her hope that the regime would grant a legal "amnesty."

Ten days later, on July 20th, Secretary Hillary Clinton stated that negotiations were going well for the reporters' release. Hopeful that their release was imminent, I took a summer family trip which I had been putting off for a long time.

I was enjoying a good time with my family in Myrtle Beach, South Carolina, when all of a sudden, national broadcasters such as ABC and CNN—and even a local Atlanta TV station—arrived in their news trucks. The plane carrying former President Bill Clinton was now on its way to North Korea, and somehow the news stations came to interview me. I couldn't be interviewed in my swimsuit at the beach, so I hurriedly bought a suit and a tie from a local clothing store. Because it was hard to find clothes that fit well on such short notice, I ended up wearing an oversized suit and looking awkward.

Finally, on August 5th, former President Clinton reached North Korea and apologized to the government using the word "apology." The two reporters were pardoned, released, and returned to their families in good health. Shortly after their release, I received a phone call from reporter Laura Ling. "I am very grateful to you Professor," she said.

The DPRK and the United States neither linked the negotiations for the two reporters' release to the nuclear issue, nor did they use it as a political means to improve DPRK-US relations. I sincerely hoped that the negotiations would serve as a catalyst for improving relations. After the two reporters were released, Secretary of State Hillary Clinton neither affirmed nor denied a reporter's question at a press conference whether Professor Han Shik Park from the University of Georgia played a role in the negotiations on behalf of the US government.

"No comment," she said, seemingly out of consideration for me.

Agricultural Exchanges between the UGA and DPRK

I visited the DPRK most frequently in the mid to late 1990s. There was a good reason. Tensions between North Korea and the United States were rising again as the 1994 Geneva Accord, reached through former President Jimmy Carter's mediation, collapsed when the United States failed to fulfill its promises even before the ink on the agreement dried up. I was also curious about what changes could be detected in the DPRK's system and society after President Kim Il Sung's death, and how Chairman Kim Jong Il was doing at consolidating power. I wanted to explore and understand these issues in my own way.

▲ In September 1997, the author led six delegates from the DPRK's Institute of Agricultural Sciences, who came at the invitation of the US government, to tour Ralston Purina (merged with Nestle in 2001), a world-renowned animal feed company located in St. Louis, Missouri.

However, what caught my attention was the reality that North Korean people were barely managing to stay alive, eating herb roots and tree bark. Chairman Kim Il Sung's promise that his people would feed on plenteous rice and meat was unfulfilled, and the whole country was crying out with groans of hunger. The food situation became most dire after Kim Il Sung's death. The dissolution of the Soviet Union and collapse of the communist bloc accelerated their economic isolation. Then, natural disasters such as drought and floods were added to the mix, causing a sudden disruption in food production. At least 2 million North Koreans died of starvation during the "Arduous March," the great famine that occurred in the mid-to-late 1990s.

With my own eyes, I witnessed emaciated children, left in daycare after their parents died of starvation, themselves now dying with nothing to eat. When I went to the Pyongyang neighborhood where I had lived for one year during elementary school, it was overflowing with people who had nothing to eat and were barely surviving by eating the bark peeled off of pine trees. Looking at them with a bitter heart, I felt regret and anger. I was plagued with guilt that I was able to live off the fat of the land in America.

The miserable sight was not unfamiliar to me. There was also a time when I had endured each day, just wishing for a taste of rice. From 1946 to 1947, as a student at Pyongyang Common Elementary School, I used to go to the racecourse nearby to buy and eat pureed soybean, which was used as feed for horses. Memories of that excruciating poverty remain vivid to this day, so I couldn't help but feel compassion for the people of North Korea.

I was always asking myself, what can I do for those who are starving?

There is an old saying in Korea that says, "Even the state cannot relieve poverty." I wasn't a government official, and I wasn't as wealthy as Bill Gates, so I wasn't in a position to help. I thought deeply about what I could contribute to increase food production in North Korea. The University of Georgia, where I was working, had an unmatched reputation in the United States for agriculture and animal husbandry. I thought it would be good to take advantage of the strength of UGA's College of Agriculture to arrange various projects to alleviate the food shortage and increase productivity in the DPRK's agricultural sector.

I suggested that North Korean officials come to UGA to learn and acquire advanced agricultural techniques which could be applied in the DPRK. The officials and researchers at the DPRK's Institute of Agricultural Sciences responded to my proposal, saying that if given the opportunity, they would like to visit the United States to learn. Although the United States is North Korea's enemy, they also envy and admire American science and advanced technology. They were pleased to come as it was not an official exchange between governments—free from any political burden—but rather a private exchange between universities and scholars.

Upon returning to the United States, I got busy promoting the North Korean agricultural delegation's visit to the University of Georgia. However, we encountered two major difficulties. The first was the expense. The North Koreans seemed unable to cover the cost of their travel to the United States. Their delegation was quite large, and the whole country was suffering starvation. I wondered how we would manage to cover the expenses of their travel and accommodation.

Another issue were their visas. Even if the expenses were somehow taken care of, we were unsure if the US government would issue tourist visas to officials from an enemy country without diplomatic relations.

I decided to start by asking the US Department of State. I called the official in charge of the East Asia desk, with whom I was acquainted. I explained the purpose of the North Korean officials' visit to the US and managed to persuade him. His wife was Korean, and he spoke the language fluently, took great interest in issues on the Korean Peninsula, and shared many views with me. Although he could not guarantee that the Department of State would issue visas in this unprecedented situation, he reassured me that they would take it into serious consideration.

While waiting for the response from the Department of State, I started earnestly raising funds to cover expenses for the delegation's travel and accommodation. As a result of asking for help from my acquaintances and their contacts in Georgia's agricultural and husbandry sector, I managed to accumulate substantial financial support. Gaining Gold Kist's support—a chicken processing company headquartered in Georgia—was particularly significant. D.W. Brooks, the founder of the company, was an alumnus of the UGA's College of Agriculture and willingly provided support because of his great interest in North Korea.

About the time I raised sufficient funds, I got the news I had been awaiting. The US government decided to allow the North Korean delegation to enter the country and to cooperate with us as much as they could during their visit. Finally, the North Korean officials from the Ministry of Agriculture and the DPRK Institute of Agricultural Sciences made their visit to the United States. Looking back now, I am grateful to a lot of people. I appreciate that I had the good luck to meet and work together with decent people. In a way, we are indebted to many people for life itself.

In September 1997, a six person delegation from the DPRK Institute of Agricultural Sciences visited Georgia. They came to acquire and transfer advanced agricultural technologies, including essential development and seed improvement to alleviate the food shortage. Their greatest interest was improving the poultry industry. They knew that the University of Georgia was at the forefront of poultry research, and that Georgia produced and supplied more poultry than any other state in the USA. (Georgia produced and supplied 28% of all U.S. chicken consumption.)

Dr. Nick Dale, an Agriculture professor at UGA, had developed a technology to raise freshly hatched chicks into broiler chickens within a month. The North Korean delegation showed great interest in Dr. Dale's research and was very excited about the prospect of being able to feed the people by rapidly breeding chickens. The visiting group attended several poultry-related seminars hosted by the UGA's College of Agricultural and toured the Gold Kist factory that had provided financial support for their visit. They were amazed to see the modern, automated chicken processing, where chickens move along an automated conveyor belt and are ready-to-cook in minutes. The

◄ A delegation from the DPRK's Ministry of Agriculture and the Institute of Agricultural Sciences toured St. Louis, Missouri, a region of the United States renowned for its livestock and agricultural industries. (Photo courtesy of Han Shik Park)

North Korean delegation was also interested in Dr. Dale's research on poultry feed. Animal feed was scarce in the DPRK, so they desperately needed to develop and supply of feed. I also guided them to tour Purina's animal feed factory in St. Louis, Missouri. The Purina personnel warmly welcomed the visiting delegation and promised to help with feed production and processing in North Korea.

The visiting group from the DPRK Institute of Agricultural Sciences made a special request to me on their way home. They wanted to bring some raw chickens to North Korea to breed and feed them to the people. However, import and export of agricultural and livestock products across borders was impossible due to strict quarantine. Their delegation was not unaware of that, but they were so desperate that they asked in spite of the restrictions. I considered their request and suggested that they carry eggs with them, instead of live chickens. They said it was a good idea. I handed over ten raw eggs for them to carry in the cabin on their flight home. When I visited North Korea the following year, I learned that five of the eggs were broken on the way home. The other five hatched successfully, but two chicks died immediately, and the other three died shortly thereafter.

With a saddened heart, I returned to ask Dr. Nick Dale what would have caused the chicks deaths and why the project had "failed." He hesitated in suggesting an exact cause; he could only speculate. Because it was difficult to determine the cause of the chickens' early death without knowing the exact soil quality and environment of North Korea, he made an unexpected request. He wanted to visit the DPRK himself to investigate what was needed for successful poultry breeding there, interact with people from the Institute of Agricultural Sciences, and transfer the results of his research to them. I was deeply grateful for Dr. Dale's amazing proposal and his sincerity.

I hastily organized a group visit from the University of Georgia to North Korea. In October 2000, I arrived in Pyongyang with a visiting delegation including Dr. Gail Buchanan, the dean of the College of Agriculture, and Dr. Nick Dale. This was the first time a US academic delegation visited North Korea. It was an exchange visit in response to the DPRK agricultural delegation's visit in 1997. Not only was the trip motivated by good intentions to alleviate the North Korean food shortage, but the delegation also harbored hopes for long-term agricultural exchange, cooperation, and trade.

During their visit to North Korea, the delegation from Georgia not only attended academic conferences, but also toured universities and agricultural sites, sharing their advice with North Korean officials from the Ministry of Agriculture. Dr. Dale, in particular, faithfully transferred poultry-related research and technology to the DPRK. The visiting delegation from the US, who initially had negative views and

▲ In May 2001, when the delegation from the DPRK's Institute of Agricultural Sciences came to the United States for the second time, they visited Coca-Cola headquarters in Atlanta, Georgia. Coca-Cola welcomed them with a huge flag. Vice President and General Manager Kim Sam-ryong is pictured. (Photo courtesy of Han Shik Park)

prejudices against North Korea, gradually began to accept it as it was. The hostile sentiments between the two countries dissolved and trust between the U.S. delegation and the North Korean officials began to grow as they spent time together throughout the visit. They were all full of expectations and hopes for future exchanges and cooperation. At that time, Secretary of State Albright also visited Pyongyang to coordinate President Clinton's visit to North Korea.

The following year, in May 2001, a group from the DPRK Institute of Agricultural Sciences visited UGA for a second time. The delegation, led by Vice President Kim Sam-ryong, took interest in sweet potatoes this time. The DPRK's food policy had previously focused on the production of white potatoes, which are less sensitive to sudden climate change and are able to thrive in harsh environments better than rice. In 2000, when the delegation from the Agricultural College at the University of Georgia had visited North Korea, they discovered that the soil and climate were very suitable for growing sweet potatoes and had promised to give some advice to increase the production of sweet potatoes.

After succeeding in researching and developing white potato-flavored sweet potatoes, the UGA's College of Agriculture was striving to cultivate and distribute them. Since there was a special order from Chairman Kim Jong Il to "remarkably increase the production of potatoes and sweet potatoes," the visiting delegation from the DPRK was more interested than ever in sweet potatoes that taste like white potatoes. The delegation wanted to take home improved sweet potato seeds, just like the last time. I understood their desperate feelings more than anyone else, so I asked the College of Agriculture to hand over some sweet potato seeds that tasted like white potatoes. (I haven't been able to confirm whether the sweet potatoes had grown well, but I hope they have been of some help in resolving the food shortage in North Korea.) The delegation returned after signing a memorandum of understanding for exchange and cooperation between GUA's College of Agriculture and the DPRK's Institute of Agricultural Sciences. They promised to actively carry out academic exchanges between the two institutions.

However, the promised exchanges between the two institutions could not continue from that point until July 2008. In January 2002, President Bush named North Korea as part of the "axis of evil." This broke the bridge between the two institutions for seven years. I cannot hide my sadness whenever I see political tensions or other issues pouring cold water on efforts for private exchange. In reality, the more inter-governmental dialogue channels are blocked, the more private exchanges are needed. This is because vital private-sector exchanges can serve to prime the pump for dialogue between governments.

In July 2008, at the request of Scott Angle, dean of the College of Agriculture, I again guided a UGA delegation to North Korea. The two institutions agreed on a long-term project to exchange knowledge and skills in the agricultural field and for UGA to support agricultural education in North Korea. Additionally, they decided to invite North Korean agricultural experts to University of Georgia every year for training, and to promote North Korean agricultural college students' study at UGA. In February 2011, a North Korean delegation visited the University of Georgia again and reconfirmed the 2008 agreement. However, it is really unfortunate that there has been no progress since then.

Receiving a Peace Prize

Morehouse College, founded in 1867 in Atlanta, Georgia, is a Black men's college located about an hour and a half drive from the University of Georgia. The mission of his school, also famous as Martin Luther King's alma mater, is to nurture African American leaders. The students were very proud of their school, and they were studying as those entrusted with developing and carrying on Rev. King's intellectual and spiritual legacy. The night that Barack Obama was elected US President, many media trucks came to Morehouse College.

◀ A glorious reunion after 35 years. The author with his aunt (right) by the Songhua River near his hometown during the July 1981 visit. (Photo courtesy of Han Shik Park)

In the spring of 2010, I taught a peace studies course at Morehouse College. My lectures and discussions with the students focused on defining peace, its necessity, and how to create it. I was eager to teach a course there because the request came from Professor Gregory Hall, head of the Department of Political Science at Morehouse College, but even more because the school was Rev. King's alma mater. In fact, when I received my doctorate in 1970 and took the job at the University of Georgia, Rev. King had a great influence. During my doctoral studies, I was fascinated by the thought and spirit of Rev. King, and was particularly impressed by his philosophy of peace and the nonviolence movement. I wanted to go to his native Georgia to better understand his life and teaching.

One day, just as I was leaving the classroom after a lecture at Morehouse, Dr. Lawrence Carter called me for a cup of tea He was a professor of religious studies and dean of Morehouse College's Martin Luther King Jr. International Chapel, established to commemorate the life and spirit of Rev. King. Since we were not well acquainted, I wondered why he had extended an invitation. As I entered his office, he told me, "I have a surprise for you."

A surprise? As soon as I was seated, Dean Carter asked me if I could free up time on April 1st. When I asked what was going on, he told me I had been chosen as the recipient of an award established by Morehouse College. However, he didn't tell me what award or why I was selected—just that I would find out more details later. This only piqued my curiosity.

About a month later, I received another call from Dean Carter. He asked me to come to Morehouse College because they wanted to paint my portrait. He instructed me to dress nicely, as the oil portrait cost up to $20,000. I inferred the portrait must be related to the award he had previously mentioned, but I wondered for what kind of prize they would spend $20,000 to paint a portrait of the awardee? I became even more puzzled.

As the portrait work was nearing completion, Dean Carter and other officials from Morehouse College came to my study. They officially informed me that I had been selected as the recipient of the 2010 Gandhi-King-Ikeda Community Builder Prize. I couldn't believe my ears. The Gandhi-King-Ikeda Community Builder Prize was established jointly by Morehouse College and Martin Luther King Jr. International Chapel in 2001. It was an award with both honor and authority, to the extent that it was called the "Preliminary Nobel Peace Prize," awarded annually to those who contributed to world peace and the nonviolent movement. Looking at the faces of past winners, it was unimaginable that I would receive this award.

In its first year, the award was shared by two people—former South African President, Nelson Mandela, and former Soviet Communist Party General Secretary, Mikhail Gorbachev. Honorable figures and past recipients of the Nobel Peace Prize—such as South African Archbishop Desmond Tutu, former Israeli Prime Minister Yitzhak Rabin, peace activist Betty Williams, and former South African President Frederick Willem de Klerk, Northern Ireland peace agreement architect John Hume, and South African politician Albert Rutully—were listed as awardees. Most of the past recipients were former heads of state or famous politicians who have achieved major milestones for the peace of humankind. It is true that I have lived my life to study, teach, and practice peace, but I was touched and solemn at the same time wondering how I—who had been a mere teacher in the countryside all my life—could receive such a great award. I still think I did not deserve the Gandhi-King-Ikeda Community Builder Prize.

The reason I think this peace prize is meaningful is not because of its past recipients, renowned individuals like stars in the night sky. There are thousands of "peace" awards in the world, but few of them correctly recognize the meaning of peace. What is peace? Defining peace as the "absence of war" is as absurd as defining men as "non-women." I would like to define peace as "harmony from heterogeneity." The state of acknowledging and accepting differences and diversity through dialogue and understanding—through the meeting of different qualities—should be the definition of true peace. True peace is a common, sacred value of mankind that transcends religious, political, ideological and cultural differences.

As the name suggests, the Gandhi-King-Ikeda Community Builder Prize was created to honor the thoughts and lives of Mahatma Gandhi of India, who dedicated his life to world peace and nonviolence movement; Martin Luther King, a pacifist and nonviolent civil rights activist; and Daisaku Ikeda, a Japanese Buddhist thinker, president of the Soka Gakkai International. This award was significant in that it embodies the common philosophy of three people who wanted to realize peace—a universal value of mankind—beyond the heterogeneity arising from differences in race and religion.

The award ceremony was held on April 1, 2010 at the Martin Luther King Jr. International Chapel of Morehouse College in the presence of 1,500 people from all walks of life. Perhaps because of the weight of the peace prize, I felt nervous and excited from the morning. I kept fixing my clothes and hair, wrote down my thoughts on winning the award, and edited them over and over again. When we arrived at the awards ceremony, the chapel was already filled with a crowd of people. The ceremony began with a tribute by Dr. Michael Franklin, President of Morehouse College. He read in detail the background of the Gandhi-King-Ikeda Community Builder Prize and reasons for selecting me as the recipient, specifically mentioning my life's work and their great appreciation of the decades I devoted to create and establish peace on the Korean Peninsula.

They placed a special emphasis, for example, on the fact that I had arranged the visit of former President Jimmy Carter to North Korea in 1994; held the "Washington-Pyongyang Track II Forum" in which Korean and US civilian experts participated to resolve the North Korean nuclear crisis in 2003; and arbitrated the release of US reporters in 2009, emphasizing that I had personally practiced mutual respect, dialogue and inclusion in those efforts. In addition, they mentioned in detail the humanitarian efforts I had made. They stressed how in the 1980s, I visited three northeastern provinces in China and interviewed Korean-Chinese compatriots to confirm if members of separated families were alive or dead and to help them reunite; induced external cooperation to resolve the food shortage in North Korea; and arranged for sending relief medicines to North Korea. The presenter added that these long-term efforts realized the purpose and significance of the the Gandhi-King-Ikeda Community Builder Prize.

What sets me apart from past winners was that I was not a politician

▲ Photo taken with students from the University of Georgia's Center for the Study of Global Issues during a tour of Panmunjom in South Korea.

or activist, but a scholar and educator. None of the previous winners have been educators. The Selection Committee of the Gandhi King Ikeda Community Builder Prize praised me for teaching peace studies to thousands of students over the decades. The committee shared the view that it is important for peace to be put into practice, but it is also urgently needed to conduct academic research and establish academic theories.

Another thing the committee paid attention to was peace education through field trips. I established the Center for the Study of Global Issues (GLOBIS) at UGA in 1995 and led over 100 American students every year to visit the Hiroshima Peace Memorial, the Dachau Concentration Camp Memorial in Munich, Germany, and Panmunjom in Korea. It was an effort to awaken students to how precious peace is by having them witness the horrors of war with their own eyes. I can still clearly remember young students weeping while looking at the dome of the Hiroshima Peace Memorial, trembling at the brutality and cruelty of war and nuclear weapons.

After President Franklin's tribute, we proceeded to the main award ceremony. The award, a trophy and a medal were awarded by representatives of the Gandhi, King and Ikeda families. Above all, the most valuable gifts I received with the prize were the writings and publications of the three men, as I was given an opportunity to study their thoughts and philosophies in more depth. Afterwards, my portrait was unveiled. A life-size portrait of me was displayed in the Martin Luther King Jr. International Chapel of Morehouse College, along with portraits of past winners.

It was my turn to go up to the podium and express my feelings about the award. Looking around the awards ceremony, everyone looked tired because the weather was hot and there were a lot of people gathered in a small space. Because I felt it would be impolite to give a long award speech, I decided to depart from my prepared manuscript and gave a brief impromptu speech, instead. I emphasized that unless we change the security paradigm that has dominated the past several centuries to a peace paradigm, there will be no way for humanity to embrace the coming of the 22nd century. The security paradigm inevitably resulted in conflict, antagonism and unrest, and military competition. The current reality is that security cannot be guaranteed no matter how much effort is put into it. The security paradigm does not guarantee security. It is the same in the United States as in South and North Korea. With so much defense spending, are we any less anxious about security? I finished my speech in 2 minutes and 40 seconds by saying that although it was an undeserved award, I would consider it a reminder and inspiration to devote the rest of my life to peace education and building peace.

Accompanied by the orchestra, the famous Morehouse College Glee Club sang a congratulatory song, making an unforgettable impression on me. Founded in 1911, this choir is the pride of Morehouse College with a tradition of more than 100 years, and is famous in the United States for its outstanding choral skills and spectacular performances. Not only did they perform at King's funeral and President Jimmy Carter's inauguration, but they built up a reputation for numerous domestic and international performances. What a great, joyous luxury it was, to hear them singing a song to congratulate me on my award.

As I listened to the choir's performance, the whole time, I was thinking about peace. I thought how the chorus—managing to blend their diverse voices together until their harmony surpassed any sense of difference—is exactly like peace. The orchestra's beautiful performance also felt like peace. Each instrument skillfully produced its original sound, and—under direction of the conductor—harmonized with the sounds of other instruments. Isn't the peace we seek similar to fantastic harmony?

While respecting and accommodating differences and diversity of race, religion and ideology, my consistent view has been that true peace is achieving harmony and coexistence, through dialogue and mutual understanding. The only way to true peace and reunification is through a series of processes in which the South and the North both understand each other's differences, realistically acknowledge the differences they come to understand, and continuously seek ways to overcome them peacefully.

My life hasn't changed since the award. I continued studying and lecturing at the university and did not neglect efforts to practice peace even after retirement. However, wherever I go, I am first introduced as a recipient of the Gandhi-King-Ikeda Community Builder Prize. It is an honor just to have my name connected with those great men who have contributed to humanity and peace.

Overseas Koreans are Assets for Reunification

I am an overseas Korean. Born as a diasporic Korean in China, I spent my childhood there. After graduating from college in Korea, I came to the United States in 1965 and have been here for more than 50 years. So, I have spent most of my life as an overseas Korean. Perhaps I will end my life as an overseas Korean.

Because I was able to gain a more balanced view from the outside, I was able to dedicate my life to work for peace and reunification on the Korean Peninsula. I was able to visit both South Korea and North Korea as needed, and—while living in a country that exerts a great influence on the Korean Peninsula—I was able to convince American mainstream society of the need for reunification and for understanding North Korea as it is.

There are often sarcastic people who tell me to focus on problems where I live in the United States rather than "poking my nose into others' business." However, I believe that overseas Koreans are the greatest asset to our nation in terms of peace and reunification of the Korean Peninsula. Diasporic Koreans have lived a life of enduring and overcoming racial discrimination and persecution in other countries, trying to preserve the identity of the Korean people, and have also learned the wisdom of living in harmony with the mainstream society of their country of residence. They are also in a position to experience diversity and to view both South Korea and North Korea without prejudice or bias. Overseas Koreans are a special asset that can serve as a bridge for peaceful reunification as a mediator and catalyst beyond the level on which one is forced to choose between two Koreas.

Diaspora originally came from the term referring to the Jews who had left Jerusalem and were scattered all over the world. Nowadays, it is commonly used as a term to refer to people groups living in foreign countries, either voluntarily or unintentionally. In Korean, we call such people "separated."[102] Considering our culture centered on extended families, our entire nation should be regarded as a separated family. The history of Koreans living abroad shares the same track with the sufferings of our nation. According to the data published by the Ministry of Foreign Affairs of the Republic of Korea in 2019, the number of Korean diaspora living outside the Korean Peninsula is 7.5 million. It is not a small number, as one-tenth of the combined populations of South Korea and North Korea lives abroad. Of the 200 countries in the world, many of them have fewer people than that number in their entire population.

About 2.5 million diasporic Korean people live in both the United States and China, and about 800,000 live in Japan. Nearly 700,000 Koreans live in Europe, and although it may sound a bit strange, there are more than 100,000 Koreans living in Central and South America, including Mexico, Brazil, and Cuba. They are called by different

---

[102] Separated, such as 이산 or 離散 in Korean and Chinese, respectively.

names as well as different migration processes and backgrounds. Those who settled in the Gando region became *Joseonjok* (Korean-Chinese),[103] and those who migrated to Primorsky Krai and settled there became *Goryeo-in*[104] after having to emigrate to Central Asia during the Stalin era. Koreans who were taken to Japan for forced labor and were unable to return are called *Jae-il Dongpo*,[105] and Koreans who were brought to the United States with the American dream after Liberation became "Korean Americans." However, all of them speak the same language, look alike, eat kimchi, and share a history that can be regarded as collective memory.

The 2.5 million Koreans living in the three northeastern provinces of China are called Korean-Chinese. Their migration process and background are deeply related to the sad history of our people. In the late 19th and early 20th centuries, many people crossed the Yalu River and Tumen River because they wanted to escape hunger, starvation, and Japanese imperial tyranny. There were also many independence fighters who devoted themselves to the anti-Japanese movement. My grandfather and grandmother also moved to Heilongjiang Province in northern Manchuria in 1906, with broken hearts from the collapse of the Korean Empire. The news of Japan's defeat and Korean Liberation was pure joy for *Joseonjok* living across the border to the north—awakening hope that they could return to their homeland—but only

---

[103] Korean diasporic people living in northeast China are called 조선족 or 朝鮮族 in Korean and Chinese.

[104] Korean diasporic people living in former USSR / Central Asia are called *Goryeo-in* (go-r'yo-een, 고려인).

[105] Korean residents in Japan are called *Jae-il Dongpo* (재일동포) in Korean and *Zainichi* in Japanese.

very few actually did return.

The division of their motherland, the horrors of war, and political turmoil shattered their hopes for returning home. The country they longed for was no longer the same as when they left. It was no longer a single country but split in two. When China became communist in 1949, the Korean-Chinese were naturally forced to accept only half of the Korean Peninsula as their homeland, and viewed South Korea only as a disease of capitalism. Since the establishment of diplomatic ties between South Korea and China in 1992, many Korean-Chinese have come to South Korea to pursue their Korean dream and became engaged in economic activities. However, neither South Korean people nor Korean-Chinese people view the other group in a friendly light.

The history of the *Goryeo-in* who settled in Primorsky Krai was not much different from that of the Korean-Chinese. They first migrated to escape famine and poverty, and even more Koreans moved there after the fall of the Korean Empire in 1910. Russia incorporated Primorsky Krai into its territory after 1860, and in the 1930s, forcibly relocated 170,000 of the *Goryeo-in* to Central Asia. Korean compatriots living in Primorsky Krai—who had already endured a life of hardship after leaving their hometowns—faced the severe ordeal of being uprooted yet again. Just like the Korean-Chinese, the Koreans forcibly relocated to parts of Central Asia—such as Uzbekistan and Kazakhstan—were forced to choose only half of their homeland. After the end of the Cold War, despite the *Goryeo-in* experiencing a sense of skepticism about socialist values and a longing for Korea's economic prosperity, they are still confused about their two motherlands.

Among the Koreans who were forcibly relocated to Kazakhstan, there was General Hong Beom-do, a well-known hero of the Battle of Bongo-dong.[106] The current unedifying brawl between South Korea and North Korea over the return of General Hong Beom-do's remains [107] for political reasons is most deplorable. Without consultation with the North Korean side, the South Korean government said that it would unilaterally repatriate General Hong's remains to Seoul, although his hometown was Pyongyang. The DPRK argued that it was an ancestral custom to return the General to his hometown of Pyongyang, characterizing the South's actions as machination and provocation. What would General Hong think of this kind of tit-for-tat? General Hong Beom-do, who dedicated his life to the independence of his country but did not see its liberation and spent his last years in a distant foreign land, would not have wanted to be buried in a nation split into halves, roaring at each other in antagonism and conflict. The country he must have envisioned when he crossed the border—wishing for national independence—has disappeared. My heart aches to think of how the General is still being forced to choose between South or North, even after his death.

In the same vein, if the remains of Patriot An Jung-geun,[108] whose hometown is in Haeju, Hwanghae Province, were discovered in the

---

[106] The Koreans defeated the Japanese in the battle of Bongo-dong (봉오동 전투, 鳳梧洞戰鬪) in Jilin, China.

[107] General Hong Beom-do (홍범도, 洪範圖) died in Kazakhstan in 1943.

[108] An Jung-geun (안중근, 安重根) was a Korean independence activist who was executed in China for assassinating the prime minister of Japan, Ito Hirobumi.

future, it is expected to cause as much controversy between the ROK and DPRK as did the case of General Hong Beom-do. Harbin, where An shot Ito Hirobumi, is the place where I was born and spent my childhood. When I was young, I grew up hearing stories about Patriot An from the village elders. When I visited China in the 1980s, I visited Harbin Station and reminded myself of An's noble will. An is also respected as a patriotic martyr in the DPRK. Just as there is his tomb in Hyochang Park in Seoul, there is also a monument to commemorate An Jung-geun at the Patriotic Martyrs' Cemetery in Pyongyang. An Jung-geun's last will was that his body be buried in his homeland. The country that Patriot An must have longed for—where he wanted to be buried—was a unified country.

The same is true for *Zainichi* Koreans who have led a tough life. Many Koreans who were taken for forced labor during the Japanese occupation did not return to their homeland after Liberation. Korea was split in two, and the horrors of the Korean War made compatriots in Japan more inclined to stay there. Despite being treated as subhuman by the Japanese, they have lived steadfastly, maintaining their national identity. What made life for the Koreans in Japan even more difficult than the discrimination and persecution was the political reality that forced them to choose between North and South Korea. For more than 70 years, *Zainichi* Korean society has been divided into two organizations, the General Association of Korean Residents in Japan (*Mindan*) and the pro-Pyongyang Federation of Korean Residents in Japan (*Chongryon*), which live in confrontation and antagonism. *Zainichi* Korean society is a microcosm of a divided nation, and the reality was that one must choose one side or the other.

Unfortunately for *Zainichi* Koreans, even after making their choice, the other side branded them either "reds" or "spies."

Not long ago, I saw a movie entitled *Jeronimo,* directed by Joseph Juhn. It is a documentary film about the story of Im Cheon-taek, a first-generation Cuban immigrant who endured a harsh life, and of a Jeronimo (Lim Eun-jo), a second-generation Korean Cuban who is troubled by his identity. Im Cheon-taek moved to Mexico as a contract worker at a Henequen farm in 1905 and then relocated to Cuba in 1921 to avoid economic difficulties. In 1926 his son, Jeronimo, was born in Cuba. The movie was very impressive in the way it calmly depicted Jeronimo's life journey as he struggled with his identity in light of the division of his country. It touched my heart that Mr. Lim and his father, shedding tears at the fall of their nation, collected money for Korean independence, delivered it to the Provisional Government, and established a Korean school to preserve their national identity. It was hard to watch that all their efforts to establish a Korean Association came to nothing in the harsh political reality of the division, and they were compelled to choose a side.

The United States is the country with the largest number of overseas Koreans. About 2.5 million Koreans live there. Korean migration to the US started in 1902, when Koreans migrated to Hawaii sugarcane plantations. Most of the immigrants living in the United States today are people who immigrated to the United States after the 1960s in pursuit of the American dream. What sets the Koreans who have settled in the United States apart from other Korean communities is that most of them were born, raised, and educated in South Korea.

Most have a strong anti-communist consciousness deeply ingrained within them, and they have the perception that North Korea is a group that cannot be dealt with. Although there are groups with close ties to the DPRK, such as the Korean American National Coordination Council (KANCC), most Korean Americans think that North Korea's collapse is inevitable and that the only way to achieve reunification is through German-style absorption and reunification. The South Korean government, through its consulates and various organizations, has consistently promoted policies in the United States that expose Korean Americans to only the southern half of their homeland. During my 50 or so visits to the DPRK, I was criticized for being pro-North Korea or a North Korea collaborator, and the South Korean government stopped me from visiting the North several times. I suffered various hardships such as restrictions on research fund applications. In a way, I was also forced to choose only half of my country.

For me, the country was and is still one. The south is the homeland, and the north is the homeland. I believe that although Korea is divided now, one day will it take the path to reunification. However, reunification will not come on its own. President Moon Jae-in's philosophy of emphasizing peace without serious consideration and reflection on reunification seemed too complacent. Peace does not bring reunification, but reunification brings peace. The only way to true peace is through a series of processes of steadily seeking reunification through inter-Korean dialogue and cooperation.

The first generation separated from their hometowns before division can all be said to be independence activists. That was the spirit of the times. Both independence fighters and writers who actively participated in independence activities wished for the independence of their country and worked hard to realize that aspiration. There were also pro-Japanese factions and those who were sympathetic to the Japanese imperialism. Still, the spirit of the times was the independence of Korea, and Liberation came through the dedication of countless independence activists who have never been memorialized.

The spirit of the times given to all of us living in this era is reunification. In the process of preparing for reunification, the role of overseas Koreans who can have access to both south and north is more important than ever. We must not be trapped in the frame of choosing between the ROK and the DPRK. With a communal sense of being Korean people and sharing one motherland, we must view both sides without prejudice or bias, and must serve as a bridge between them. The 7.5 million Koreans living scattered around the world have more diverse experiences than any other ethnic groups, historically, politically, ideologically, and culturally. This rich experience will be of great help, not only in the process of reunification, but also in designing the blueprint for a unified country.

The process of reunification must be carried out in accordance with the "principle of national independence." However, we desperately need to diplomatically convince neighboring countries that our reunification will serve, rather than undermine, their national interests. In that sense, diasporic Koreans are at the forefront of reunification diplomacy. Of the 7.5 million overseas Koreans, two-thirds, or 5 million, live in the so-called "G2," the United States and China. Considering that the cooperation and support of these two great powers is indispensable for the reunification of the Korean Peninsula, the role of our compatriots in the United States and China is of utmost importance. We must make efforts to increase our political power, move public opinion in our countries of residence, and to fulfill the key role building bridges between the homeland and the nations where we live.

Peace Studies at a Crossroads in My Life

In the fall of 1967, I began my doctoral studies at the University of Minnesota. After completing my master's degree at American University in Washington DC, I drove my wife and infant daughter 17 hours to University of Minnesota.

The weather in Minnesota is similar to that of Harbin, Manchuria, where I was born and spent my childhood. The summers are not hot, but the winters are cold and long. There is frequent snowfall, sometimes piling up higher than a grown man. In fact, at the University of Minnesota, you find two types of maps—the first displays buildings and roads above ground, and the second displays the paths underground. Due to the long and frigid winters, there are underground passages linking buildings and parking lots. You may think of medieval monasteries or catacombs when you have a look at the map showing underground passages between buildings and classrooms.

Despite the long, cold winters, I chose to attend the University of Minnesota for an important reason. While pursuing my master's degree, I read a thesis entitled, "The Place of Classical Political Theory in the Study of Politics: The legitimated spell of Plato."

Professor Mulford Q. Sibley's thesis became a turning point in my life. From the moment I read his thesis, I knew I wanted the author to supervise my PhD studies. I decided, *I must learn from this person!*

Professor Sibley was teaching at the University of Minnesota.

Since my bachelor student days at Seoul National University's department of Political Science, I have been interested in using Plato's ideas and philosophy as a means of seeking peace. At that time, I was obsessed with Plato's famous work *The Republic*. I read and re-read the wisdom of a Western philosopher who lived 2,400 years ago, longing to find answers for the modern age. I read both the Korean and English translations. It wasn't easy. My English ability prevented me from fully understanding Plato's thoughts, and the Korean translation had significant errors that made it even more difficult to understand. However, I could still vaguely guess what Plato was talking about. The book contained rich, in-depth descriptions of how human-to-human relationships should be established in society, how to define correctness, and what kind of society is the most ideal. My desire to study Plato further led to my discovery of Professor Sibley, a Plato expert.

So, I wrote to Professor Sibley, telling him how I became interested in Plato and peace, conveying my desire to study with him, even discussing Plato's work. Professor Sibley was very impressed with me, and after corresponding with him for some time, it wasn't difficult for me to gain admission to the University of Minnesota. The challenge was financial, as I had no official confirmation that I would receive a scholarship.

I was penniless and could not pursue a PhD without a scholarship. PhD programs are usually filled with graduate students who also work part-time as office workers. They are both students writing their own dissertations and academic colleagues, conducting joint research with their professors. Therefore, it is common for doctoral students to receive a small monthly salary along with a scholarship covering their tuition. In my case, several schools, including the University of Illinois, had already offered me full scholarships. I had to decide. I wrote to the University of Minnesota and Professor Sibley, inquiring about a scholarship, and the unofficial answer was, "I cannot give you a definitive answer yet, but I will find out about scholarships and a teaching assistantship once you're in the program."

After much deliberation, I decided to go to Minnesota. Fortunately, from the beginning of my first semester, I managed to receive a full scholarship.

However, arriving at the University of Minnesota, my doctoral studies got off to a disappointing start. Professor Sibley would not be giving lectures or even advising me on my doctoral studies. I felt as if dark clouds descended around me. The only reason I had come all the way to Minnesota was to learn from Professor Sibley, so the news hit me like a bolt of lightning. I began my PhD in 1967, at the height of the Vietnam War. Professor Sibley was an ardent anti-war activist and a well-known pacifist in academic circles. He led anti-war protests across the United States and served as president of the National Association of Professors Against the Vietnam War. During the McCarthyist craze in the early 1950s, he was even blacklisted for his public support of socialist and pacifist ideologies. He published many articles and books on pacifism, idealism, and civil disobedience. Yet, due to such involvement in the anti-war movement, he did not have the mental and physical energy to take on the role of being my academic advisor.

I was devastated at not being able to study with Professor Sibley. However, it did not dampen my desire or persistence in pursuing peace studies. I considered all the professors in the politics department, but no one studied Plato and Peace except for Professor Sibley. Most of the professors believed in the "behavioralism" approach that was so prominent in the field of politics at the time. So, I started looking into professors in the adjacent fields of sociology and philosophy, where I found two professors who could possibly supervise my studies. One was Professor Don Martindale and the other was Professor Herbert Feigl.

Professor Don Martindale, who focused in sociological theory, was famous for his academic work about Max Weber. He was so immersed in Weber's writings that he had not only translated several Max Weber treatises and books into English, but people even called him Max Weber's disciple. Until meeting Professor Martindale, I had only a superficial knowledge of Max Weber. Listening to his lectures gave me new insight on Max Weber's work and enabled me to recognize how influential it was in shedding light on human behavior and social phenomena within the academic culture of the time, so steeped in behaviorism.

Most illuminating of all was the philosophy of science. The

philosophy of science is a branch of philosophy that pursues epistemological inquiry into the scientific method. In other words, it is a study of how we know and how to assure we do in fact know what we think we know. Herbert Feigl, one of the world's leading philosophers of science, was in the Department of Philosophy. Professor Feigl was born in Austria and immigrated to the United States in 1930. He was also known as an early member of the Vienna School, known for introducing logical positivism.

Looking back now, I was very fortunate to have met Professor Feigl. During my time as his student, I visited him whenever I could to discuss his lectures with him, asking endless questions. Taking lectures from Feigl and his student May Broadbeck, I realized that this is what science should do, and I became more immersed in the philosophy of science. After completing my doctoral studies for 3 years, I was equipped with enough academic knowledge and perspective to explore the methodology of political science as a philosophy of science on my own. (After graduation, I was hired as a professor at the University of Georgia to teach Philosophy of Science and Methodology in Politics.)

The three years studying for my PhD at the University of Minnesota were the most passionate years of my life. I worked hard, read a lot of books, and discovered a variety of perspectives. I studied and attended lectures in fields as diverse as philosophy of science, sociology, social psychology, and political philosophy. Although, in recognition of my masters' studies, the doctoral program required only 90 additional course credits, I completed 120 credits in 3 years. My doctoral studies provided the foundation for lifelong learning and research, broadening my perspective of the world.

In the more than 50 years I have served as a professor in the United States, I have taught many Korean students. At times, I was saddened to witness young people studying abroad without a sense of purpose, wasting their prime for the mere purpose of obtaining a degree. I would like to ask Korean students who come to the US to have a clear sense of purpose about what they want to study and why.

I was able to break free from the stereotype that peace studies should only be conducted within the confines of political science. You can study war in politics, examining the causes of war and ways to prevent it. However, as I have always emphasized, peace is not the simply the absence of war, neither does the absence of war necessarily bring peace. Peace is the harmony of heterogeneity, and peace studies is a discipline that first learns and then educates about how to harmonize heterogeneity. I came to realize that interdisciplinary research alongside adjacent disciplines is essential for true peace research.

My disappointment in being unable to study with Professor Sibley turned out to be a blessing. If Professor Sibley had become my advisor, perhaps I would have lived my entire life confined within the thoughts of Plato. Professor Martindale and Professor Feigl—gifted scientists and my teachers—passed away long ago. Once again, I would like to express my gratitude to them both for treating me warmly throughout my PhD years.

Why I Chose the University of Georgia

Life is a series of choices. As you go through life, you will be faced with many choices ranging from everyday choices, like choosing your lunch menu, to important choices that change the direction of your life. The summer of 1970, I faced the most important moment of my life. Drawing near to completing five years of study to receive my doctoral degree, I had to decide whether to return to South Korea or stay in the United States.

The choice wasn't difficult at all, to the degree that it seems ridiculous to say it was the most important decision of my life. I did not need to rack my brain or stay up all night. Returning to teach in the ROK would not have been difficult. At that time, news that a Korean had received a doctorate from an American university was rare enough to be published in the newspaper with a commemorative photo. Some professors in the Department of Political Science at Seoul National University even advised me to return to train younger students, but I had already decided to stay in America.

I had actually decided to stay in America long before I got my PhD. More than anything else, my passion and aspiration for learning led me to stay. Because American universities had a more free and creative environment, I could devote myself fully to academics and research. I thought that staying in the US would be much more helpful for my studies than returning home. In South Korea those days, the main political news was that Major General Park Chung-hee, who seized power in a military *coup d'état* on May 16, 1961, took off his military uniform, directly participated in civil affairs, and became President. He was moving toward dictatorship and long-term rule with a three-term constitutional amendment. I had no desire to study in a suffocating environment where academic freedom and freedom of expression were suppressed. If I had returned to the ROK at that time, I might have lived a life of suffocation in the midst of a dark political reality, repeatedly imprisoned and released after being branded as a red or a spy.

Another reason I decided to stay in the United States was because I thought that the longing for peace that had afflicted me since childhood could not be cured in South Korea. It was virtually impossible to study North Korea, peace, and reunification in an environment where anti-communist ideology had seized the national consciousness. I did not want to live in Korea, where I would be forced to choose one of the regimes, desiring instead to live outside and see both sides of the Korean Peninsula from a more objective and balanced perspective. And, as mentioned earlier, I also preferred to stay in the United States from where I could visit the south or the north as necessary.

Having decided to stay in the United States, I needed to find a job to earn a living for my family. In the winter of 1969, I started applying to various American colleges and universities by mail. Luckily, I received offers from three universities: the University of Georgia in the southern United States; York University in Toronto, Canada; and Angelo State University in Texas. Perhaps because I had taken many sociology courses and sent a letter of recommendation from Professor Don Martindale, who was considerably influential in the field of sociology, York University's offer came from the Sociology Department, not the Political Science Department.

Needless to say, I made up my mind to go to the University of Georgia (UGA). As a foreign student, I felt unworthy to work at UGA, the first public University established in the United States in 1785. I particularly liked the fact that the campus was located in Athens, Georgia, very close to Martin Luther King Jr's hometown of Atlanta.

However, my advisors at the University of Minnesota generally cautioned me against going to the University of Georgia, as the "Deep South"—also known as the Bible Belt, Sun Belt, or Dixieland—was not a place "for a person like me" to go. The professors at the University of Minnesota generally had a negative view of the South. To them, the South was still dominated by a backward culture, where white supremacy and racism prevailed. I was told several times that it may be difficult for a small Asian like myself to survive there.

I appreciated their sincere advice, but I had a slightly different view. As much as I was determined to settle in the United States, I wanted to know more about American society. The United States is a massive land where a racially and culturally diverse society coexists. Each region has its own unique characteristics. I felt I could at least vaguely grasp the culture of most regions, without having to directly experience them, except for the Deep South.

For example, the culture of New England, in the northeast, closely resembles British culture. Boston, similar to London, was a community where Anglo-Saxons (having immigrated from England) were the mainstream. English pronunciation, architectural style, and Ivy League schools were also influenced by British white culture. The Midwest region, where the University of Minnesota is located, was home to many immigrants from Scandinavia such as Norway, Sweden, Denmark, and Finland. It is characterized by people's large size and slow movement and seemed to have adopted Nordic culture. The western region, whose population is centered in California, was a region where many Asians, progressive, and pioneering people live and where various races and cultures coexist. The southern regions, including

Texas and Arizona, have many Mexican immigrants and Latino cultural influence and are inhabited by many indigenous peoples, including the Navajo.

If I wanted to fully understand American culture and values, the way of life and behavior of the people, I thought I should go to the southeast. It seemed impossible to really know America without experiencing the Deep South firsthand. Because of my special interest in racial inequality, I wanted to study America more closely by living where slavery had been prevalent and its effects still remained.

As much as I was curious about the regional culture, I was even more drawn to the University of Georgia because it was the Reverend

Martin Luther King Jr's homeland. I have been fascinated by Gandhi's ideas since my college days, and since coming to the United States in 1965, I had a growing interest in Rev. Martin Luther King Jr. I had a deep yearning and admiration for his rich knowledge and profound ideas.

▲ Rev. Martin Luther King, Jr. (second from right), Rev. Jesse Jackson (second from left) and other human rights activists, speaking to a crowd from the balcony of Lorraine Motel, room 306, in Memphis, Tennessee on April 3rd, 1968–the day before Rev. King's assassination. (Photo courtesy of the Martin Luther King, Jr. Museum)

Ironically, I became more immersed in his thoughts and spirit due to his death. On April 4, 1968, I was sitting in the classroom waiting for class to begin, when Robert Holt, professor of comparative politics, entered our classroom. He suddenly burst into tears. Not knowing what was going on, all the students were bewildered. They had never imagined seeing a professor weep in front of the class during lecture time. Wiping his tears with a handkerchief, Professor Holt informed us that Martin Luther King Jr. had just been assassinated in Memphis.

Rev. King spent his life advocating for human rights, equality, and peaceful coexistence. He was a contemplative activist, sympathetic to the vulnerable and communities of color. I was fascinated by Rev.

King's ideas and philosophy of peace and particularly impressed with the paradoxical logic of employing nonviolence and love to overcome violence. The idea of confronting the ruthless oppression of violent white people with nonviolence—a qualitatively different method— has inspired me and guided my research throughout my life. I also embraced Rev. King's famous teaching about one human family[109] being the only avenue to peace. I will cherish this belief for the rest of my life. When I think of how he left behind so many famous speeches, I can't help but marvel at his ability to know such profound truth and communicate such wisdom at a young age.

Rev. King's life ended tragically before he reached his 40th birthday, but his achievements and legacy live on in human history. In light of the racism still inherent within American society, which we saw acutely in the aftermath of George Floyd's death, Rev. Martin Luther King Jr's thoughts and philosophy are more relevant than ever. I am proud to have taught peace studies at Morehouse College, Rev. King's alma mater, and receiving the Gandhi-King-Ikeda Community Builder Prize was an infinite honor. My choice so many years ago— to stay in his homeland to better understand his life and thoughts— was a wise one.

In the spring of 1970, I was excited to visit the University of Georgia for a campus interview. The faculty recruitment processes at American universities are quite similar. The first round of the application process is review of submitted documents, and the second round—for shortlisted candidates—is a phone interview (by video call

---

[109] The "beloved community"

these days). After the phone interview, three or four applicants are invited to campus for a face-to-face interview. Campus interviews are also an opportunity for applicants to explore and learn about the school and surrounding area. What is different from Korea is that one's academic connections, blood ties, and regional networks do not give a particular advantage. The campus interviews are usually in-depth interviews over the course of 2 or 3 days, and the candidates are marched from appointment to appointment according to a very tight schedule. My campus interview at the University of Georgia lasted 3 days and 2 nights, including a guest lecture to students and research presentations. Meetings with fellow professors as well as other faculty and staff were tightly scheduled. I ate six times with school officials, including the political science professors.

What stood out to me in the campus interview was the fact that everyone around me was white. At UGA at that time, there was reportedly not a single faculty member of color, let alone African American. The student population was the same. All the students were white. The University of Georgia was famous for American football, but there was not a single Black player on the football team.

Not surprisingly, it was only in 1961 when UGA first allowed African American students to attend. After winning a three-year court battle, two Black students, Charlene Hunter and Hamilton Holmes, were able to attend the University of Georgia. When you consider that the police accompanied them on the first day of school to protect them—in case of any accident—it was not surprising that there were no African American students on campus. Charlene Hunter became a prominent journalist and human rights activist and is still active today. The only African American people that stood out to me at UGA were all cleaners and groundskeepers. To me, they seemed to still be bound by the submissive and obedient culture of slavery. (I later realized that progressive and forward-looking African Americans were more likely to leave the south to settle in other states.)

Everyone was kind throughout the interview, which put me at ease that I wouldn't have any worries even if I was hired. However, I became a little worried thinking of my children who would later attend Georgia public schools. Shortly after returning to Minnesota from Georgia, I received an offer from UGA. I gladly accepted the offer, teaching and researching at the University of Georgia for the next 45 years, from 1970 to my retirement in 2015.

Traveling Through the South in 1970

To be honest, the journey to Athens, Georgia in the summer of 1970 was filled half with anticipation and half with anxiety. I was full of joy at finding a job and relief that I could now take responsibility for my family's livelihood as the head of the household. I was also confident that my doctorate qualified me to do research freely. Yet, behind my excitement and fluttering heart, there was also some fear. My family and I were still unfamiliar with the Deep South, where the remnants of slavery were still entrenched and where racism and inequality were tolerated throughout society.

It was not easy to find a place to live in Athens. In the age of the internet, it would have been easy to check online listings for homes, locations, photos, and neighborhood information, but in 1970, it was very difficult to find real estate information from other far away states. All I knew about the area was what I saw during the 3 days and 2 nights of the campus interview, and I was at a loss as to what kind of house to find or where. I called the political science professors at the University of Georgia and got some information about safe neighborhoods, commuting time, proximity to supermarkets, etc. I was introduced to three or four prospective rental homes. After communicating with the landlords by phone and mail, I signed a monthly rental agreement for one of those houses, paying $75 a month.

I rented the house sight unseen, and when I actually moved in, the house was as shabby as can be.

Our car was also a problem. The one I drove in Minnesota was old, and there were several repairs to be made. I had only used it for commuting to and from school, so there had been no major inconvenience. However, traveling all the way from Minnesota to the University of Georgia—six times the distance between Seoul and Busan—was a different story. Living on a tight budget, we couldn't afford a new car. Instead, I bought a sturdy, second-hand van at a good price. The van provided ample space to move our belongings. We had only modest household items, but we took them all with us, thinking it may be difficult to buy things in an unfamiliar place while still adapting ourselves to the new environment. I laid down all the rear seats, loaded in the luggage, then—with my wife and eldest daughter in the passenger seats and me in the driver's seat—we headed off for Georgia. My wife was 8-months pregnant with our second child.

Even today, it takes 17 hours to drive from the University of Minnesota to the University of Georgia. Moreover, crossing the Appalachian Mountains at altitudes higher than 1,000 meters makes it a difficult journey. In those days, the road conditions were much worse than they are today, making it impossible to reach Georgia in one day. Had it been possible, it would have been too much for my pregnant wife and three-year-old daughter. We set out on a two day road trip, stopping at the midpoint to stay overnight. The day before departure, my wife and I reviewed a US' atlas to get a rough idea of the interstate highway information. At that time, the passenger in the front seat had to serve as navigator. My wife gave directions the whole way, never putting the atlas down. She did not dare to take her eyes off of the map to prevent going the wrong way and wasting a lot of time.

I drove non-stop all day, thinking we should travel most during the daylight. Then, as it was getting dark, I saw the gas tank's indicator light appear. I pulled into a gas station to top up and to request information on where to stay for the night. I think we were in either Kentucky or Tennessee. As I stopped the car alongside the gas pump, the fuel attendant slowly approached me. I rolled down the window a bit and asked him to fill up my tank. The attendant said, "Ok," nodded his head, and picked up the nozzle. But when he was about to start refueling, he glanced at my car's license plate and suddenly said that he would not sell me any fuel. I was embarrassed to ask his reason, but his reply was even more amazing. They were not allowed to sell fuel to "Yankees."

The word "Yankee" carries various meanings depending on the original context. Outside of the United States, it is used as a term to refer to Americans, and within the United States it is generally used as a term to refer to people from New England. During the Civil War, the Confederates used it as a derogatory term for the Union Army, and used it to refer generally to all the States located in the northern part of the United States. The Minnesota license plate on my car seemed to have misled the fuel attendant to think that I was a Yankee from the North traveling South. I turned on the interior lights, lowered the window, put my face out, and shouted loudly after the attendant who was returning to his office without fueling, "Do I look like a Yankee?"

The fuel attendant returned to my car, looked me in the face, and abruptly changed his attitude. He said he was sorry, and filled the car with completely transformed, kind manners. He even told me about a clean place to stay overnight. I wondered if so-called "Southern hospitality" was harsh to Yankees and discriminative against African Americans, but kind to foreigners. On the way home, I was reminded of the scars and resentment left on American society by the Civil War, which ended 100 years ago. In fact, the scars that the Korean War left on our people are no less than that of the American Civil War. Isn't the Korean War also the source of hostility, antagonism, and resentment between South and North?

My family and I arrived at the University of Georgia at sunset the next day. I had a map of the interstate highways, but I couldn't find a map of the city of Athens. It was not easy to find our rented house on a dark night with nothing but the address. As soon as I entered the city of Athens, a brightly lit neon sign at McDonald's caught my eye. (That McDonald's is still open in the same place.) We happened to be hungry, so we went into the store to eat and to ask for directions. I looked around and saw two, hefty police officers having a late meal with big burgers and a plate full of fries. As local police, I thought they would know directions well, so I explained our situation to them and asked for directions.

For a long time, I had a negative preconceived notion about police officers. When thinking of police, the first thing that came to my mind was the image of a Japanese patrol officer. I particularly feared police due to their tyranny, ruthless oppression, and abuse of authority during the April 19th Revolution. However, hoping to encounter southern hospitality and friendliness to foreigners, I had the courage to approach them. As if to live up to my expectations, the officers immediately finished their meal and, very kindly, told me to follow them in my car. Escorted by two police motorcycles, ignoring and moving straight through traffic lights, our family made it home in no time.

I was tired from the long drive, but I left the house early the next morning and headed to school. I wanted to finish the administrative procedures quickly, such as stopping by the political science department to greet professors, find the human resources department, and completing my application form. I still remember my commute on the first day of work—well-manicured green lawns, clear weather, and beautifully crafted pathways on campus that connect the buildings. Students had not returned from vacation, so there were hardly any people on campus. My eyes saw a young, African American man dressed in a suit, walking somewhere. I was surprised to see a Black man in a neat suit at the University of Georgia, where there were very few African American students and faculty. The young man entered the political science department.

I entered the political science department office, greeted the staff, and asked about the man I had just seen. The staff seemed to know him well. He was a 25-year-old man named Guy Gibson Smith, the son-in-law of Professor Dean Rusk, who joined the University of Georgia law school that year.

I looked in the library for an article about the wedding of Professor Dean Rusk's daughter, Margaret, and Guy Gibson Smith. I couldn't help but wonder how Professor Rusk, a white native of the southeastern state of Georgia, who served as the U.S. government's Secretary of State for eight years, allowed his daughter to marry a Black man. Their wedding was a hot topic in America, big enough news to make headlines in every newspaper. No wonder, the wedding took place in September 1967, just three months after the U.S. Supreme Court ruled that laws in 16 States banning interracial marriage, particularly between white and black people, were unconstitutional.

I came to admire Secretary Rusk's personality for supporting his daughter's marriage to a young African American man in the 1960s, when racial inequality and discrimination were rampant. He even submitted his resignation to President Johnson to prevent burdening the administration with his daughter's wedding. Professor Rusk and I developed a close friendship that lasted into his retirement from the law school in 1984, sharing many opinions about the situation on the Korean Peninsula.

On my way home, I stopped by a bank to open an account. The people I met at school and the people who worked at the bank all spoke English with strong southern accents. Additionally, the English spoken by African American people was markedly different from the English I had heard before, not only in pronunciation, but also in vocabulary, expressions, and manner of speech. I realized I was entering a new land, even though I was still in the United States.

At home, I found my wife busy unpacking our things. Thus, the first day in Athens, Georgia came to an end. Now, I have been living in the suburbs of Athens for more than half a century.

The Purpose of my Study

If you climb one hill, another is waiting for you, and when you think you have reached the end, life brings you to a higher hill. When I first moved to the U.S. for my studies, I thought I would be all set once I got my doctorate. Yet, after completing my degree, I was worried about finding a job. Then, even with my excitement at becoming a professor, another big mountain lay before me at the University of Georgia, and it was called "tenure."

The tenure system in America is designed to guarantee a university professor's job for life. This system is intended to guarantee academic freedom. By ensuring professors' employment, they have freedom to research and teach without fear of undue pressure or retaliation in form of dismissal. Tenure is decided by a tenure committee at the department or college level, usually five to six years after a professor is hired. Regardless of tenure's original purpose in guaranteeing freedom for academic activity, research, and expression, ironically, a professor's qualification for tenure is actually evaluated based on work performance and other records.

The more deplorable reality is that there are very few scholars who deserve protection in line with the original purpose of the tenure system. In other words, university professors rarely conduct research or teaching requiring protection from the tenure system. The sad reality is that few professors either advocate academic theories outside the mainstream or rigorously criticize government policies. Throughout my tenure at the University of Georgia, I was branded as Marxist or pro-North Korean, and on multiple occasions endured external pressure for dismissal from my job. However, thanks to the tenure system, I was able to continue my research and teaching.

Tenure is mainly determined through rigorous screening of performance in three areas, namely research, teaching, and service. If you do not achieve tenure, you might as well just pack your bags and move (though it is seldom so simple), or you may spend the rest of your life as an assistant professor, working on annual contracts without job stability. In fact, it is not easy to achieve adequate performance in all three areas required for tenure. If you focus on research, you may neglect your lectures; yet, if you spend a lot of time preparing your lectures, your research performance may be insufficient. Also, the service requirement mainly relates to research and lectures offered outside the university context, which can become cumbersome and require a lot of time investment. Beginning my first year as a professor, I got busy physically and mentally preparing for tenure.

I had little concern about my research performance. I had a solid vision and philosophy of what and how I would study. And, if we equate achieving a doctorate to obtaining a driver's license, I also had the confidence that I could "drive" properly; I knew I was capable of conducting creative research to my heart's content.

From my perspective, research and scholarship's main purpose is problem solving. Because behavioralism dominated American political science in the 1950s and 1960s, focusing only on explanation or prediction of political phenomena, political science neglected both deep thought on the various problems of society and prescribing solutions for those problems.

In December 1969, as I neared completion of my doctoral dissertation, the Journal of the American Political Science Association published a significant article. Although it was a fairly short paper, it made considerable impact on the world of political science. The article, entitled "The New Revolution in Political Science," pointed out the limits of behavioralism and warned that political science, as a science, was in danger of survival. Even more shocking to political academia was the author of this warning—David Easton—the scholar who led the behavioralism revival of the 1950s.

Easton suggested post-behavioralism as a new path for political science. He briefly argued that from the approach of behavioralism, science is value-neutral, but norms and values can never be neglected or ignored in the study of human and social phenomena. He also pointed out that because behavioralist research focused only on observable and quantifiable problems, it tended to focus on local or trivial problems for which data are readily available. Easton's argument was that politics should be able to focus on bigger and more important problems facing our society. In addition, he said the study of political science had become too far out of touch with the real world, and he urged political scientists to carry out the proactive task of researching and solving real problems.

It was not that the behavioralist academic tradition had made no effort to solve such problems, however, we should consider the historical background in which post-behavioralism emerged. As mankind entered the 1970s, facing the transition to a post-industrial society, market expansion led to significant problems risking human survival. For example, food shortages, wars, epidemics, and environmental degradation were universal and unavoidable problems affecting everyone and threatening the survival of mankind. As a result, in the political science community, voices of self-reflection grew louder, and David Easton sounded an alarm. Just as Professor Sibley's thesis on Plato led me to the University of Minnesota, Professor Easton's paper advocating post-behavioralism guided me in my first steps as a scholar.

My lifelong understanding of science was problem solving. I believe the purpose of science and the calling of scholars is to identify large and small social problems, find their causes, and suggest remedies. To discover problems, you have to have an idea of what an ideal society without problems would look like. However, proposing an ideal society is both normative and philosophical, which are thoroughly rejected in behavioralism.

In the same way, before a doctor treats a patient, he must know the standard of a healthy body to discover the pain and diagnose the disease. Without knowing normal body temperature and blood pressure, it is impossible for the doctor to know where and how a patient is sick. I believe that the purpose of science is to present the image of an ideal society without problems. It is therefore the role and responsibility of scholars to design such a society. I have come to the conclusion that an ideal and desirable society is one in which our problems are solved, and only such a society can be called a "developed." I decided to focus on studying, teaching, and researching the theory of political development in order to design such a society. After creating my own theory of political development, I published a book called *Human Needs and Political Development* in 1984.

Most people know me as a North Korea expert. This is partially correct. Throughout my life, I have observed and studied North Korean politics and society in terms of political development theory, but I did not study the nation itself. From the perspective of the political development process, the United States, China, the ROK, and the DPRK can all be located somewhere along the spectrum of development into an ideal society. North Korea is a "developing society" trying to solve various inherent contradictions and problems. The most urgent problems it faces are national security and feeding its people. Ideas such as socialism and *Juche*, even nuclear weapons, are simply tools being used to solve these problems as political development progresses.

Teaching students is as important and rewarding to professors as is research. More than imparting knowledge, the most important part of my teaching has been helping students learn wisdom on their own. During my first lecture, I would always ask my students two questions. First, "What kind of society would you like to live in 30 years from now?" Second, "What kind of society do you think we will have in 30 years?" The first question is a normative and philosophical one, and the second is empirical. I taught my students to always keep these two questions in mind, and to consider how they may realistically contribute to building a good society regardless of what job they take after graduation. In other words, my educational philosophy was to teach people to contribute to solving social problems.

I have been teaching diligently since my first year as a professor in 1970. I labored over my lectures and taught a wide variety of subjects, some courses which were already in place and other courses that I created. I taught seven subjects, including the theory of political development and the methodology of political science, my main areas of study, at both undergraduate and graduate levels. According to the needs and requests of the Political Science Department, I also lectured on American politics, comparative politics, international politics, human rights theory, and East Asian politics. As I created and taught such a variety of courses, my fellow professors nicknamed me "Utility Player."

As I stood at the lectern for 45 years, thousands of students have learned from me and graduated from my program. I have felt like a rock, rising in the midst of a river; students were like the water flowing through the midst of the rocks. I do not even remember most of my undergraduate students' names, although each doctoral student is still vivid in my memory. Not long ago, I received a call from a former student, a certain Professor Kazuya Fukuoka from St. Joseph's University in Philadelphia. He told me the good news that he had been promoted to full professor. I felt most grateful.

I taught countless doctoral students until retirement, many

American students and many who came from abroad. Many international students attended the University of Georgia because it is known for providing a quality education at an affordable price. We had students from Europe, India and Africa, and since I am Asian, quite a few international students from China, Japan, and Korea asked me to advise them on their research theses.

▲ Meeting with the audience at the University of Georgia in September 2009, after a special lecture on negotiations to release the two American journalists detained in the DPRK. (Photo courtesy of the University of Georgia)

I worked especially closely with Korean students studying abroad to help them see Korea correctly. I taught them that certain things which were difficult to see from within Korea are more clearly perceived from the outside, and that by comparing Korea with other countries, including the United States, they would be better be able to identify Korea's problems. I taught them to take interest in issues of war and division, and to constantly ask, thoroughly consider, and answer how to create a peaceful society and under what circumstances peaceful reunification should take place. However, I had no intention of forcing Korean students to solve problems for peace and reunification on the Korean Peninsula or of instilling in them what I had studied. I thought it was the teacher's role to help students find their way by showing them the process of solving problems for themselves.

I believe introducing students to different perspectives was my greatest contribution as a professor at the University of Georgia. Until the 1990s, no professor at an American university would assign students to read Marx. It's hardly different now. As a result of the Cold War, there were no academic exchanges or communication between the US and Soviet camps, and the prevailing thought in American society and universities was that liberal democracy was superior to any other ruling ideology. No one studied communism or lectured on how it came into existence, except that it was bad and should be eliminated. There was only black-and-white thinking—the logic of good versus evil. I taught students to embrace differences by introducing them to the various political institutions and ideologies that exist outside the United States.

From the perspective of my political development theory, it would be absurd to perceive democracy as a more advanced system than outdated communism. Instead, whichever system fulfills human needs and desires more effectively is a more developed system. For example, survival is the most basic human need. To survive, humans must consume water and food. That is a universal human need. However, whether to eat bread or rice to survive, or whether to use chopsticks or forks, is entirely determined by the history and culture of a society. Ideologies such as democracy and socialism are merely means to an end, and neither can be said to be a more developed or superior system.

To briefly recount an example I often gave my students, political development is like mountain climbing. There is only one mountain peak, but there are many ways to reach the top. In the end, scholars and academics take the humble attitude that the goal is the same, but there are various methods and paths by which to achieve it. To give a concrete example, American students tend to view North Korea as "evil." However, I taught American students to take a balanced perspective, to understand it as it is, for North Korea is also a political system. Most of the students I taught began to take a different perspective.

Public service is also important for achieving tenure. As a scholar studying political development and peace, I pondered what contribution I could make for peace on the Korean Peninsula. I started specific activities for peace and reunification on a visit to the DPRK in 1980, but I had been preparing for those activities much earlier, since being appointed to the University of Georgia in 1970. My efforts gradually began to bear fruit in the 1980s.

In 1976, I successfully achieved tenure, and the University of Georgia gave me a professor's highest honor, the title of "University Professor," in recognition of my research, lectures, and contributions to peace on the Korean Peninsula.

A Scholar Designing Reunification

As a scholar, the problems I chose to tackle were the division of North and South Koreas, military confrontation, and how to reunify the Korean Peninsula. It is no exaggeration to say that when I began my academic career as a student in the United States in 1965, I was already determined to contribute to reunification.

Though my efforts are limited, I have been doing my best all of my life, believing it my responsibility as a scholar to design and present a society capable of resolving both the division of North and South Korea and the military tensions. Any efforts that emphasize only the improvement of inter-Korean relations and creation of peace, without serious consideration and reflection on reunification, are short-sighted and have obvious limitations. Since liberation over 75 years ago, inter-Korean relations have been dominated by challenges to legitimacy and regime competition. Therefore, I question whether true peace can come without reunification. I repeat, peace does not bring reunification, but reunification is the way to achieve peace.

Reunification can not come by itself. Since childhood, we grew up singing the song, "Our wish is reunification." Yet, we have still not reunified. Desire alone cannot achieve reunification. It is absolutely necessary to prepare a realistic "roadmap," a reunification plan to guide our aspiration to its fulfillment. It is the responsibility of scholars and theorists to design this roadmap.

The studies of a scholar who ponders and designs a blueprint for reunification can be compared to the creative work of a composer completing a melodious piece of music. The process of using knowledge and inspiration to compose a beautiful tune is time consuming and arduous, only achieved through multiple drafts. The same is true of the efforts of scholars studying reunification. A song born through hardship is nothing more than a dusty sheet of paper until an orchestra brings the beauty to life, pleasing the ears of rapt audiences around the world.

▲ The author gave a farewell lecture on peacebuilding at his retirement ceremony at the University of Georgia in December 2015. (Photo courtesy of the University of Georgia)

A good performance requires a conductor with the insight and wisdom to interpret the composer's intentions. The conductor must have the ability to draw out harmonies, so that the sound of each musician's instrument contributes to the whole, without creating dissonance. In reunification, the government's role is the same as that of an orchestra's conductor. Similar to how an orchestra embodies the art of music through harmony, so the government implements the path of reunification, following the scholars' blueprint to harmonize each part of society's various capabilities.

I propose "dialectical reunification theory" as a blueprint for reunifying the Korean people. Dialectical reunification theory begins with an accurate understanding of the peculiarities between the two Koreas and a realistic recognition of the remarkable "heterogeneity" between the ROK and DPRK. The only desirable path to reunification is to identify and harmonize the two nations' heterogeneity, while discovering and continuously promoting their homogeneity. This effort requires much observation and study of both South and North, particularly the North, which is exactly why I have made more than 50 trips there since 1980.

▲ The author, introduced as "The Peacemaker," on the cover of *The University of Georgia Magazine* in 2011. (Photo courtesy of Han Shik Park)

The biggest obstacle I encountered when I started visiting the DPRK in 1980 was the lack of infrastructure. Financially, it was very challenging for an individual scholar to visit every summer to observe, study reunification, and communicate directly with officials. Not to mention that arranging and facilitating exchanges between the United States and the DPRK in an academic or quasi-governmental capacity was too much for an individual professor. In this uniquely challenging situation, government-level dialogue between South Korea, North

Korea, and the United States required some structure—that is, physical assistance—to provide the human, financial, and administrative support to make "Track II Dialogue" possible. This is why I established the Center for the Study of Global Issues (GLOBIS) at the University of Georgia in 1995.

It was surprisingly easy to establish GLOBIS. University of Georgia officials gave their full support, granting approval as soon as my proposal for the center was submitted. The school provided more support than I expected, including a two-story building and a generous budget to hire two full-time employees and several doctoral students as research assistants. Many Korean doctoral students with financial challenges came through this Center. Additionally, thanks to GLOBIS, we were able to conduct various academic conferences, debates between public figures, and international events—such as inviting a delegation from the DPRK to conduct Track II diplomacy—without great difficulties. Moreover, GLOBIS was able to receive helpful donations and contributions for these events, unlike those I had personally funded and promoted before the Center was established.

Although my main research area concerned North Korea, inter-Korean issues, and reunification, I did not want to name the institute anything like the "Korean Research Institute" or "Center for Reunification Research." I definitely wanted to include the word "global." At that time, the word "global" was not in such wide use as it is now, and I particularly liked how it effectively connoted a common fate or shared destiny for all mankind.

The Cold War ended with the collapse of the Soviet Union in 1990, reopening possibilities for East-West exchanges that had been blocked throughout the Cold War. Globalization accelerated. Additionally, with the collapse of the Soviet Union, United States' hegemony reached its climax as there were no other great powers to compete with her militarily, economically, or culturally. Due to this international phenomenon, it is no exaggeration to say that the globalization which occurred beginning in the 1990s was the "Americanization" of the world. Globalization, which accelerated under the unilateral influence of the United States, caused a new and diverse range of world problems to emerge. Terrorism is one prime example. Military and nuclear tensions between Korea, the United States, and North Korea can be understood in the broader context of US-led globalization. From this perspective, Korean reunification is not only a challenge for Koreans, but also a global issue.

When establishing GLOBIS, I also focused on promoting global education. I wanted to instill in American students a recognition and accurate awareness of global problems caused by globalization (or the world's Americanization). Most American students have limited exposure to the world. Foreign travel rarely extends beyond Britain, Canada, and France, and there is more ignorance and indifference about other countries and cultures than one might imagine. I actually think the world needs the United States to succeed. If the US collapses, I do not know if the world will be able to sustain itself properly. I believe that in order for the US to thrive, it must have a global conscience, understand and accept other cultures, and free themselves from ignorance and sense of superiority. I believe that started with education.

Since 1995, through GLOBIS' short-term overseas training program, I have conducted international educational trips with more than 100 American students every summer. By seeing and experiencing things firsthand, I intend that American students feel, realize, and learn about peace and world issues for themselves.

We selected four locations from around the world for the overseas training program. In Munich, Germany, students toured the Dachau Concentration Camp Memorial Site to learn about the murderous atrocities of the Nazis against the Jews. In Japan, students visited the atomic bomb dome of the Hiroshima Peace Memorial to remind them of the brutality and cruelty of war and nuclear weapons. During the trip to South Africa, students stopped by the Nelson Mandela Museum to learn about the injustice of racism, and in South Korea, on a tour of the DMZ at Panmunjom, I tried to impress the students with the necessity and justification for peace on the Korean Peninsula.

GLOBIS was a precious project for me. I cared about it as if it were my own child, and many people still call it the "Han Shik Park Institute." I founded it and poured all my passion and energy into its development until my retirement in 2015. Without missing a single day, I went to my office at GLOBIS, researching and writing at my desk—for 20 years. When I retired, I was very sad to clean up my office and move out. However, I believe that another director will sit there to faithfully continue conducting global education and research on global issues, continuing GLOBIS' mission.

After a modest retirement ceremony in December 2015, I stopped going to GLOBIS. After coming to UGA in 1970, I taught and researched for 45 years. I was on active duty much longer than others, retiring at the age of 76. Even then, I wanted to be on active duty a little longer! I have often seen people around me suddenly grow old or even die soon after retirement, which is why I thought about delaying my retirement. And, although I have no particular diagnosis, my doctor recommended I should retire. There was also some writing I wanted to finish if I had enough time in retirement. These were my reasons for retirement.

▲ A glorious reunion after 35 years. The author with his aunt (right) by the Songhua River near his hometown during the July 1981 visit. (Photo courtesy of Han Shik Park)

I wanted to write a book on globalization, but before retirement my lectures and work at GLOBIS did not afford me ample time and energy. Writing a book requires a lot of serious desk time for contemplation. In the end, I allowed considerable time for work after my retirement, and after two years of hard work, an extensive book, called *Globalization: A Blessing or a Curse?* was published in English in 2017, second enlarged edition in 2022.

At the retirement ceremony, the University of Georgia expressed their deep gratitude for my efforts toward peace and global education through GLOBIS. They also presented me with an undeserved retirement gift. In return for my passion, dedication, and contribution to peace over the past 45 years, they created an "endowed chair professorship" in my name, called the "Han S. Park Professorship of Peace Studies." Such awards are usually named after the person who donated to a fund, but this was the first time that the University of Georgia has created a fund chair professorship named after a retired professor. It was a gracious and glorious retirement gift.

Convening Private Experts from the US, DPRK, and ROK

In 2011, the situation on the Korean Peninsula was intense and grim. Due to the March 2010 sinking of the South Korean ship, *Cheonan*, and the subsequent May 24th sanctions against North Korea, relations between the two Koreas were at a standstill. And, since North Korea's second nuclear test in 2009, the United States and North Korea had been through a whirlwind of talks with no significant breakthrough. It was incredibly frustrating to witness how the windows of communication between governments had closed so tightly without any sign of immanent breakthrough. I was convinced that in the middle of this suspension of official inter-Korean and US-DPRK dialogue, communication through private channels was essential to gain the necessary insight to resolve the pending issues between these nations.

From October 17th to 20th, 2011, after more than a year of preparation, I hosted a "Trilateral Track II Conference" through GLOBIS. Private, civil sector experts from the ROK, DPRK, and the United States participated in this conference for four days. It was the second Track II meeting I hosted, following the November 2003 "US-DPRK Forum (Washington-Pyongyang Track II Forum) for

▲ October 2011, 30 private experts from South Korea, North Korea, and the United States gathered at the University of Georgia for three-party Track II dialogue between ROK, DPRK, and the USA. Front row from the far left podium, moderator Han Shik Park, Asia-Pacific Peace Committee Vice President Ri Jong Hyok, Seoul National University Professor Emeritus Baek Nak-cheong, Democratic Party lawmaker Park Ju-seon, U.S. Representative Curt Weldon, and Asia-Pacific Peace Committee Director Han Song Ryol. (Photo courtesy of Han Shik Park)

Resolving the North Korean Nuclear Crisis and Improving US-DPRK Relations," which I organized for breakthrough in the Six-Party Talks.

Track I dialogue is direct communication between governments, while Track II is dialogue among private experts who can influence the government and its policy. Through the 2011 Track II summit, I wanted to prepare a place to promote close and sincere dialogue between three Parties—South Korea, North Korea and the US.

Track I dialogue between government officials aims to persuade the other party. They make the claim that their own views and policies are more rational or convincing than those of their counterparts, while actually prioritizing achieving favorable results for themselves through negotiation and implementation of their own policies. This posture makes it difficult for them to bend their hardline positions, often leading to breakdown in talks between countries.

The purpose of Track II meetings, however, is entirely different from Track I meetings. Track II does not exist because Track I will not go well, nor is Track II a substitute for Track I or merely a supplement to Track I. Track II exists to understand the other party through honest and candid dialogue. According to etymology, the English word "understand" means to put aside one's own words and stand under the other to listen to what he has to say. I wanted to provide an opportunity for private experts from the ROK, DPRK, and the United States to clear up misunderstandings and listen to each other's honest opinions.

▲ The DPRK-US Track II Dialogue held at the University of Georgia in December 2003. From left: Counselor Shin Song Chol and Deputy Ambassador Han Song Ryol from the DPRK Mission to the UN, Professor Han Shik Park, former U.S. Ambassador to the ROK Donald Gregg, U.S. Representative Curt Weldon, Director Cho Song Gu from the DPRK's Institute for Disarmament and Peace, and U.S. Democratic Senate staff Frank Jannuzi, Republican Senate staff Keith Luse, Director of the Asia-Pacific Peace Committee Kim Myong Gil, and Interpreter Shim Il Gwan. (Photo courtesy of Park Han-shik)

Dialogue involves listening to the other person's story as it is shared, without prejudice or judgment and with an open mind. Only such dialogue can make it possible to understand the other party. When we understand each other, we can embrace each other's differences and heterogeneity. When heterogeneity meets and embraces each other, a higher level of homogeneity is created. This is harmony and peace. It is unbelievably tragic that the South and the North have adhered to systemic competition for the past 75 years, that only clings to their own views and repeatedly claims that their respective regimes are superior. Reunification and peace will never come without understanding and sincere dialogue with each other.

In 2011, during the three-party Track II dialogue between South Korea, North Korea, and the United States, I set three of my own principles to preserve the original purpose of Track II. The first was the principle of informality. As much as possible, I excluded inviting participants who officially represented their country or held positions in government. Government officials in public office would be obliged to represent their government's position, making it very difficult to speak freely and confidently. The second principle is that of non-disclosure. These events inevitably get some attention from the media, so it is customary to invite them, advertise, and use the event for publicity. However, in my opinion, it is much better and more effective for Track II closed-door meetings to occur privately, without media disclosure. In such private sessions, participants can engage in free exchanges of fresh ideas, but only if the discussion is confidential and not disclosed to the media. Therefore, only the opening and closing ceremonies of the meetings were disclosed to the media, while the principle of non-disclosure was strictly observed during the four days of plenary sessions. Finally, there is the principle of non-responsibility. In order to create an environment in which participants could openly express their thoughts and discuss them freely, I established this principle so participants would not be responsible for any remarks or claims made at the meetings. We closely followed these principles throughout the Track II meetings, which served as a cornerstone to broaden our mutual understanding through candid and open dialogue.

Another important issue in determining the success or failure of Track II conversations was the face of meeting participants. It was not easy to determine who to invite to the meetings and by what criteria to invite them. Although I cannot disclose all the names and titles of the participants here, I will share my three criteria for inviting participants, like the aforementioned three principles for conducting the meetings.

The first criterion was that the participants should have passion and commitment to peace and reunification. I only invited those who agreed and sympathized with the premise that peace and reunification should be achieved through dialogue and mutual understanding. The second criterion was professionalism. Because I believe only expertise can influence society—be it through academia, art, or civic engagement—and that only people with expertise could play an ongoing, significant role in society during and after reunification, I invited recognized experts in various fields.

The final criterion was personality, and this was the most important to me. Whether from North Korea or the United States, I invited people with character transcending systems and ideologies, in other words, trustworthy people. I was convinced that participants would be able to understand each other much better if people of good character spoke candidly about their societal system and life experiences. During my dozens of visits to South and North Korea, I closely observed the character of the people with whom I interacted. Others might find this off-putting, but I made a habit of rating the character of everyone I met. People invited to the Track II meetings had excellent character, with a personality score of at least 8 out of 10 according to my standards.

Of course, it was not easy to prepare for these meetings. The task of contacting a total of 30 attendees, male and female, from each country, checking whether they were able to attend, and receiving their confirmations alone required considerable time and energy. I could not delegate that task to anyone else. Participants from the North did not have access to the same real-time communication as the participants from the South or the United States, so it took a long time to correspond about their schedule and confirm their attendance.

Another big challenge was meeting expenses. Although most people from the United States and the South expressed their willingness to attend at their own expense, it was impossible for the participants to bear the entire cost, including accommodation and meals for 3 nights and 4 days, in addition to transportation costs. It was very difficult for the North Korean participants to bear the expenses of a large delegation traveling to the United States, particularly at a time of great hunger at home. I earnestly set out to fundraise the necessary budget to host the conference. I first submitted the "Track II Meeting Plan" to the University of Georgia, officially applying for a budget. I personally met with the president to explain the purpose and significance of the meeting and the need to secure a budget. Thankfully, through GLOBIS, the University of Georgia provided considerable financial support.

Additionally, we received significant funding from ABC, a broadcasting company with which I have a longstanding relationship. From 1994 to 2008, I was a North Korea commentator for their news broadcasts. In the 2000s, I arranged for a group of ABC reporters, including ABC's president David Westin, to provide on the ground reporting inside the DPRK. I took them to North Korea several times. After Track II, as a reward for their financial support, I conducted an exclusive interview with ABC to explain the significance and achievements of the meetings in detail.

Another challenge to achieving these talks were the visas. It is not easy for a delegation from North Korea, an enemy nation without diplomatic relations, to visit the United States. The key question was whether or not the US government would grant their visas at such a sensitive time. Fortunately, I was close to John Merrill, then director of the State Department's East Asia desk. He stepped up to help. I was lucky to get to know and interact with people of character like John. John himself had strongly hoped to attend the meetings, but at the last minute the State Department refused, so he had no choice but to turn around at the Atlanta Airport.

The journey of the North Korean participants was not only highlighted in the media, but also drew attention from the FBI in the Atlanta Airport. The FBI kept an eye on the itinerary and every move of the North Korean participants, even watching them in real-time from a helicopter. I asked the FBI not to approach the meeting room so as not to interfere with open discussion, and each evening, I personally briefed them about what had been discussed and the mood of the day's meetings. Although the FBI presence may have been unpleasant surveillance for the visiting delegation, I deeply appreciated their close surveillance. I felt reassured that their service was thorough protection for the North Korean visitors in case of any unforeseen accidents.

During four-days of meetings, we had serious, sincere discussions on various concerns. Rather than simply having private experts gather and haggle, they discussed specific ways to confirm each other's heterogeneity and homogeneity, how to reconcile heterogeneity, and how to encourage homogeneity. In addition, there was a broad policy discussion about what advice each country could contribute to the current environment.

But the best moments of all occurred during the shared evenings with participants from South and North Korea and the United States, after all the daytime sessions. It was overwhelming and heartwarming to see participants getting to know and understanding each other through friendly, casual conversations as we ate and drank a glass of medicinal wine together. A Korean participant said, "This is the first time I have talked at length with North Koreans. It was a good opportunity to talk openly and broaden our understanding."

On last evening of the meeting, I invited all the attendees to my house for dinner. I served an abundance of Korean food, Western food, and my very own barbecue chicken recipe. Alcohol flowed, and the participants, who had grown closer over the four days together, shared stories freely. The friendly mood was enhanced by a performance of "Träumerei" by world-famous violinist Ahn Yong-gu.

In the middle of the warm atmosphere at that dinner, I went down to my basement study and, together with representatives from each country, wrote a joint statement from the meetings in Korean and English. After we finalized the agreement, I read the six paragraph statement all the participants. As soon as I finished reading, one of the participants immediately suggested that we all sing "Our Wish" together. Everyone held hands and, forming a large circle, began to sing to Mr. Ahn's beautiful violin melody. It was a heart-warming moment. As I sang, I felt that moment was peace, and that was how reunification would come.

Although we worked hard to establish permanent or regular ROK-DPRK-US Track II dialogues, they have not recurred since 2011. As mentioned before, Track II is a model of private exchange that can enhance inter-Korean dialogue and broaden mutual understanding and trust. Track II dialogue is an indispensable starting point, particularly when direct dialogue between governments is at an impasse. Experts in various fields from South Korea, North Korea, and the United States continuously carrying out track II dialogues is key to the process of seeking reunification and peace on the Korean Peninsula.

The role of Track II cannot be overemphasized in implementing measures agreed upon in the past Inter-Korean Joint Declarations (June 15, 2000; October 4, 2007; April 27, 2018). Considering how current inter-Korean relations have been drifting since the North-South Joint Liaison Office was bombed in Kaesong in June 2020, Track II dialogue is more urgent than ever.

Our Reunification is not German Reunification

We often hear of public opinion polls on reunification conducted by media organizations or research institutes. Unfortunately, the first question on the questionnaire is always, "Do you think reunification is necessary?" or "Why do we need to make reunification happen?"

It does not make sense to ask or answer such questions without presenting a desirable "path to reunification" or suggesting a political and social system for a unified Korea.

There are various existing theories for reunification, which all have serious inherent flaws. In Korea, people who hate North Korea claim that war is the most "realistic" way of achieving Korean reunification. However, the theory of reunification by force is an extremely "unrealistic" method because war's overwhelming destruction would destroy the very purpose of reunification. The theory of armed reunification is nothing more than a self-destructive, self-negating, and self-hypnotic "mirage" that feeds into hatred of North Korea.

Also, when talking about reunification in Korea, many people think of German reunification, revealing that Korea's understanding of reunification was secretly constructed around the case of German reunification. However, we must clearly recognize that Germany's "reunification by absorption" is not a suitable model for the Korean people's reunification because East-West German relations before reunification and current inter-Korean relations are significantly different historically, economically, culturally, and politically.

Prior to reunification, East and West Germany were overwhelmingly more homogenous than heterogenous, thanks to the longstanding "Ostpolitik" policy, while inter-Korean relations now reveal more heterogeneity than homogeneity. Nevertheless, if Germany's absorption-style reunification is forced upon Korea as a model for Korean reunification, the Korean Peninsula is highly likely to fall into chaotic turmoil, similar to the political chaos immediately following Liberation from Japan. Korean people's reunification should not be planned based upon external cases, rather it should be prepared by accurately understanding the peculiarities between the two Koreas through careful consideration and meticulous understanding. Only a reunification plan uniquely designed to fit the Korean people could be stably established on the Korean Peninsula.

There is a perception that the younger generation and the older generation to a smaller extent are increasingly abandoning the idea of reunification. Believing it better to live separately as South and North, the plan is to conduct economic, sports, and cultural exchanges and to give up on political reunification. This discourse on abandoning reunification was born out of the 75-year history of division. However, the Korean people lived as one unified people for thousands of years, before foreign powers divided the Korean Peninsula. Thus, maintaining this division is the same as voluntarily surrendering our national autonomy.

I propose "dialectical reunification theory" as an alternative to overcome the various deficiencies existing reunification theories. The "dialectical reunification theory" prioritizes realistic acknowledgment of the ROK and DPRK's remarkable heterogeneity. Furthermore, because there is always an undercurrent of homogeneity, this acknowledgement will form a blueprint for Korean reunification, seeking a way for the south and north to coexist peacefully. I am confident that reunification will occur naturally only when the Koreas reach a higher level of homogeneity, that is, a new consensus. This will come through understanding, realistic acknowledgment, and work to peacefully harmonizing the heterogeneity between them.

During my more than 50 visits to North and South Korea since 1980, I have focused on observing the heterogeneity between the two nations from an objective and balanced perspective. As a result of the 75-year division, there are many differences. The heterogeneity I felt most strongly can be summarized into three differences:

The first is the difference in the capitalist and socialist systems. Socialism is based on the absence of private property, whereas capitalism is based on private property. The DPRK is a society based on a cost-of-living economy rather than a consumption economy and on public property rather than private property. This system also emphasizes just distribution of resources according to socialist ideology.

In North Korea, labor is neither a commodity nor a means of accumulating wealth. Work is a considered a sacred right of the people, and the State has the responsibility to provide its people with stable and non-exploitative jobs. Wages are paid according to the price of individual labor, a concept quite different from the salaries received in capitalist society. In the DPRK, the money earned by working for a month is called a living expense, and is distributed according to the needs of each worker. Because living expenses are distributed based upon needs, there is no big difference between households.

Once, while discussing North Korean economic theory with a political economy professor at Kim Il Sung University, I asked explicitly about the living expenses. He said living expenses are distributed justly to the extent that senior professors are not compensated any more than double the living expenses of new instructors. Doubtful, I stopped by the souvenir shop of the Koryo Hotel, where I often stayed, and asked the same question to the female staff. They told me there is very little wage difference between a female clerk who sorts items on the shelves and a manager who oversees the store's operation. The DPRK is practicing just distribution with the goal of equality.

While the DPRK is an idealistic society with metaphysical values, the ROK is a materialistic capitalist society based on the principle of private property. There is a lot of corruption because of this system of private property in South Korea, and everything is driven by private property. Accumulating wealth is a virtue and supreme value, and the measure of wealth distinguishes people and society. Distributive justice does not exist, and the gap between rich and poor was formed and justified in the name of freedom. The value of labor has declined, while the gap between the rich and the poor widens day by day. Class mobility has become impossible to achieve through an individual's hard work, as evidenced by the fact that all of South Korea is caught up in get-rich-quick schemes, real estate speculation, and stock frenzy.

Some South Koreans want to go north to invest in real estate after reunification and have even asked me to connect them with North Korean officials. Their thinking is sheer nonsense. In South Korea, money is power and status, but accumulating personal wealth in North Korea is rather a matter of caution. Accumulating wealth in North Korea leads to investigations by the authorities, along with accompanying hardships. Jang Song-Thaek, who was executed in 2013, was charged with substantial corruption, including accumulating personal property.

Also, to judge the DPRK by comparing South and North Korean economic power is to make the mistake of forcing a capitalist perspective on the DPRK. In June 2020, President Moon Jae-in declared this in his speech to commemorate the 70th anniversary of the Korean War:

> Our gross domestic product is more than 50 times that of North Korea, and the amount of trade is more than 400 times that of North Korea. The systemic competition between the South and the North has long since ended. We have no intention of forcing our system on the DPRK.

It was an expression of his determination and will to pursue mutual prosperity and peace between the two Koreas, but from the North Korean perspective, it could also be understood to mean that DPRK-style socialism as a political system has already fallen out of competition and has been defeated. North Korea may vigorously oppose such statements. Such arguments are not at all helpful for dialogue and reunification between the two sides.

If the gap between rich and poor is an inherent contradiction in the ROK, the biggest contradiction the DPRK faces is that of its people's hunger. Compared to the South, the North is an equal society, yet everyone is poor. From a human empirical verification perspective, social and historical development begins by overcoming self-contradiction. According to my dialectical reunification theory, South and North Korea must each begin by finding their own contradictions. Once the two societies acknowledge their own contradictions, I am confident that we could proceed through the process of overcoming self-contradiction through recognition and will naturally be able to reach a "synthesis."

The second great difference I discovered between South and North is the difference between individualism and collectivism. While South Korean society is changing to become an individualistic society, North Korea is still thoroughly collective, operating from a foundation of collectivist thought. The North Korean nation is an extended family which thoroughly rejects individualism and liberalism according to the principle of collectivism. "One for all, all for one." This society is dominated by the perception that the interests of the State, the party, and society take precedence over individual interests and desires. Only when individuals contribute to the interests of the collective can they become a true "socio-political living being" and transcend base biological human existence.

North Korean society is based on the principle of resource distribution according to need, but there is another method of distribution—according to "social contribution." Those who have contributed to the workplace, the Workers' Party, or the nation are rewarded according to this system. The government rewards its people with gifts—from small badges of Kim Il Sung and Kim Jong Il to large appliances such as refrigerators and TVs, or even houses! One day, when I was invited to eat at an acquaintance's house, I saw a large refrigerator with Kim Il Sung and Kim Jong Il badges in his kitchen. When I asked about it, out of curiosity, they were proud to explain. They said it was the pride of the family, explaining that the refrigerator was gifted to them by the Party.

All North Korean people wear the Kim Il Sung badge (portrait badge) on their left chest, and the type of badge may indicate the wearer's status. Once, I saw a person on the street who was not wearing a Kim Il Sung badge. When I asked my guide about it, he explained that if that person did something wrong at work or in society, his badge could be confiscated for a certain period of time, as a form of probation. He added that people without badges would be humiliated by others.

Another significant difference between the South and North is their understanding of human rights. The horrendous situation of human rights abuses and oppression in North Korea has been the subject of international condemnation, illustrated in the UN Human Rights Council's 20 consecutive years of resolutions on North Korean human rights since 2003. When South Korea agrees to those resolutions, it often causes internal conflict within South Korea, not to mention inter-Korean conflict on the peninsula. However uncomfortable it may be to hear, the DPRK does have a definition and concept of human rights. There are a significant differences between how the North and South understand human rights.

Among the dimensions of human rights, South Korea prioritizes the right to choice-making, which is a political freedom, as the essence of human rights in capitalist society. However, the right to equality is the core of the socialist system in North Korea. As a socialist system, the DPRK prioritizes and values the State's sovereignty over individual human rights. This is because the State deigns that individual human rights can only be guaranteed when State sovereignty is guaranteed. Among the six dimensions of human rights that I classified earlier, the DPRK relatively neglects the right to choice-making, which is emphasized in the ROK's concept of human rights, while emphasizing the right to survival, the right to belonging, and the right to equality. Those three are relatively weaker in the ROK's conception of human rights.

Is it possible to reconcile capitalism and socialism, or individualism and collectivism? It is not an easy task, but I believe they are not unalterably opposed and can be reconciled. How, to what extent, and in what shape should they be harmonized? This in the most important question for discussion in the process of forming a unified State and drafting a unified Constitution. Additionally, efforts to discover and steadily promote the homogeneity that the south and north share is just as important to reunification as the harmonization of heterogeneity.

I believe we must present a desirable and ideal model for reunification before debating the necessity of and justification for reunification. Only then will we all be able to find a proper answer and overcome the controversy and heated discussions surrounding why reunification is necessary.

Finding Homogeneity Between North and South

Over the course of 40 decades of visiting the DPRK, my feelings about the nation's system, society and people slowly began to change. During my first ten visits, I often thought about how people were living. Like us, they think about their groceries every evening, anxiously anticipate receiving their children's report cards from school, and plan family outings on Sundays. On a summer evening, the Daedong Riverside comes alive as a popular dating spot for young men and women. Rather than demons with horns on their heads, I discovered ordinary people in North Korea, living normal lives, not so different from our own. Therefore, my ignorance and prejudice, a product of South Korea's anti-communist education (or brainwashing) and the United States' demonization, fell apart.

When I had visited around 20 times, I couldn't shake the thought that North Korean people lived there. The striking differences between the DPRK system and people was tangible. People's lives were thoroughly directed by DPRK-style socialism and built on *Juche* ideology. By abolishing private property, adopting collective ownership, and practicing need-based economic distribution, they were trying to achieve just distribution according to the goal of

◄ On April 27, 2018, President Moon Jae-in and Chairman Kim Jong Un met without an interpreter at the inter-Korean summit and went for a walk on the Panmunjom Bridge. (Photo courtesy of the Panmunjom Joint Reporting Foundation)

equality. They were also thoroughly indoctrinated into a form of collectivism that prioritized the interests of the group over individualism and liberalism. They lived their daily lives under an anti-American and anti-capitalist nationalism. Furthermore, because of their international isolation and economic poverty, North Korea displayed a radically evolved form of nationalism.

However, in spite of the ROK and DPRK's heterogeneity, which appeared as incompatible as oil and water, the more I visited, the more I could feel in my heart that North Korean people were fundamentally the same as South Korean people. Despite our long-standing conflict, antagonism, and division, I also observed and felt the considerable similarities that the south and north share.

Efforts to discover and steadily promote such homogeneity is as important to the reunification process as is harmonizing our heterogeneity. Reunification education that informs the Korean people about their same-ness through the media, social education, and the school system is the core of building a culture of reunification. Reunification culture is not to be created after reunification, but to be formed in the process of reunification. The culture established during the reunification process will provide stability and support the survival of the political system jointly established between the ROK and DPRK. Furthermore, beginning to create this reunification culture now is indispensable to achieving true and complete unity after reunification.

Despite 75 years of separation, North and South Korea are the same ethnic group with a common identity. Their homogeneity is inherent in the nation's ethos (heritage and customs); it has not been created rapidly and artificially through education and socialization, like capitalism and socialism. A nation's ethos is a system of beliefs, values, and norms, formed collectively over hundreds or thousands of years. The longstanding ethos—or spirit of a nation—cannot be abolished or changed by a single individual or government.

The homogeneity I felt between the south and north can be summarized in three main points. Firstly, they share a common language. From an epistemological and philosophy of science point of view, a shared language means a shared way of thinking, structure of consciousness, and similar values. One thing I worried about while visiting North Korea was what I should to do if I found communication difficult. My middle and high school anti-communist education in South Korea had taught me that the language between north and south was so different that communication with people from the north was difficult.

However, when I went to North Korea and spoke with normal citizens as well as with DPRK officials, I could understand every single word. Also, all the people I met there managed to understand my strong Gyeongsang-do accent. Undeniably, certain words and expressions vary between north and south. For example, what we call a "restroom" in South Korea is called a "sanitary room" in North Korea,[110] and what is called "reciprocal relationship" in the south is called "mutual relationship" in the north.[111] People also use slightly different words in North and South Korea to express, "I will be right back."[112] But all these small variations are understandable in context.

One proof that we communicate in the same language, despite 75 years of separation and the ensuing generation gap, was the 2018 occasion where President Moon Jae-in and Chairman Kim Jong Un were able to talk together for 30 minutes on the foot bridge in Panmunjom, without any staff accompanying them for translation assistance. Having the same language is an asset and cornerstone for reunification, as it facilitates communication, harmony, and mutual understanding.

Secondly, the ROK and DPRK share a long history. Such shared national experience can give citizens a sense of belonging and pride in their nation and serves the function of integrating its members into a united whole. Not only does shared history justify reunification, but it confirms that north and south are the same people. In north and south,

---

[110] The word for bathroom in the south (화장실) is different from that in the north (위생실).

[111] The phrase meaning "reciprocal relationship" in the south (상호관계, 相互關係) is different from that in the north (호상관계, 互相關係), simply by changing the order of the first two Chinese characters.

[112] The phrase meaning, "I'll be right back," is said slightly differently in the north (인차 돌아오겠습니다) and the south (곧 돌아오겠습니다), using different adverbs for the word "right"—*incha* and *got*, respectively.

everyone is educated about our shared history from the Gojoseon, Goguryeo, Three Kingdoms, Goryeo, and Joseon dynasties clear through to the current division.

We see a particular example of our single nation's shared history if we consider the October 3rd National Foundation Day celebrations in the DPRK and ROK. Both countries regard the myth of Dangun[113] as a historical fact and commemorate this holiday as a unique national celebration of the birth of our people through the establishment of the Korean Peninsula's first nation-state. In the north, Dangun's tomb was excavated in 1993 and renovated the following year into a 70-meter-high, nine-step pyramid to inspire the spirit of the nation. I visited that location twice, before and after Dangun's tomb was built. South Korea and North Korea even held joint National Foundation Day celebrations at Dangun's tomb several times, although the last joint celebration was held in 2014.

The ROK and DPRK's deep-rooted homogeneity has been preserved through language and history, and is remarkably shared in terms of customs and linguistic convention. First of all, consider that both Koreas use two words to distinguish subtle differences in their expression of the concept of a "human being" and a fully human "person." [114] On one occasion while I toured the outskirts of Pyongyang, I witnessed a young child sprinting through a gate, running away from his scolding mother. I saw the mother following

---

[113] Dangun (단군, 檀君) was the legendary founder of the first Korean kingdom, called Gojoseon.

[114] A living human being is called *ingan* (인간, 人間), while a mature and developed human being, a fully human person—is called *saram* (사람, a pure Korean word without Chinese characters).

behind the child, shouting, "When will that human being become a full person?"

This linguistic subtlety—in which a human being is only regarded as *fully* human, "a person," when they have reached moral, social, and qualitative perfection—exists in both North and South Korea.

"Conscience" is also a shared concept in both Koreas. Even in the DPRK, I often heard the question, "Does that person have no conscience?"

In both north and south, conscience is a duty that governs mature people's thoughts and actions. Conscience is a higher concept than democracy or the *Juche* idea. In the DPRK, no matter how heavily armed one may be with *Juche* ideology, a person without a conscience cannot be treated as a fully human "person."

If I could add one more similarity, among the countless cases of homogeneity in both places, it is that Korean food is the same in both places. North Koreans still eat foods like kimchi and soybean paste, and they taste almost the same. Survival according to a similar diet requires living a similar lifestyle. Additionally, because food is always prepared where people meet, sharing the same food creates a feeling of home and comfort. Many Koreans living in the United States come together to exchange food and even cook together. As a shared medium, food is an important part of our lives and a big factor that helps us feel the same-ness between south and north.

If you focus only on the differences between the Koreas, you may doubt reunification is possible. The road to reunification will open with profound efforts to dialectically overcome heterogeneity and to discover and promote homogeneity between the ROK and DPRK. Similarities will be a direct catalyst for uniting Korean people, so efforts which steadily expand the horizon of homogeneity is part of creating a reunification culture. If established in this way, such reunification culture will be a pillar in the stable construction of a reunification system and constitution, jointly prepared and agreed upon by the ROK and DPRK.

History teaches us that institutions are only stable and survive when they have a strong cultural foundation undergirding them. For example, Mao Zedong's socialist revolution succeeded not through the imported Western ideas of Marx and Lenin, but through Mao's ideas that were intentionally rooted in China's traditional, agrarian culture. It is self-evident that socialism also succeeded in the DPRK— not through pure Marxist or Leninist ideology—but through ideology that actively reflected the customs and cultural reality of Korea.

Alexis de Tocqueville also expressed this insight in his book *Democracy in America,* saying that laws not rooted in the customs of a nation are incomplete, for only customs can sustain resistance in the lives of a people. He went on to say that the American people were only able to operate a stable democratic system because their customs firmly supported it. In the *The Protestant Ethic and the Spirit of Capitalism*, Max Weber argued that capitalism and its spirit originated in Christian ethics and customs dominating Western society at the time.

Therefore, to achieve reunification of the Korean Peninsula in our own way, we must build a culture of reunification based on south and north homogeneity. Who will play an important role in creating and fostering such a culture on the Korean Peninsula? I think we should note that in 1636, only 16 years after they came to the American Continent, British Puritans established the first American university, Harvard University. They did this as soon as they had established a minimal livelihood. In a similar vein, I propose the establishment of "Kaesong Peace University."

Similar to how the Puritans at Harvard discovered, studied, and continuously educated themselves in their perception of an "ideal Christian lifestyle," I am confident that Kaesong Peace University can play a leading role in creating a reunification culture for a future, unified Korean State.

Fulfilling the Dream of Reunification

Working toward reunification has never been easy. Despite the ROK and DPRK's continuous efforts toward this goal, inter-Korean relations are currently at a standstill, and the prospect of reunification is still so distant that it provokes sadness and frustration. So far, the best path to reunification that the two Koreas have mapped out together was the "June 15th Joint Declaration." It states, "The South and the North have agreed to resolve the question of reunification on their own Initiative and through the joint efforts of the Korean people, who are the masters of the country. Acknowledging that there are common elements in the South's proposal for a confederation and the North's proposal for a federation of lower stage as the formulae for achieving reunification, the South and the North agreed to promote reunification in that direction."

In accordance with the spirit of that June 15th Declaration, the Kim Dae-jung and Roh Moo-hyun Korean administrations both reduced military tension on the Korean Peninsula and promoted exchanges between people of the ROK and DPRK. However, the successive Lee Myung-bak and Park Geun-hye governments' anti-North policy reversed this earlier trend, brought military tensions on the peninsula to dramatic new heights, and inter-Korean exchanges to a grinding halt. Keeping this historical pattern in mind, although inter-Korean relations have been improving under the Moon Jae-in administration, the situation is highly likely to return to a crisis phase if another so-called conservative government comes to power again in the ROK. In short, the June 15th Declaration had obvious limitations that South Korea's conservative camp could not accept. If inter-Korean engagement continues repeating this historical pattern, it seems reunification will be delayed indefinitely. This context explains why Moon Jae-in's government sought to ratify the April 27th Panmunjom Declaration during the 21st session of the National Assembly.

I highlighted earlier that East-West German relations and current inter-Korean relations have distinct historical, economic, cultural and political differences, therefore, German absorption and reunification is not a suitable model for Korean reunification. If we examine reunification policy, there are clear differences between West Germany and Korea. In West Germany, the progressive Social Democratic Party's "Ostpolitik (Eastern Policy)," implemented in the early 1970s by Willy Brandt, continued even after the conservative Christian Democratic Party, the political opposition, came to power.

Despite their different political believes, both progressive and conservative parties in West Germany shared the vision and values of German reunification, therefore, they were able to consistently pursue the Eastern Policy for 20 years despite the regime change. However, in Korea, the so-called progressive and conservative governments do not share the vision and values of reunification; in fact, their respective views on reunification are in sharp conflict. Whenever a conservative government comes to power, there has been neither reason nor will to continue pursuing the June 15th Joint Declaration, a product of past progressive governments.

In order to continuously implement reunification policy regardless of Korean regime changes, we must establish a view of reunification that both liberals and conservatives in the ROK, the regime in the DPRK, and overseas Koreans can share. There are currently about 8 million Koreans living abroad, but they tend to be excluded from much of the discussion about reunification. However, their accumulated experiences are an asset to the nation, so diasporic Koreans should play a leading role in work toward reunification.

In order to prepare a view of reunification shared by all Koreans, I believe we must embrace the urgent task of forming a "pan-national committee to promote reunification" (tentative name) in which both liberal and conservative South Koreans, North Koreans, and diasporic Koreans participate. This pan-national committee will be able to create a view of reunification that can be shared by all Koreans and elevated above political changes in the ROK and DPRK. I propose the pan-national committee seriously considers the "One nation, two states, and three governments" reunification model, as well as the establishment of a "Peace and Reunification University."

Understanding reunification as a desperate national task, there are plans to form and establish a third government, that is, a "reunification government," while the existing systems of the two countries, ROK and DPRK, relate to one another with mutual respect. While the ROK and DPRK work faithfully to overcome their internal contradictions (the ROK's unequal resource distribution and gap between the rich and the poor; the DPRK's poverty and international isolation), the third government will be a new, experimental type of government to harmonize their heterogeneity while promoting homogeneity to build a unified, ideal village. Although the third government does not possess strong powers, such as that of diplomacy and national defense, it can form a low-level federal government with independent territory and legislative, judicial, and administrative authority far beyond the level of the inter-Korean iaison office.

I also believe that the Demilitarized Zone (DMZ), a scar of war and symbol of division, can become a valuable asset toward Korean reunification. The 3rd government could govern the DMZ as its own territory, granting citizenship to separated families, overseas Koreans, and anyone who wants to come and live there, essentially creating an

▲ Lecturing at the 2018 Atlanta Korean Association. (Photo courtesy of the Atlanta chapter of the Advisory Council on Democratic and Peaceful Unification)

autonomous "independent government." It would be essentially a reunification government that experiments with and practices unification. The ideal unification village, designed and built by the third government, will overcome heterogeneity between ROK and DPRK through chemical bonding, as opposed to physical bonding. This ideal village will guarantee human rights, realize justice, and establish a Korean community where people lead pleasant and prosperous lives in an eco-friendly, residential environment.

Under the Armistice Agreement, the DMZ is currently under military control of the UN Command (UNC). If South and North Korea convert the Armistice Agreement into a Peace Agreement and agree to establish the based on the birthright, non-transferability, and shared responsibility mentioned above, third government, South and North Korea will have a legal basis to demand the withdrawal of the UNC from the DMZ. Of course, establishing this third government in the DMZ will not be as easy as it sounds. However, it is not wise to give up without even trying on the assumption that the difficult is impossible. Establishing a third government is a huge project requiring a lot of effort, wisdom, and thorough study. I think presenting, designing, and planning an ideal third government is an urgent reunification task, therefore I conclude that establishing the University of Peace and Reunification is the most urgent next step.

Ideally, the University of Peace and Reunification would be established in the Demilitarized Zone, but realistically, that is impossible without consent of the United Nations Command, overseen by the US military. Kaesong, an alternative location to the

DMZ, holds geographical, historical, and cultural significance to the Korean people and was the capital of reunified Goryeo in the 10th-13th centuries. Although the Industrial Complex located in Kaesong was a limited economic collaboration between the ROK and DPRK, it was a practical reunification experiment that lasted more than 15 years. Therefore, Kaesong is the perfect location. I am confident that the Kaesong University of Peace and Reunification will be able to play a leading role in creating a political system and a culture of reunification that can lead to the reunification of the Korean people.

I suggest the Kaesong University for Peace and Reunification, a new and unfamiliar organization, as an opportunity to reflect on our more than 70-year division. The past 75 years have been full of intense conflict and confrontations between south and north. Inter-Korean and inner-ROK conflict has built a culture of division into that history. The fact that inner-ROK conflict could be provoked by the Kim Dae-jung, Roh Moo-hyun, and Moon Jae-in administrations' reconciliation posture toward North Korea proves that our history of division has calcified into a strong, structural inertia.

Even if after much effort, the Moon Jae-in and Kim Jong Un governments had reached a political agreement for the peaceful reunification of the Korean Peninsula, it is highly unlikely that such an agreements could be continually implemented due to the deep divisions that exist in South Korea. In order for a joint reunification policy and system to be implemented and successfully take root in the Korean Peninsula, we must first grow a deeply rooted reunification culture that accepts joint policies and systems.

The Kaesong University of Peace and Reunification can philosophically dismantle the culture of division and contribute to replacing it with a new reunification culture. By pioneering the mission of establishing and promoting reunification culture, I am confident the university will provide cultural soil in which the Korean people's reunification policies and system can take root and grow unhindered. Furthermore, I believe this university will play a leading role in promoting peace and the culture of reconsiliation to a world at war.

In a phrase still engraved on a plaque at the entrance to Harvard University, the Puritans who came to the United States from England explained their motives for establishing America's first university as follows:

> After God had carried us safe to New England and we had builded our houses provided necessaries for our livelihood reard convenient places for Gods worship and settled the civil government one of the next things we looked for and longed after was to advance learning and perpetuate it for posterity dreading to leave illiterate ministry to the churches when our present ministers shall lie in the dust.

Considering Harvard University's acclaimed position in the United States today, I deem their decision to have been a wise one.

Although we long to enter the unexplored world of a unified Korean nation, philosophically deconstructing division- oriented lifestyles, fed by our divided culture, is a major task that will determine the success or failure of a unified nation. We must urgently establish a new reunification-oriented lifestyle, one that corresponds to a unified nation. I believe that an educational institution comparable to Harvard University is absolutely necessary to seek reunification of the Korean Peninsula, which will be as difficult and complex as it was to build the United States.

I propose the Kaesong University of Peace and Reunification should be composed of five colleges, as follows: First, a College of Health that creatively combines Western medicine developed in the ROK and traditional Korean medicine developed in the DPRK. It will play a role in harmonizing treatment-oriented Western medicine and prevention-oriented traditional Korean medicine and spread its results internationally. Second is the College of Art. Art is essentially the harmony of heterogeneity. I am sure that if both Koreas work together to open up new artistic horizons and make efforts to spread them around the world, they will also cultivate a harmonious culture of reunification between North and South. Third is the College of Political Science. The ultimate goal of politics is to embody just distribution. The main task of the college is to study theories and methods that realize just distribution by creatively harmonizing capitalism in the ROK and socialism in the DPRK. Fourth, the College of Humanities prepares for cultural reunification of the two Koreas. It will conduct research to establish theories and methods for creatively harmonizing South Korea's materially -oriented culture and North Korea's ideologically-oriented culture. The college will also conduct research that promotes various human rights, based on human dignity, by developing a theory of world peace and putting into place a foundation for practical implementation. Lastly, there should be a

College of Socio-Ecological and Environmental Studies. Reckless environmental destruction threatens the survival of mankind, and the outbreak of infectious diseases such as coronavirus has reached a state where we cannot guarantee human survival. The main purpose of this school will be to research and compile wisdom in the organic symbiosis between humans and the environment.

I am confident that a Kaesong University of Peace and Reunification, dedicated to the reunification of the Korean people, will be able to play a leading role in creating our culture of unification.